Accounting 101: Learn Cost Accounting From A To Z

Gaurav Sanjiv Kalangan

Published by Gaurav Sanjiv Kalangan, 2024.

Also by Gaurav Sanjiv Kalangan

Learn Options Strategies Options Basics & Greeks For Stock Trading By Technical Analysis
Bitcoin, Altcoins & ICOs Learn the Basics of Digital Coins from Zero
Time Management This Is How I Work 300 Percent Faster
How To Build And Implement A Winning Pricing Strategy
Networking For Introverts: Gracefully Exiting A Conversation
Accounting 101: Learn Cost Accounting From A To Z

Table of Contents

Copyright

Published by Gaurav Sanjiv Kalangan

Distributed by Gaurav Sanjiv Kalangan

Accounting 101: Learn Cost Accounting From A To Z

Design and composition by Gaurav Sanjiv Kalangan Cover design by Gaurav Sanjiv Kalangan For permission credits.

To offset the number of trees consumed in the printing of our books, Gaurav Sanjiv Kalangan donates a portion of the proceeds from each printing to the Arbor Day Foundation. Gaurav Sanjiv Kalangan has replaced over 50 trees since 2022.

First Edition

I dedicate this to the dreamers, healers, and givers who deliver value through art and invention, expression, and creation. With all my love.

About

Are You An Accounting Student?

Are You Already In The World Of Accounting, Perhaps an AP clerk or Accounting Manager?

Do You Want To Quickly Learn and Understand The Entire Accounts Payable Cycle?

Do You Want The Top Tricks and Methods To Make Your Accounts Payable Function Work Perfectly?

If You Answered "Yes" To Any Of The Above, Look No Further. This Is The Book For You!

Accounts Receivable is where all the sales you made turn into actual funds and cash in the business. As such, it is a very important part of any company, and a solid understanding of the accounts receivable function is very important. Increase your accounts receivable turnover, collect funds quicker and put in place the best practices in the industry.

In this Book we will learn the basics of accounts receivable, the accounts receivable cycle, the best practices that should be used, fraud prevention, collection methods and much more!

At any point if you have a question, please feel free to ask through the Book forum, I'd be happy to answer any and all questions.

Receivables Introduction

This chapter we will take a look at receivables. The major two types of receivables and the ones we will be concentrating on here are our accounts receivable and notes receivable. There are other types of receivables we may see on the financial statements or trial balance or chart of accounts including receivables such as rent receivable and interest receivable. Anything that has a receivable in it basically means that someone loses something in the future. We're going to start off talking about accounts receivable that's going to be the most common, most familiar, most used type of receivable. And that means something someone, some person, some company, or a customer typically owes us money for a transaction that happened in the past. Typically some type of sales transaction.

So if we record the sales transaction that would typically be the way accounts receivable would start within the financial statements. Meaning if we made a sale we would credit the revenue account we'll call it SALES If we sell inventory. It would be called SALES If we sold something else it might be called fees earned or just revenue or just income increasing income with a credit. And then the debit not to go into cash but go into accounts receivable. This is a transaction that should be fairly familiar that there's going to be a transaction that happens fairly often. We made a sale on account and Of course if we made that sale on account and it was inventory then under a perpetual system we'd have the second component to that which would be cost of goods sold.

The expense related to the inventory we sold some amounts less than the receivable and the inventory going down the assets going down. So we Of course we are focusing on here and this receivable amount and talking about what that means for us and what it means to the company. And are there some types of problems with receivables that we will have to deal with. And one major problem with receivables and one that many people see when we start to learn the accrual accounting we start to say hey we recorded a receivable here. We're talking about balance sheet accounts . For example, we have cash and we have total receivables of 45000 while the cash is pretty concrete.

We have that in the bank and therefore there's not much question about the cash. Cash is cash. However , many of us start to question the accrual principle especially when we start to first learn the accrual principle and say hey is it really fair for us to record this receivable of 45000 when we have not yet gotten the cash. We're recording it as an asset, a current asset almost equivalent to cash in some ways in the same chapter of the balance sheet as an asset when we don't have the cash yet. What can we do about something that seems like we might overstep the financial statements and that's the question here.

Will we be able to collect on this is the question with the receivable the problem with the receivables just because we made the sale just because we earned the revenue by doing the work completed in our case getting the merchandise in order to complete the sales process and earn the revenue and therefore be entitled to the receivable. It is the fact and the case that some receivables won't be paid in will differ from industry to industry. So that's what we'll talk more about as we go through future chapters. How can we value this? One way to do it is to have an allowance method and say hey this is people that always money how much is owed to us. We're going to estimate how much of that is not going to be collectible.

We cannot write down the receivables directly because we don't know who's not going to pay us yet but it would be reasonable to tell our readers that someone is reading the financial statements. They would want to know the receivables we got to put on the books so we can't remove them. We can't be that conservative in that in that we're going to take it off the books not recognize any assets at all 45000 of what is owed to us is significant readers to financial statements want to know that number however in order to be as fair as possible on the balance sheet side we would also want to say hey we know that based on past history that it's likely that a certain amount of these receivables would not be collectible and therefore the net receivables is what we really think should be recorded as an asset.

And so we cannot write down the receivables directly. We don't know who's not going to owe us but we can make this contra account and that's what we'll talk about in the allowance method. There's also a problem related to the receivables on the income statement side of things. And whenever we talked about receivables we talked about the debit to accounts receivable and the other side of that is Of course sales when we record the revenue and the receivable.

And we have the same question or similar question on the revenue side. Did we really earn this money? Is this sales or is this revenue that we recorded as earned when we made a sale on it account for a certain time period.

That really sales that we can record in other words it's not exactly a sale even if we delivered the goods. If we're not going to get paid in the future and we need to question this on the income statement site which again is another area where a lot of people when we learn accrual accounting we start to really question as this question comes up a lot as to who will how can we record a sale aren't we recording the sale that we may not actually actualize and therefore be overstating sales. And the same thing is the case here that we have to record the sales because the readers of the financial statements do want to know that we earned the revenue by completing the work and therefore earned the revenue.

However we also need to tell the reader that hey some of those sales possibly will not be collected on and therefore do a similar type of fashion on the income statement side not only increase in the sales but also decreasing it with the amount of those sales that we believe are going to be uncollectible something we typically called bad debt expense. So this would be dealing with the matching principle so that the net income effect here we think should be something netted out between these two in order to be as fair as possible under the allowance method. This number here and this number here are just going to have to be estimates which is another area of problem in and of itself because estimates are estimates there's a range and it is guesswork that we have to do there.

But you can see why we would need to do these things because we need to record the receivable we need to record the sale because those are important to the readers of the financial statement. We cannot eliminate it. We can't go to a cash basis and not record sales on account or accounts receivable. However it would also be useful for us to try to look at past experience and give the actual number that we think is receivable on the balance sheet and that we think was actually earned on the income statement and that will take a bit of guesswork.

The other type of receivable we have is notes receivables so a note receivable is going to be different from an accounts receivable in that it's typically a bit longer term and time frame usually has a larger dollar amounts and therefore is often put in writing and often has interest than attributable tribute to it. So an accounts receivable may not have the formal notes documentation to record the transaction and the notes whereas the note receivable were typically going to have the formal notes transaction because of the longer time period. The bigger dollar amount and probably having the interest being charged on that when we're considering notes receivable we're going to consider notes receivable of time periods that are typically shorter than a year when we're talking about our receivables here. They could happen for a couple of different reasons.

We might make a sale and we might have that the period be a longer period and or more money and therefore want a more formal documentation and or charge interest and therefore make a note receivable rather than run through accounts receivable when we have a note receivable. We're not going to put it into account. See saveable and track it in the subsidiary Ledger to accounts receivable. We are typically going to have possibly our own accounts on the trial balance for each note that we make for each individual customer or we'll have a notes receivable account on the trial balance and then we'll have the supporting documentation tracking the note receivable as well as the interest that will be generated from it.

So a note receivable document will have something like this will have the amount of the note receivable on the note receivable the date of the note receivable the date it was generated so we will have the due date. So the due date might be formatted such as 90 days after the date of the note I promised to pay to the order of. And then we have the pay. So that's going to give the terms of the note which is going to be 90 days in effect of the due date of the note and then it's going to be paid to the order of the pay. Then we're going to have 1000 No cents dollars for value received with interest at the annual rate of 10 percent. So in other words we're typically going to have the principal amount that will be due in some time period 90 days.

In this case from the date of the notes to pay each and then we're going to have the interest rate in this case being 10 percent then we're going to have the maker of the notes signature here. So when we think of the note remember that the maker is going to be the one that you can think of as creating this note. If we had a business transaction say we sold something to a customer then the customer would be the signer as the maker of the note. Now Of course we would probably be that one as the business generating the note for the custom then sign in that circumstance. But note that this is in essence a promise to pay so you can think of this actually being written out by an individual making a promise.

And that would be the person purchasing something would be writing out the note saying you're giving me something of value and purchasing something from your store. I'm going to write you a note here saying that I'm going to pay you 90 days from this time period to pay you the amount of one thousand plus 10 percent interest and then signing the note as the customer then gives the note to the company or the store that is providing that good or service. So if we go through the terminology of this one more time we could see that the amount here is going to be the principal. So when we consider the amount of a note we typically consider it two components of it. When we get paid at the end of that time period we're going to receive the original principal and that's what we gave the customer in value.

So if the customer purchased something $4000 the sticker price of what they purchased was a thousand and they didn't give us money they gave us a note. This note is receivable and therefore the principal of this note's receivable is the thousand. We're going to get more than that because we loaned them that money. We in essence rented them the money and therefore are going to also generate interest. So the final payment we will receive can be thought of as having two components of it. One a principal component and to an interest component and then we're going to have the due date. Now this is the date of the note here that the due date is actually this item which is the promise to pay within 90 days.

And that does provide a bit of a complexity because when notes are worded this way we do need to figure out when exactly that is when it's 90 days up and make sure that we get the correct due date on the note and then we've got to Of course pay e the pay is the person who's going to get paid. And in our case we're going to say that that's going to be the company or the company making the sale. Receiving the note from the customer. Again obviously if you go in somewhere and you purchase something on account that you're going to get financed and you go through the financing process the company will typically help out with the financing process and be the one that generates the note.

But you can think about this note clearly being a promise from the purchaser the person purchasing the customer to the store the seller in order to purchase something a promise to pay. And so that means that the pay e is going to be the person paid the store providing the goods or the service was going to be paid the principal plus interest at the end of the term. So this will Of course be the interest amount, the interest amount being the 10 percent. Note what we have to do here with the note receivable is see what the principal is saying what the interest rate is but it doesn't say specifically one what the actual due date is it just says it's 90 days we'll have to figure that out.

And that's like the case with many notes the way the note will be formatted and written. And that's one reason it makes it easier to formalize a note or make it a standard no copy if our standard note is 90 days. Then it's easy for us to just say 90 days from whatever date the signature happens and therefore we can have just a template of the note for that type of sale and make it pretty easy to do and the interest rate will be the same type of concepts if we say that whatever the interest rate is typically 10 percent then you know whatever the dollar amount.

We can basically have the interest rate there but we're not generating here. Isn't is an amortization type table or a table to show us the calculation of interest that will be due at the term or the end of the note. And also note that if we could have many different types of notes set up this is going to be a fairly simple type of notes where we're going to pay simple interest and the principal at the end of the term period at the end of the 90 days we could make a note as complex as we want. We can make a note that pays monthly. We can have the compound of interest be different so note that the complexity of a type of note can differ greatly.

But at the minimum we're going to need these components typically in a standard note in order to create a standard note. And oftentimes when you look at the note it doesn't give the total amount that will be due at the end of the term it only gives you the interest rate and gives you the principle and it gives the time frame for the note. And therefore we're probably going to want to go through the process of figuring out what is actually going to be due at the end of the note which Of course will be the principal amount plus some type of interest.

Now then Of course the maker of the note once again is going to be the person who is promising to pay. So this is the person who is signing the note and therefore promising to pay for services rendered or goods rendered so if we purchase goods and we're the customer we purchase goods we got something of value of $1000 in terms of goods and services. We're making this promise to pay back that amount. Some points in the future.

Accounts Receivable Journal

Within the accounts receivable journal entries chapter of the Book we will be taking a look at normal journal entries related to our accounts receivable. This should be a bit of a review if we haven't seen the accounts receivable journal entries. We may want to go back to a prior Book about the accounting cycle and look through the full accounting cycle. But we will review the accounting journal entries for accounts receivable because we're going to focus on those accounts receivable. And we want to know what the normal cycle is. That being typically that we're going to make a sale on account debit accounts or sealable credit some type of revenue account and then we're going to have a payment on that in which case we're going to debit cash and credit accounts receivable.

Accounts Receivable Journal Entries

Hello in this chapter we will be recording journal entries for business transactions related to accounts receivable otherwise known as the revenue cycle. We will be recording these using debits and credits. At the end of this we will be able to list transactions involving accounts receivable record transactions involving accounts receivable using debits and credits and explain the effect of transactions on assets liabilities, equity revenue expenses and net income. We're going to be recording these transactions up here on the left hand side constructing those journal entries in accordance with our thought process.

Our list of questions to most efficiently construct the journal entries we will then be posting them not to the general ledger but to this worksheet here so that we can see the quick calculation of the beginning balance and what is happening to the individual accounts as well as account types in that we have the accounts categorized as is the case for all trial balances accounts being in order. That order being assets in this case in green the liabilities in orange of the equity light blue and the income statement accounts of revenue and expense type accounts first transaction performed work on account for $10000.

First question we will always ask is the cash effect in this case. No we didn't get cash. And the key term here is on account be aware of that key term in real life. We would know what would be happening here, meaning we did work for her bookkeeper, we did the bookkeeping and then we sent out the bill, but we have not yet received the cash in a problem that's in a book. They have to indicate that in some way often a very generic type of thing here we're just a service company. And we did work. And the key term being on account on account will mean either accounts receivable or accounts payable when working with the accounts receivable or sales cycle as we are here. The account when you see on account will be accounts receivable.

Some books might use the term on credit and in practice you might hear the term credit. The reason many books avoid that term is because we don't want to confuse it or the book doesn't want to confuse it with the idea of debits and credits mixing up the meaning of what a debit and a credit is. But when you hear that term in real life you have to know what the distinction is when someone says they're going to have something on credit versus debiting or in credit in a journal entry if cash is not affected and then we're going to ask what we received and what we got. In this case is an IOU we've got people owing us money we got a promise to pay at some point in the future. That's going to be our accounts receivable account. It's our second favorite asset account.

Not as good as cash but we like people owing us money. Therefore because it's an asset that has a debit balance we need to make it go up because people owe us more money. So how do we make an account go up? We do the same thing to it as it's normal balance. It being an asset having a normal debit balance means we will do the same thing as another debit. So we're going to debit the accounts receivable and that means we are going to have to credit something for the same amount.

Why are people going to pay us 10000 in the future? Because we did the work today we performed the work today and therefore earned revenue or income the credit going to revenue or income. We already know that if we know that it's going to be revenue or income that we will be crediting it because we debited the accounts receivable. But we want to think through that. Remember that revenue is an income statement account revenue and expenses being the income statement accounts and income statement accounts only go in one direction. Revenue accounts going up in the credit direction.

Therefore we're going to do the same thing to it which in this case is another credit. Also note that according to the revenue recognition principle we're recording revenue here. When the work was done although we have not yet received the cash. And typically this would be like an invoice transaction the transaction would be recorded when invoking the client as is shown here. So if we post this out we're going to say that the account will go from zero up in the debit direction by 10000 to 10000. The revenue starts at zero and goes up in the credit direction by ten thousand to ten thousand.

Remember here that we are representing debits and credits in two columns and the credits with brackets on the journal entry. But when posting We're showing the credits as in numbers only not in a separate column and debited numbers without brackets. This will save a lot of room when we post to a worksheet like this and that's why we will be working with this in practice. It will save a lot of time if you're working with Excel which I highly recommend doing. Then it'll save a lot of functionality in the formulas as well.

The effect on the accounting equation as it's increasing as cash goes up liabilities are remaining the same and the equity going up because net income is going up net income going up because revenues going up. Net income calculated as revenue minus expenses net income increasing equity. Here we see that that net income is increasing due to revenue increasing net income starting at zero going up by that 10000. Calculated as the 10000 minus the zero minus the zero.

Remember that that bracket does not mean a negative number for us. When considering this in the format of debits and credits it represents a credit. It represents revenue over the debits the credit of revenue over the debits of expenses by net income of 10000 next transaction receives cash on account 10000. The first question we're going to ask is cash affected. We're going to say yes we're going to receive cash. Is it going up or down? Up keyword received. How do we make something go up? We do the same thing to it as its normal balance which in this case would be a debit to an asset account which has a debit normal balance increasing in cash.

Now when first seen this many times when we start working with journal entries we start to think wait a sec is cash really affected in this because I also see the key term on account and I started to think that when I see on account that means cash isn't affected it means that some other accounts receivable or payable thing is happening here. And when we are purchasing something on account that will be the case because we purchased in the last example we purchased something on account. And in that case we did work on account and therefore the on account was affected rather than cash.

But in the second half of that transaction what's happened is we're going to receive cash for the amount that was owed to us in this case what was in the on account account of accounts receivable. So bottom line don't let that throw you off. If it says received cash then we received cash. Think about that first and then we'll think about why we got cash. We got a credit for something . What are we going to credit? We can't credit revenue because it says on account and that indicates that we didn't do the work at this point in time that indicates that we did the work some time in the past and if we see this this transaction without having first seen the prior transaction we've got to be able to look at this and say what must have happened in the past what must have happened in the past is that prior transaction.

That's how the accounts receivable works. We do work on accounting and we invoice the clients. We put that money into this account called or that receivable that IOU into this account called accounts receivable it represented here with this ten thousand. Now once we get paid that 10000 needs to decrease so the credit is going to go to that accounts receivable. It's going to reduce that 10000 back down to zero. So if we post this out we see the ten thousand debits to cash increasing cash from zero up by 10000 to 10000 accounts receivable then going down with a credit to it being a debit account we do the opposite thing crediting it bringing that balance down to zero. The effect on the accounting equation as it's going up however as it's also going down one asset increasing one asset decreasing.

In essence we're getting a better asset and losing the worst are assets. We're losing the fact that people owe us money. And given the fact that we have now got the money there is no effect on the liabilities and no effect on equity for looking at the net income. No effect on net income. Note that although we got the cash now we already recorded the net income in the past and therefore in the current transaction in the middle column nothing's happening to net income and we are remaining at 10000 represented in net income calculated as revenue minus expenses we are now able to list transactions involving accounts receivable record transactions involving accounts receivable using debits and credits and explain the effect of transactions on assets liabilities equity revenue expenses and net income.

Debits and Credits Accounts Receivable

Hello and it's chapter we will record transactions related to the accounts receivable or sales cycle. We will be focusing on the accounts receivable account recording transactions for work done on account meaning we do work and have not yet received the cash. And then we will then receive the cash. Therefore we're working mainly with accounts receivable revenue and cash. It's helpful to work by cycle here rather than just by date because it will let us see what is happening in terms of a particular process, a particular process within the accounting department. So it's good to work on a few problems by cycle. And then a few problems that's just going to be by date not necessarily by cycle working on the entire accounting transaction whatever happens to happen at any particular date.

Bouncing around from department to department we're going to record these journal entries in the general journal on the left hand side. We will then post them not to the general ledger but to this worksheet later on we will post to the general ledger. But for now we will be working with a worksheet because it will provide quick information for relatively few journal entries in order for us to see the impact on each account. And on net income very quickly we will then go to the accounting equation and see the effect of each transaction on the accounting equation as well.

Note that we do have the accounts in order of the accounting equation of assets rather than liabilities than equity then revenue and expenses we're going to start with zero balances at this point in time. We're then going to record our transaction's year end result and Indian balance after every transaction, hopefully always remaining in balance. Let's take a look at the first transaction we have to perform work on account and invoice the client. So we're going to do work and invoice the clients.

Therefore the first question is cash affected. We're going to say no not in this case because we invoiced and we have not done work. Key word for many book problems will be on account in real life Of course we would know that we basically invoiced the client and have not received cash at this time and recording this transaction would be probably routine we probably might not even know the journal entry or whoever is processing this may just send an invoice out. Not really knowing the journal entry but in a book problem and in real life we want to know what's going on so that if there is an issue we can go and kind of see what the system is doing.

And a big problem is going to have to tell us in words that we didn't get money we got something on account typically using the word on account they may use the term on credit. The problem with the term on credit is that it mixes up what a debit and credit is and having credit terms. So a lot of times books will avoid that by saying on account. So let's record those trends that we're going to say. Cash is not affected. Then I would focus on what we received and what we got.

And in this case we got something intangible. We got an IOU. We've got a client. All we know is money that's going to be accounts receivable.

It's not as good as cash but it is still an asset. It's our second favorite asset. We expect that to be converted into cash within 30 to 60 days. Therefore it's still a pretty good thing. So we're going to say it's an asset and as assets have normal debit balances we need to make it go up to people owing us more money therefore we're going to do the same thing to it which in this case is another debit. So I don't put my cursor here on E-6 Can I copy this. Gonna put that on the transaction. I'm going to put it right on top and the five right click and paste it. Not normal. I don't want to change the format of the text but one two three.

Just the values only so that half of the transaction. And you could just type it in there but I would recommend copying and pasting that helps me from avoiding errors and spelling errors and whatnot at least reduces those greatly. Then we're going to say that we have 13000. So we're going to just type that in see five thirteen thousand I'm not going to put any commas or any kind of other reference here. And when you select enter then the Excel will put those commas and references in there in accordance with the format of the cell.

Now we've worked last time with these transactions are going to represent negative numbers with the credits and I'm going to try to use a formula here I could just type in negative thirteen thousand but I'm going to go ahead and use a formula to try to connect as much as possible so I'm going to say if this is a debit this needs to be a credit and instead of saying it equals negative if I just start this I'm going to delete that if I just start with a negative that's going to tell Excel if I point to anything else it's like an equal sign it's going to try to take that sale so I'm going to point to this 13 and it's going to say OK you want that see five thirteen thousand and it's going to flip the sign basically in essence multiplying at times negative 1.

So that's one way that we can kind of have a formula and I'm just including one more formula. You don't need to do that, you can type in a negative 13000. But the more formulas we have the better off we usually are the less work we typically have in the long run especially if we have to make adjustments for errors. Now we just need to know what the other side of the transaction is and when people owe us 13000 or was it because we did work and when we do work we earn revenue according to the revenue recognition which is an accrual principle we recognize reg of revenue when work is completed when it is done.

And that's typically that point in time close enough to when we send out the invoice. So we know that we're going to credit revenue. Now we already know that I'm going to copy that. I'm going to put that in the B-6 right click paste. One two three. Here's our journal entry. I want to indent this a little. I might double click on it and spacebar three times and indent it like that. So there we have it. Now we might want to double check why we are crediting revenue. We know we credit it because we debited the accounts receivable However we might actually want to ask ourselves if I hadn't you know debited receivable would I know that I could credit revenue. To answer that we would say wolt revenue.

If we look at our cheat sheet it would be a normal balance of credit revenue that never goes down. Meaning the clients or customers never pay us. We pay the clients or customers and therefore we're going to increase revenue. How do we increase something? We do the same thing to it as its normal balance. So revenue has the credit normal balance we will then increase by doing the same thing to it by crediting revenue. So let's post this. This is the beginning balance. This is going to be the column we will post. So I'm going to say revenue or accounts receivable is here I'm going to go to sell G-6 and say equals and then point to that 13000 that's it's going to pull that number over. It'll go from 0 up by 13000 to 13000.

Put us out of balance by 13000 and there we have that no and no effect on net income from that part of the transaction. Then we're going to post the revenue side. So here's revenue there. Here revenue starts at zero. We're going to be recording in cell G 12 in Silje 12 and say the goals and then point to that 13000. We will then go from zero up in the credit direction by 13000 to 13000. Put us back in balance here meaning that we'll go to zero and net income will go up in the credit direction. There we have that. Now note that I'm recording debits and credits over here not with two columns just with one column but the debits equal the credits in that the debits are positive and the credits are negative therefore the debits minus the credits are zero.

Over here I'm recording them in a kind of more traditional fashion in that debits on the left credits on the right. And I'm recording the credit as a negative number or bracket number. Therefore if I highlight both of these I can say debits minus the credits equals zero. This format of putting credits has negatives is very useful in practice so that's what I'm going to introduce. I think a lot of textbooks don't give the benefit of telling people that because they think it might confuse plus and minus and debit and credit. But the idea of the reality of the world is that if you're learning to debits the credits you're going to get mixed up and have to differentiate. No matter what between what a plus and minus is because we're going to be adding and subtracting debits and credits.

So no matter what you do you're going to have to figure out what the differences between those two things and it's very functional and reasonable and what worth doing to start using if you're using software which I highly recommend doing like Excel to recognize that credit can be used in this format and you'll see it often times. So what that does for us here is it allows us to condense a worksheet like this from six columns that we would need if we had a separate debit and credit column for each to three columns. And so hopefully you can see kind of the functionality it'll it'll also allow us to shorten up some of these formulas and just do a quick calculation so that Excel will do all the work for us although we can see all the work being done by Excel as it's been done because we can see what the formulas are doing. So hopefully I can convince you of that.

But in any case net income means net income is increasing because that's a credit. So the credit is increasing that income that's not a loss. That means the credits of revenue are greater than the debits of expenses. What's going to happen to the accounting equation? Well we know that the assets went up the green accounts went up with receivables so that's going to increase. Nothing happened to the liabilities here. So liabilities will then remain the same. And then we see that equity is increasing. That's not a decrease, that's a credit direction and equity accounts have credits therefore it is increasing. We also know that it must be increasing because assets went up.

Therefore the other side must as well go up to the next transaction we're going to see what we have been to receive cash on account for work performed in the past. So the first question I would ask is: Is Cash affected? And in this case we're going to say yes it is affected because it says received cash. Now this is one question that people often get mixed up because it also says on account and people often think well if it says on an account that typically means that cash is not affected that something happened on account meaning accounts receivable. And when we purchase something or when we make a sale on it, then that is the case because we're not getting cash and we're recording receivables as we did in the first year lottery.

But the second journal entry in the cycle of accounts receivable is affecting both cash and receivable because we got cash and were paying off the receivable owed to us. So when you see the term received cash however we can really just start there without even knowing anything else that's going on. OK we received cash. That's pretty clear language, let's just record that first. There's 13000 of us who received cash. Well, cash is an asset that has a debit balance. We need to make it go up. We therefore will do the same thing to it which in this case will be another debit. So I'm going to copy Cashman to right click on cash on e five cell E-5 copy.

We're going to put that in V8. So in-cell be 8 right click paste 1 Three 3 and yes you can type in cash there. It's not a very long word so I'm not too worried about misspelling that one but I'm just going to copy and paste as much as possible so it's going to be thirteen thousand in-cell C-8. No formatting is going to type that in. And then I'm going to have a negative or credit 13000 over here in D 9. Now again I could put a negative 13000 or use a formula which would be negative of this cell. So I want to take whatever is in that cell and get to flip the sign on it and that'll be it. So we get a debit and then our credit then we just need to know what the credit will be if we got cash from a client or customer.

You would think that we would then credit revenue. However we have not yet received it. I mean we already recorded the revenue up here. So the credit is not going to go to revenue. Instead it's going to go to accounts receivable because we have this money here. People owing us money that needs to go down. This is really just tracking you can think of this receivable later on. We'll talk about a subsidiary ledger which will break this receivable down by customer. So you can think about this as kind of like the lump sum total of the list of accounts reporting who owes us money. And so people over 13000 if we think that that is just one person then we're going to say now they paid us 13000.

That then needs to go down. It's an asset. Assets have normal debit balances. We're going to make it go down by doing the opposite thing to it which in this case is to credit someone to copy that right click copy and paste that and so benign is benign right click paste. One two three. I'm going to double click before I'm in the cell space three times. And there we have it. Now we'll go ahead and post this out so we got cash for's to the debit to cash in a post that in the cash account I'm going to in-cell. G 5. So within the cell G-5 equals and then pointing to that 13000.

Then once I hit enter that zero will go up by 13000 to 13000 and then we have the accounts receivable here. Here's the accounts receivable on the trial balance. We're going to post it to G 8 or G-6 and I'm going to double click on it because there's something in it so see 5 in the formula bars in it. So if I double click on it I'll see that there it is. And I'm going to go to the end of it and say plus and then point to this 13000 credit. This is a debit balance account. That is a credit. Those are opposites and therefore this balance will go down. Once we hit it or put us back in balance.

No effect on net income. So it's important to kind of see what's happening all across the board here. Assets went both up and down. So we think about our accounting equation. We could say what assets went up because cash went up but assets also went down because receivables went down and there's actually no net increase there. No net increase in liabilities , no net increase or decrease in the capital. So this is one of those kinds of funny accounts where two assets happened from a debit and credit standpoint. It actually kind of makes more sense because we have a debit and credit from an accounting equation standpoint. The net of these is zero meaning assets, liabilities or equity are not affected at all.

Although we got cash as well. We didn't get any revenue in the second journal entry. We recorded revenue in the first journal entry because this is when we earn the revenue. This is when we receive the cash. We didn't do any work on this date. We did the work on this date. So that's when we recorded it under the revenue recognition principle. C says performed work on account and invoiced the client. So we're going to say cash perfect isn't going to say no. We did work on account. So we invoice the client and typically that's going to be the driving document later on when we start talking about accounting software it's an invoice that's going to drive this transaction and we're going to say that cash isn't affected.

Therefore what did we receive? We got an IOU. We got an accounts receivable. Accounts receivable is an asset. Assets have debit balances. We need to make it go up. Therefore we will do the same thing and debit accounts receivable. So I'm going to copy accounts receivable. To put that in. So be 11 or right click and paste one two three. Put the dollar amount in see 11 of that dollar amount being 650. We then know that we will credit something. I could put in just a negative 650 but I'm going to start using that formula. So I'm going to say negative and then point to the 650 there and that will pull over the number and flip the sign.

Now we just need to know what this account will be. Why are people going to pay $650? Because we did work, earned revenue and invoice the client expecting to be paid in the future. Therefore the credit is going to go to revenue. So here's the revenue account money to copy that to get a pace that can be 12 right click pastes one two three again you could just type it in there but I'm going to copy and paste is a bit faster bit easier bit easier to learn Excel. Double click on that cell I'm going to end in three times on the spacebar and there we have that. Now if this form if this worksheet weren't locked you can go over here and you can indent using the Home tab alignment group and increase indentation.

Now we knew we were going to credit revenue because we debited the receivable and we had to credit something. But if we think about it right once again double check revenue has a credit balance account. We need to make it go up because the revenue always goes up and we get more revenue and therefore we will do the same thing to it as its normal balance, its normal bounds being accredited, resulting in us crediting the net in order to increase it. Now we'll post this we're going to say receivables Here is an asset. Here's the receivables account on the trial balance. We are going to record it in the blue chapter in column G. So we are on G-5 double click on G-5. We see the activity.

I'm going to go to the end of this and say plus and then point to the 650. Now I know this formula is getting a bit complex. So you could just type in the formula as long as you have these in the exact same cells on the worksheet we are working with. Or you could if something gets messed up and this gets deleted then you're really just going to go back and point. Say equals and point everything with receivables including this has a receivable plus. And then I'm going to point to this as a receivable plus. And then this had the receivable and enter that brings the receivable back up to this 650 and it puts this out of balance by the 650 until we record the other side down here in the revenue or income. Again something is in it therefore we will double click on it.

I'm going to go to the end of it and say plus and then point to the 650 over here that's going to increase our revenue. Put it back in balance and increase the net income. Remember that net income is calculated as revenue minus expenses. Revenue is increasing here. Nothing's happening to expenses that is not a loss for us. It's representing the fact that revenue has a credit balance and went up in the credit direction. Credit's being represented with brackets. What happened to our accounting equation. We know that assets went up because the accounts receivable went up.

So when you say assets are increasing We know that nothing happened to liabilities nothing's happened to liabilities in our entire process. So far so far. And then we know that the equity too is increasing for a couple of reasons. One is that the revenue went up increasing equity any time revenue goes up or net income goes up. That will increase the total equity. We also know that if assets went up on the left hand side of the equal side then the equity too must be going up on the right hand side. If equity is the accounts affected on that side go into a transaction be performed work on account and invoiced the client.

So that same accounts again we're working on the same accounts receivable account so is cash affected. We're going to say no we did work on account. Key term on account. Therefore we're going to say what we received. And in this case we received an IOU that YOU being represented by the receivable account it's going to go up to is a debit balance normal balance account. The way to make any account go up is to do the same thing as its normal balance which in this case is another debit. So I'm going to copy the receivable. We're going to put that in the 14. Right click and paste one two three will then enter the dollar amount of that dollar amount of 780. So it's going to be 780.

I'm going to credit 780 as well so we have an equal number of debit and credit. I'm going to do that with a formula by saying negative and point to that 780 and enter. Now we just need to know what that account will be. And if we did work then we earned revenue under the revenue recognition principle and a cruel principle. Therefore we will recognize that revenue is here. I'm going to copy that to get a piece that in-cell is 15 by right clicking and pasting one to three values only. I'm going to double click on the revenue and an interspace space three times to have the indentation. Now we already know that we were going to credit revenue because we debited the receivable. But let's think through it.

Revenue has a normal credit balance and revenue only goes up. Net income goes up and down however revenue only goes up and therefore we will increase revenue by doing the same thing to it. That same thing is a credit. OK so now we're going to post this. We got a debit to the receivable. So I'm going to scroll up to the receivable that's in cell G 6 is where we need to post this. Something is in that cell therefore we will double click on that cell go to the end of it and say plus and then point to that 780.

So these are the accounts Of course now that are included in the accounts receivable and enter. So now we are up to 14 31000 430 which includes this 650 and this is 780 than what we record. The second side which is the revenue side of that is here. So it's in G 12. I'm going to double click on G 12, go to the end of it plus and then point to that 780. That will increase revenue, put us back in balance and increase net income. So revenue goes up and net income goes up and we are back in balance here. We will then take a look at the accounting equation. It is going to be the same transaction here where accounts receivable went up and count receivable is an asset. Therefore assets are increasing. Nothing happened to the liabilities so none.

And then we're going to say that equity is increasing. So that's going to be an increase in equity. And that's what we have so far. Next we have it. E says received cash on account for work performed in the past. So the first question is cash affected. And we're going to say yes the key term is to receive cash. So cash is going to go up because we received it. Don't let this on account terminology throw you off. We know that cash went up because we received it. Cash has a debit balance. We're going to make it go up by doing the same thing to it which in this case would be another debit. So I'm going to go ahead and copy cash. We're going to put that on top.

It's on B-17 right click and paste one two three. Within the debit side we're going to put six hundred and fifty and then we're going to credit something for 650. We could type in negative 650 or negative and then point to the 650 and that will bring the balance down. Now we just need to know what account will go with that. And if we normally get paid we would say it should be in revenue. But Of course we had already recorded the revenue in the past up here and this account we recorded the 650 revenue and here we know that we are reducing the asset, reducing the receivable and reducing the amount that people owe us that account reflecting what people owe us is accounts receivable.

How do we know that with the term of the text? Because of that on account. So we know that received cash means cash is affected. We know on account means either accounts receivable or accounts payable is affected and this case receivable. Therefore the receivable here needs to go down. So we're going to decrease the receivables. I get a copy of the accounts receivable or at a pace that year in the 18 right click paste one to three going to DoubleClick before that a space bar three times and there we have that. Now we know we're going to credit the receivable because we debit it cash.

We also want to think about it and say accounts receivable is a debit balance account. It needs to go down because it represents what money is owed to us by customers and after payment from customers then the amount owed to us will go down. Therefore we need to decrease the receivable receivables our assets have debit balance normal balances and we need to decrease it. Therefore we will do the opposite thing to it which is our credit. So let's pose this out now we've got the cash. First I'm going to go up to the cash account to sell G-5 something and it's going to double click on it then go to the end plus scroll back down. We're going to get to this 650. I know it's kind of in two different sales here.

But then enter and there we have it. Now if you want to just type it in there you can just type in equals C 8 plus C 18 but I highly recommend using formulas in this because it will really help you go back and try to say what's in the cell and you can just see by looking at the highlighted cells here and see what's in there that's really helpful. We are now out of bounds by 650. We're going to go to the accounts receivable. So here's accounts receivable in-cell G-6 something's in it therefore we will double click on it go to the end of it plus scroll down just the tab going to point to that 650. Once we hit enter it's going to go back down the receivable, put it back in balance and there we have it.

Now there's still 780 in the receivable because we haven't received this amount that was recorded in D yet. Note that there's no impact on our net income from this transaction because we had recorded the increase in revenue up here in transaction see transaction see the date of the time when the work was actually done. We'll then go over here and we will record the increase or decrease in cash going up but our council seat is going down. Both assets therefore have no effect on assets, no effect on the liabilities and no effect on the equity. So that's going to be one of these weird transactions again where there's no effect on any of it as revenue is recognized when we receive cash.

We're going to say no, not necessarily. It's recognized when we earn the revenue when we do the work is recognized as revenue when we have earned it whether cash is and we're going to say yes. So that's the revenue recognition principle that's one of the major points that we want to get from working at an account with accounts receivable or the receivable cycle. Note that if you were working with a company that was on a cash basis they wouldn't even have a receivable account and this receivable account depends on the industry as to how important it is. If you're in an industry that always gets cash at the same time work is done.

It may not be as important as any industry such as the legal industry or if you're a bookkeeper or any industry that does work but for they get paid and then they build the client to be paid at a later time. We'll need this cruel account of receivable because this is the account that helps us track who owes us money. We're going to back this account up later with a subsidiary Ledger with a list of clients who owe us money. And so that's going to be very important depending on the type of industry that we are in.

General Ledger Accounts Receivable

Hello and this chapter we will work on a problem related to the accounts receivable cycle similar problem that we had in the past. However now we will be recording the transactions here as we did in the past but not posting them directly to a worksheet but rather to the general ledger building the general ledger as we go. Then using that General Ledger in order to construct the trial balance which will then remain in balance. So as you can see this is going to be a bit longer of a worksheet. This is kind of the traditional type of worksheet that we would work out. However we're going to set up this worksheet a bit differently than many book problems in that we will be posting the journal entries as we go to the general ledger and then building the trial balance as we go.

So just putting a system together like this whenever possible because it's going to save you time in that if you do everything at once over here and then post it to the general ledger and then post it to the trial balance it's very likely that you will be out of balance and not know where to go where to go back where to start to see where and how to fix things. And if we do something in this format where we put it together as we go it'll be a lot easier for us to know when an error happened and know where to go in order to fix it rather than going back to the beginning. I also recommended using Excel as much as possible just to learn Excel and as well as it's just a great tool to learn these types of problems. All right.

First activity we can say performed work on account and invoice invoiced the client.

So we did work and invoiced the client. Our first question is always is cash affected. We're going to say here that no cash is not affected because we invoice the client and have not yet received any money. Therefore I would think about what we have received. Second question and we received an IOU accounts receivable counsel. Siebel is an asset that has normal debit balances. We're going to make it go up by doing the same thing to it which is another debit. So I'm going to copy the accounts receivable and sell E6 right click and copy that cell in E-6 going to paste that to sell be five. So in the 5 or right click and paste it's one two three then we're going to put the dollar amount of 13000. So that's going to be in the sea. So in C5 we will type in 1 3 0 0 0.

No commas, nothing else. That's it. Once we select enter it will then include the comma and then we're going to put our cursor in D6. We know that we will then credit something. I'm going to do this with a formula being negative of this number that'll take the 13000 debit in-cell C5. Multiply it times negative 1 in essence and flip the sign. So I'm going to represent the credits we're going to represent the credits with brackets and or negative numbers in Excel. And in this case in the credit column as well then we just need to know what this account will be. Why are people going to pass 13000 in the future because we earned it we earned revenue and therefore we're going to have the revenue account down here revenue or income.

I'm going to copy that we're going to put that over here right below in B-6 right click and paste it one two three then we're going to double click right before the R and space three times in depth. That's three four and three. It For The indentation. Now we know that we credited the revenue because we debited the accounts receivable. But if we think through it we're going to say revenue has a normal credit balance and revenue only goes up. Customers pay us, we don't pay customers and therefore we will do the same thing to it which in this case is another credit so that we can double check that we are credited in that account. Two different ways.

Now we can post this. Remember that this is the general journal of this whole sheet. This is the journal entry that we posted into the general journal. The active us recording the journal entry as Journalizing the journal entry in the general journal. Now we will be posting in the journal entry. This is the process of posting to the general ledger. So we're first going to have these accounts receivable here. Here it is on the trial balance. Second account. Here it is on the general ledger. Second to account. So we are on the debit side. So here's accounts receivable debit side since cell J 16. We will use a formula to record this highly recommended using formulas because it will tie your worksheet together.

So NJ 16 I mean to say that equals and then just point to this thirteen thousand. That's going to make this amount go up by 13000. It will also pull that total over here to the trial balance and that will Of course put us out of balance by that 13000. So there we have that then we're going to post the other side's revenue in order. The accounts on the trial balance assets and liabilities and equity then revenue. So revenues are going to be over here a bit. Therefore I'm going to try to make this a bit smaller so we can see more of this big spreadsheet and one page.

I'm going to use these bars down here you could hold down control and scroll down. I'm going to use icons. You can see what I'm doing and I'm going to take it down from 130 to 120. And now you can see at 110 we can see the revenue. Remember it's in order of assets , liabilities , equity then revenue. We over here have a credit to revenue. Therefore we are going to credit revenue over here. So here's the revenue account. We're on the credit side and we're just going to be right here in the cell at 9 9 9. That equals that I'm going to point to this 13000.

Once I select enter it's going to increase this amount to 13000 credit direction. That amount will also pull over here and the revenue will put us back in balance and we'll have a net income of thirteen thousand. So there we have that 13000 here 13000 there back in balance net income at thirteen thousand net income calculated as revenue minus expenses. Remember that this is revenue and we're seeing it as a credit so that credit means we have net income this isn't a loss. We're not working with a kind of a plus and minus income statement. We're working with a debit and credit and income statement and here the credits are greater than the debits.

Next activity we said we receive cash on account for work performed in the past. Note I just updated the worksheet a tad here so this is going to be the thirteen thousand thirteen thousand It's going to be beat meaning we received cash on account for work performed in the past 13000. We're going to say our first question is cash affected. We're going to say yes we received cash. Key word here being received. Remember that you might get mixed up with this terminology in that we see both the idea of receiving cash and on account and wouldn't you see on account you might just think hey that means cash is not affected it means something else like receivable is happening.

And that would be the case like it was in a. But in this case Of course both of those things are happening meaning accounts receivable is happening and the cash is happening and it will be able to think that process through if we first think about the cash. So just the idea that we have received cash will tell us that cash is going up. So we're going to say cash is an asset. Cash has a debit balance we need to make it go up. So we're going to do the same thing to it as its normal balance which is a debit. So I'm going to copy cash. I'm going to make this a bit larger too. I'm going to scroll back down here Bachtiar plus back to 130. Scroll back over so I just copied cash. I'm going to put that fear in so be 8.

So right click and paste. There we have it. The amount then is going to be that 13000 again. Thirteen thousand and if we debit something 13000 we will credit something for 13000. I'm going to do that without a formula negative of that. So there we have that now we just need this amount here or this. This account here and that account you would think if we got cash from a customer you would think revenue. But clearly we had already recorded revenue in the past. That being the time that we earned it, that is therefore the time that we recorded under that revenue recognition principle. So this time we're actually going to credit the receivable, Of course the receivable having 13000 in it representing people owing us money.

Now they have paid us therefore that receivable needs to go back down to zero representing the fact that people don't owe us money anymore. So I'm going to copy that. I'm going to put that on the bottom and sell the nine right click pastes. One two three. We're going to double click in front of the a. And then three times on the spacebar and enter. Now we know we're going to credit the receivable because we debited the cash. But we want to think through it. Double check it. We know that the receivable has a debit balance. We know that it needs to go down because people paid us and they no longer need to have an account representing that they owe us therefore we will do the opposite thing to the receivable as its normal balance that being a credit.

Then we'll post this journal entry. We Journal lies in the general journal which we will now post to the general ledger. So we have cash up top that's going to be the first one that's our first account on the trial balance. Our first account on the general ledger we debited over here. Therefore we are going to put it on the debit side over here in cell J 9 equals. I highly recommend using formulas here. We're going to say equals and then point to that 13000 in sales C-8 you could just type in equals C-8. That's easier as well as you can say equals and then look over here and say that C-8 and do that and that's going to increase once we select enter it will increase this so to 13000.

It increases the accounts receivable to 13000 and it puts us out of balance by 13000. The second account is accounts receivable accounts receivable as our second to count up here and therefore will be our second to count down here. We're going to be on the credit side and some on the credit side. We are in so key 17 remember that you always want to keep skipping a row whenever possible because it really should be an order by date. Some book problems will try to squish everything together and put the credits right next to each other right next to a debit wherever there's room.

But you really don't want to do that because typically a general ledger will be in order by date and each date should have its own line item so we shouldn't really have a debit and credit on the same line item. So we are on K 17 equals. We're going to select equals and then point to the accounts receivable here in D 9. And once we select enter it should bring it back down to zero. It will bring that to zero over here two accounts receivable put us back in balance. No effect on net income. So there we have those zeroes here. We're back down to just cash and the revenue that's all that's happened so far during the activity of this problem number see or let her see perform work on account and invoice the client.

So this should sound familiar. We'll go through a bit quicker here we're going to say it is cash affected. No we build client therefore got an IOU that accounts receivable count Sibyl's and assets. We need to make it go up. We'll do the same thing as its normal balance. Its normal bounds being a debit means that we will then debit it again, copying receivables, put it on top in so b 11 or right click paste one to three the amount then six hundred and fifty. We're going to credit something for 650 with a negative of that number. So there we have that. Now we just need to put the account here. Why are people going to pay us six hundred and fifty in the future? Because we earned revenue we earned revenue that's going to be this account either 10 or right click copy. We're going to put that and paste it in the 12 Right-Click and he used one two three then we're going to double click right before the R and space bar three times and enter.

So we know we were going to credit the receivable because we debited the and we're going to credit the revenue because we debited the receivable But we also can double check it in our mind we could say that revenue has a normal credit balance. It only goes up if customers pay us, we don't pay them. Therefore we need to make the revenue go up by doing the same thing to it which is another credit. So here's the receivable account we have a debit here it's our second account on the trial balance. Second account. Therefore on the general ledger we're going to post this 650 to the receivable G.L. in the debit side down here in J 18.

So within J 18 we're going to say that that equals and then point to this 650 and that should bring this balance up to 650. We should be able to record that Schir 650 will then appear here and the trial balance and put us out of balance so there's that side of it. Now we're going to record the revenue side of it and notice that revenue is way down here. It's always in order of assets , liabilities , equity and then revenue. Same order on the general ledger. So in order to see that I'm going to try to make this a bit smaller again so we can see more on one page I'm going to select this negative and bring it down to 100 and 10 percent rather than 130 percent as you do this. Note that some of the sales might get too small for it and that means it will show a bunch of like number signs.

If that happens just just make it bigger again and they'll go back away. All that means is the cell is the ROE became too small for the cells. And typically it'll correct itself as you adjust the screen back to whatever the default was that you were working with. OK. Second side we're going to have here is the credit side, which is going to be right here in S-10. So within 10 I'm going to say that equals and then point to this 650. Once I select enter this is going to increase by 650 and it'll also pull that balance over here. It'll put us back in balance and it will increase net income. So there we have that we have 13 650 now here and that's increasing net income because we have no expenses and therefore we have revenue minus expenses of just the revenue of 13 650. Remember that is revenue that is not a loss although it has brackets around it it is a revenue account. Okay.

We perform work on account and receive an invoice the client performed work on account and invoice the clients. So the same type of activity and we're focusing on that receivable cycle. So we're looking at that receivable cycle so is cash affected. We're going to say no we performed work and invoice the client no cash has happened at this time. We're going to say then that we got something. We got an IOU that I or you being represented by accounts receivable are going to go back down over a year. I'm going to make this a bit larger again. I'm at 110 going to bring it back up to 130. And we have this receivable. So the receivable is going to go up people. It was more money.

We have a debit balance in the receivable. We're going to increase it by doing the same thing to it as its normal balance which in this case is a number of other debit. So I'm going to copy that. We're going to put that on top. We're here in B 14 right click and paste one two three. The amount then is going to be 780. So 780 then we're going to credit something by 780. So I'm going to go ahead and record that now it's going to be a negative of that number and enter and then we just need to know what that account should be. And if we are going to get paid in the future then it's for work that we have done now. So that's going to be the revenue account revenue that has a credit balance and we're going to increase it.

So I'm going to copy revenue but on the bottom right click paste one to three then double click in front of the R and space it three times. Now we already knew that we're going to credit revenue because we debited the receivable that's why we worked on the receivable first. But we can double check ourselves by saying that revenue is a credit balance account. It only goes up and therefore we're going to do the same thing to it which in this case is a credit being a credit to a normal balance account. Then we're going to record this.

So we've got accounts receivable. Seven hundred and eighty. That's the second account on our trial balance and therefore second account on the general ledger. And we're going to just go to the next line down.

That is Engy 19. So we're in accounts receivable. We're on the debit side and we're in line J 19. So will J 19 and we're going to use a formula equals and point to this. Seven hundred and eighty that's going to bring this balance up 760 plus 780 to 14: 30 that 14:30 also will be pulled over to the trial balance as we go. And we are out of balance by the 780 until we record the second half that has been the revenue half. Now the revenue is going to be in order again. So it's an order of assets , liabilities , equity and then revenue. So it's in the same order on the gold meaning revenue is going to be towards the end. So I'm going to make this a bit smaller again and bring it back down to 120. So we can see this revenue account. Note that revenue only goes up in the credit direction and we don't see any debits in the revenue account.

There are no credits and debits in the revenue account. Something funny happened. So we're going to say that the revenue is a credit here and therefore we will put it on the credit side here in sales as 11 and say equals and then point to this as seven hundred and eighty. Once we select enter it's going to increase this side here. It will pull that amount over to the trial balance over here and put us back in balance. So there we have that we're at 14 for 30 and net income now has increased to 14 430 last transaction and make this a bit larger back up to 130 over here going to scroll over to the left hand side and we are now on e received cash on account for work performed in the past. So the first question is cash affected.

And we're going to say yes it said received therefore we received cash. Note again that it also says on account which probably might be triggering in your mind hopefully at some point it's going to be triggered in accounts receivable which might make you think that cash isn't affected. But remember this is the second transaction. So both the well and cash will be affected. So let's start with cash as always and we're going to say Cash has a debit balance. We got more of it. Therefore it's going up. How do we make something go up? We do the same thing to it as its normal balance which in this case is a debit. So I'm going to copy cash and put that on top right next to the E here or right click and paste.

One two three. The amount will then be six hundred and fifty and then we're going to credit something for 650. I'm going to do that with a formula that formula negative of the cell taking that cell flipping the sign for a negative six hundred and fifty. We're then going to say what we are going to credit. What accounts? We just need this account now. Now you would think maybe revenues since we got money for work we have done but we did the work in the past and had already recorded the revenue up here. Therefore we're not going to credit revenue but accounts receivable we are decreasing the receivable. So I want to copy the receivable. We're going to put that down here in between right past one two three.

We're going to double click in front of a space three times and we know that we credited the receivable because we debited the cash and therefore must have credited the receivable. If we think through it then we would say well receivable represents the money owed to us. Now we have two people basically owing this money. Later on we'll work with a subsidiary ledger that will tell us exactly who those two people are. But we can tell that it happened from these two different transactions. So we probably have two different people that owe us money there. Now one of those individuals from this transaction has paid us and therefore the account representing people owing us money should go down.

So this is a debit balance. We're going to make it go down by doing the opposite thing to it which in this case is a credit. Now we just need to post this out. So cash is here the first account first account here first account on the general ledger. So we're in the cash account. We're going to credit cash and we're going to go to the next line. I'm sorry. More on the debit side. It's a debit to cash debit cash where in-cell J 10. I'm going to say equals and then point to the 650 that 13000 will then go up by 650 to 13000 650 which will then be pulled over to the trial balance as well. Then we're going to credit the receivable. So here is the receivable. We're going to credit the receivable account. Down here it's the second account on the trial balance.

Second account on the general ledger we are on the credit side of. Therefore we're going to be in the credits column and we're going to be down here in sales. Kate 20 where we will say equals and then point to this 650 that's going to bring this balance 14:30 down by 650 to 780 that 780 will then be pulled over to the trial balance and it'll also put us back in balance at this point. Note that if we look at the receivable account here we'll see kind of a story of the receivables this is what will count. Basically it always looks like we're going to have to invoice the client and then we receive a check and then we invoice the client and we receive the check.

We invoice the client here and have not yet received the check. So note that the invoice in this check receipt may not be right next to each other on a date such as this but that will typically be the pattern we should see. We should see invoicing and then payments being received. Note also however that we might be invoicing and then receiving like installment payments or something like that which could make the picture look a little muddier. But whenever we look at the receivable side of it we're going to have both debits and credits that represent the work we did as billing the clients usually with the documentation of an invoice and then credits represent payments usually in the form out of checks we have received for work done in the past.

That's going to be the typical thing you will see in the receivable cycle. If we look at the revenue side of things. Note that there's typically less activity in revenue than Of course the receivable because the receivables are going to have twice as many transactions one for the billing of the invoicing and one for the receipt of the check but the revenue account only goes one way. Notice it's only going up in the credit direction. You're not going to see any debits in the revenue account not until we close it out and that will typically be the case.

And what we will see within the general ledger of the revenue accounts. So note that these general ledger accounts are telling kind of the story: they're telling the history by transaction broken down to each individual account and then that story is being condensed to one number that is then shown on the trial balance and then we can basically see that we can tie all that out. All those ending balances to zero in a similar way. So this is kind of condensing the data that is being found on the general ledger to just the ending balances of all the G.O. accounts.

Multiple Choice Questions - Accounts Receivable

In this chapter we will take a look at multiple choice questions related to receivables. First question: the person who signs a note receivable is a maker b e c holder d receiver e owner will read through this again and see if we can cross off some options with the process of elimination. The person who signs a note receivable is now a note. If we look at a note receivable you might first start thinking well maybe both parties should be two people signing the note receivable. But typically it's only required oftentimes for one individual to sign the note receivable and for that reason we need to know that the notes receivable is basically kind of like a promise.

So a note receivable is is an individual promising to pay it in the future at some point so we can imagine if we have a debt that is due and we say well I'm not going to pay you now but I'll write this little note here and give a formal note telling you that they will pay you in the future. That's what's going on here. So who's going to be the person who signs it? The one who's making it. So if we look at this as the maker and so that sounds good right the maker it seems like a technical term you might not hear or think of the maker of the note. But that's going to be a technical term.

Typically that looks like a good term to use and it's what it's probably going to be the it's going to be pay me now the difference between the pay and the payoff is a little bit confusing we just have to know the terminology P E and then the pay or the pay or is going to be the one that eventually pays the payment. At the end of the note term and then the payee is going to be the one that's going to be receiving it. So the payee may sign the notes but not really required to sign the note. The one who's making the promise to pay it is going to be the one that needs to sign that's going to pay or the holder of the notes.

The holder of the note is probably going to be the one that is going to get paid at the end. The payee is the one that's going to hold the notes and again they're not the one that really needs to sign it. The one that needs to sign is the one making the promise that is good then giving the note to the holder that will be able to use it for collection in the future. I'm not sure that's exactly a technical term there. The receiver of the note I think. But that sounds more even if it were more of the holder of a note. And again the holder of the note is not the individual that is signing the notes per se or is required to sign it the one that is making it is. And then the owner is not really an owner of a note.

And so the note doesn't know you could say that the holder has possession of the note but I don't think that term really applies here. So it looks like the maker is what we are left with. So the person who signs a note receivable is the maker of the notes receivable next question. A credit sale results in a debit to accounts receivable account in the general ledger and in the customer accounts and the customers account in the accounts receivable subsidiary Ledger the credit to the accounts receivable account in the general ledger and to the customer's account in the accounts receivable subsidiary

Ledger see a debit in the accounts receivable account in the general ledger and a credit to the customer's account in the counter saveable subsidiary Ledger d a credit to the accounts receivable account in the general ledger and a debit to the customer's account in the accounts receivable subsidiary ledger and E a credit to the sales and a credit to the customer's account in the accounts receivable subsidiary ledger.

OK so one more time we'll see if we can go through this with the process of elimination. A credit sale results in. Now this one since it actually has a journal entry we might first want to just record the journal entry. I would say Write it down. It doesn't have a dollar amount. You may say that's ok we can still write down what the debit and credit would be and that would typically be a credit sale we made a sale and we didn't get cash we got our accounts receivable. So I can just put a dollar sign or something for the dollar amount or just put an amount of 100 or something like that to show us that that represents some type of amount we don't know they didn't give us that that's OK. And then the credit is going to go to something like income or revenue or sales whatever the income account is so that's the normal journal entry. Now they're talking about this subsidiary Ledger type thing.

And remember that that really is going to be supporting backing up the accounts receivable accounts. You've got the accounts receivable account and then some type of subsidiary ledger which will give us the same information. By order of the customer. So then says a debit to the accounts receivable that looks like a good account and the general ledger. This journal entry is going to be posted to the jail, the general ledger and the customer accounts and the accounts receivable subsidiary Ledger. So that would be also a debit to the city or Ledger.

That sounds pretty good because that's really what's happening here we're debiting both the general ledger and the subsidiary that you look at the rest of them though. BS says a credit to the accounts receivable account in the general ledger of credit and debit in the general ledger for accounts receivable. So that's why that one's not right. See says a debit to the accounts receivable in the general ledger. So a debit to the calcium that looks good in a credit to the customer's account in the accounts receivable subsidiary Letcher. Now we wouldn't be crediting the subsidiary ledger. We're basically doing the same thing to this journal entry. We are in essence posting the same A-S debit both to the G.L.

general ledger and to the subsidiary Ledger the subsidiary Ledger being the same thing as the general ledger except that it's ordered in a different order rather than being just in order by date it being ordered first by a customer. So that says a credit to the accounts receivable account and that's not correct. We're not credit and debit in the accounts receivable and e says a credit to sales and a credit to that customer account in the accounts receivable subsidiary ledger. We will credit income to our sales whatever that account is. But we're going to debit accounts receivable which in essence is the subsidiary Ledger and the geo Leger's. So we're not going to credit the accounts to see what accounts.

That's why that is incorrect. So it looks like our correct answer. Once again a credit sale results in a debit to the accounts receivable account in the general ledger and a customer account customers account in the accounts receivable subsidiary ledger. Next question. A promissory note is an investment for the Maker be a written promise to pay a pacified amount of money at a certain date see an asset to the maker D and installment receivable. He can never be used in payment of an accounts receivable. So we'll go through the process of elimination. QUESTION: One more time.

A promissory note is an investment to the maker. You may have a question on who the maker is. So I'll leave that one for now. I mean you could think of a note as a kind of investment. B says a written promise to pay a specific amount of money at a certain date and a promissory note. That sounds pretty good. It sounds like a pretty good definition. And then C says an asset to the maker. So once again we've got this maker term here. So let's leave that one for now. DS says an installment receivable and not necessarily an installment type sale unless it says it was an installment. So going to cross that he says a can never be used in payment of accounts receivable and it's possible actually to do that.

We could say OK we can't pay you the accounts receivable. How about we sign a note receivable and they might accept that because the note receivable would then charge interest. So that might be we could actually use a note receivable as payment for an accounts receivable. So we're left with a B and C.. So a promissory note is a he says an investment to the maker and C says an asset to the maker. Now note that those two kinds cancel each other out. In some ways they can't both be correct. And even if we didn't know what the maker is if something was both an investment and an asset they would both be. And you know if it was an investment it would have to be an asset typically. So that's one reason.

Just looking at the multiple choice format we could say those two don't look right and we can kind of cross those out now. Who is the maker? That's the one that is actually signing the notes. So the maker is actually the one that is making the promise of the notes so that's usually the customer. In other words now that's a little deceiving of a term because oftentimes the person who you know writes The note will be the business because that's what they do. They make a standard note but you can think of the note as a promise being made by the maker of the one the customer is promising to pay in the future and therefore one that's going to sign it as if they made as if they wrote up the notes and I'm going to promise you to pay whatever I owe you in the note and sign it and give it to the other individual that be in the business.

So the maker then it's not an investment to them it's kind of like a liability to them. And so that's not correct here and that's why it's not an asset to the maker. It could be an asset to the receiver or the holder of the notes. So be Looks like our correct answer. A written promise to pay a specific amount of money at a certain date. So once again a promissory note is B a written promise to pay a specific amount of money at a certain date.

Accounts Receivable Subsidiary Ledger

Within the accounts receivable subsidiary Ledger chapter of the Book we will be discussing the subsidiary ledger as it relates to accounts receivable. We're focusing in on this Book in the valuation of accounts receivable and we want to know what the cycle of accounts receivable is as well as the detail to make up the accounts receivable the subsidiary Ledger being that detail which breaks out the accounts receivable by customer rather than by date as does the general ledger account.

Accounts Receivable AR Subsidiary Ledger Explained

Hello when this chapter we're going to talk about the accounts receivable subsidiary Ledger the subsidiary Ledger being the ledger that will be backing up the account of accounts receivable showing on the trial balance with 27000 in it. In this case accounts receivable beyond that account that represents what is owed to us if we were the owner of the company we might ask our accounting department how much money do people owe us. In this case it would be 27000 would be the reply. Next follow up question would most likely be who owes us that money and have we called them when we are going to get paid that money in order to answer that question. We cannot look at the normal backup balance for all accounts. That being the general ledger accounts if we look at the G.L.

we do get some detail in terms of the activity that has happened. However that activity is not going to be in terms of who owes us the money it's in terms of dates. So every account has the general ledger which does give very good detail but not the detail we need. In this case what we will then need is that information broken out by a customer which will be in terms of a subsidiary Ledger such as this for example it might say that Smith owes us 5000 and Ryan owes us 15000 and Adams owes us 7000 for a total of that 27000. The accounts of the Siebel subsidiary sledger matching the general ledger matching the trial balance which Of course would match the balance sheet. It's important to note that this information is all put together using the same data. So the general ledger is often thought of as how we create or put together the information which the end result will be reported in terms of the trial balance.

We can put that same data and the same general ledger data into the subsidiary Ledger. That's what we'll do in this process. Also important to note that because of that relationship when we look at the end result meaning the accounts receivable account in terms of the trial balance or the balance sheet we can sort that data and backup that data in terms of a general ledger or a subsidiary ledger. Let's take a look at some transactions. First transaction is a familiar one. We've seen it before we're going to inform the clients so we're going to do work on account. Therefore our council is going to go up the IRA you're going to go up with a debit and we're going to credit the income account I'm going to post out the income account. I'm not going to post it to the general ledger account. It would have one.

But we want to focus on the G.L. for the receivables so if we post out that income first income would increase increasing revenue for that time period when the invoice was issued counts receivable we're going to first post to the general ledger so the general ledger for accounts receivable increasing by that 35000 which would then increase the total in the accounts payable jail to 35000. And Of course the same would impact on the trial balance increase and the trial balance to that 35000. We can see then that after this journal entry we have 35000 Siebel.

We have thirty five thousand in the general ledger but we also want to see that information in terms of who shows us the money. And in order to do that we have the subsidiary Ledger broken out by client by customer and we want to post the same information, that same 35000, to the information by customer. So it's the same as the jeel except it's a bit more detailed in that it's by customer and then by date. And if we post that out we see the 35000 is owed by Smith. Now we have a total in the subsidiary ledger of 35000 total in the general ledger of 35000 as well as in the trial balance. And what would be on the balance sheet of that 35000. That relationship always has to be their next transaction. We're going to assume that we paid so the customer then paid us.

We're receiving cash, cash is going to increase and we're going to credit the accounts receivable not revenue because we didn't do the work we did the work last time or credit in the receivables that one as it's going up one asset it's going down. I'm going to post the cash first because I don't want to focus on cash we're not going to be looking at AGL for cash. I was going to say cash is going to be a debit increase in the cash and then we'll focus on the receivable which we will post to the general ledger. So that's going to bring the balance down. We can think of that in two ways, one the running balance.

Thirty five thousand debits minus the new activity which is a credit bringing the balance down to zero or summing up the debits 35. So up the credit 35 debits minus the credits would then equal zero. Same activity, same thing would happen to the trial balance bringing the balance down to zero. Meaning trial accounts now at zero. General Ledger now zero subsidiary ledger. Need that same information. So we're just going to post that same information on the same thing. That will be impacting the account ledger. However it will be there by client or customer bringing that balance down. We're back down to zero on the subsidiary ledger for A-R and the general ledger for A-R and the trial balance for our new customer and a new customer.

We're going to invoice a new customer. We did work and the envoy went out. That means did accounts receivable credit the revenue account we're going to post the revenue first. Again because we're not really focusing on revenue. So although it has a general ledger account like all accounts do we're just going to post it to the trial balance increasing revenue then we're going to focus on the receivable. We're going to post that out to the G.O. What would that do to the G.O. debit to the G.L. the general ledger for accounts that people go up by that 14 that would bring the balance up to 14. Calculated in one of two ways we can say its zero running balance was 0 before plus a debit bringing it up in the debit direction.

Or we can say that debits 35 plus 14 minus the credits of 35 bring us to the 14. Same thing what happened to the account Siebel up here. So we're saying accounts for the bounces go up to 14000. Now we see that we have 14000 in that trial balance for accounts to see what we see. We have 14000 in the general ledger for accounts receivable and we need to post that same 14000 of the same 14000 needs to be posted to the subsidiary ledger but by customer in this case and that customer being Adams here. So Adams is going up by that 14. Now we have zero plus 14 plus 0 brings us to that same 14.

The subsidiary leads your time out to the general ledger timed out to the trial balance then we're going to have another invoice we're invoicing another customer. We did the same work invoice in the customer accounts as he was going to go up with the debit of that 27000. We're going to credit the revenue I got. I 'm going to post the revenue first not to the general ledger although it does have a general ledger account but we're not focusing on the G.L. for this particular count but revenue would then increase in the credit direction.

Now we'll post out the receivable is going to be another debit to the receivable in this case increasing the receivable we can think of that two ways the 14 prior balance plus the 27000 current activity brings it to the 47 or 35000 debit plus 14000 plus 27000 debit that total minus thirty five thousand credit total would also bring out to that 41000 that's the T account format. And this is the running balance format for both out to the trial balance we see the same activity the 14 plus to 27 bring us to that. Forty one thousand.

We can see that then the 41000 on the trial balance is equivalent to the general ledger account for accounts payable 41000. We need to post that same 27000 to the accounts receivable subsidiary ledger but by customer Breon Ryan in this case bringing the balance up to twenty seven thousand. Now we have a balance of 41 total including the fourteen thousand atoms 0 for Smith. Smith paid off the balance and 27000 for Ryan. Point being that subsidiary ledger is the same data in essence as the general ledger. It's just posted in a bit more detailed fashion. We want to be able to know that relationship so that we can build the trial balance. And also we need to note so that if we are using software we know that we can store this data one by G.L.

by date but also by customer and then date. And that's also why much of the software when we work with accounts receivable will require a customer every time we post to the receivable the software saying hey I can't make a subsidiary Ledger unless you assign a customer therefore we're not going to let you both do this to the receivable account unless you assign a customer.

Accounts Receivable Subsidiary Ledger 700 Part 1

Hello, during this chapter we will work on certain journals in transactions. Right here we're going to generalize those transactions here and then we're going to post them to three different places one being the equipt posted to the trial balance in this entry chapter so we can see the activity in a quick and easy way and see what the effect is on the trial balance. Then we're also going to post it to the subsidiary Ledger. So these are going to affect accounts receivable. Much of the time and accounts receivable is representing what is owed to us and therefore we also need to know who owes us the money. So we're going to start recording that to the subsidiary ledger which will be in order by client or customer in this case and then we're also going to record it to the general ledger.

So we want to see all of the type of activity that would happen when we're recording these transactions focusing on the accounts receivable cycle. So we're going to see the quick reaction here to the trial balance directly. Analyze that then recognize the fact that we do want to sort this by customer in this case Biek. And that would be done through the accounts receivable subsidiary ledger. And then Of course we have the general ledger and we're only including the general ledger here for the accounts receivable account. So we're not going to recorda every general ledger account Of course every other account here would have a general ledger account but we're focusing in on accounts receivable and therefore we're just going to record at the general ledger account for receivable to distinction and to have a distinction between that and the subsidiary ledger here.

So Of course we have our balance right here and that's going to have our assets are going to be in green. We've got our yellow or orange or liabilities. The equity count in the light blue. And then we got the revenue and the expenses on the bottom. We know that we are in balance because the debits minus the credits equals zero. And we're going to post our activity here. We also can see that net income is actually income not a loss because it's the revenue unless the expenses and we have the income here. And then Of course we have our counting equation up here where the assets are the green ones. And then the liabilities. Notice there is no negative sign here because we've flipped the sign. And then all of this is the equity of that nasty equity. Right.

So now this records these hours and the first one says perform work on account and invoice the client and the client. Smith In this case. So we got thirty five thousand. We did work and we invoiced the client. So is cash affected in this case. No because we did the work on account and we sent out an invoice but did not yet get the cash. Therefore we did get something, we got an IOU that are accounts receivable. So we're going to say it receives what we have received in this transaction and that it is an asset account. It's just under cash and assets have debit balances. We need to make it go up. How do we make something go up?

We do the same thing to it as what it is which in this case would be another debit. So I'm going to debit the accounts See going to copy that right click copy 1 to copy and they're going to put my kids there and see five and then right click and paste it one two three so paste and just the values not the formulas just the values here to keep the cells looking like they are and that blue color. And then going to put the amount 35000 every debit is going to have an equal number of credits for every transaction. We're going to have at least two accounts so we're going to have a credit here. We will be represented in the credits with negative numbers or bracketed numbers in the Excel worksheet.

So we're going to have negative thirty five thousand and I'm going to enter and Of course it'll format that cell for us with brackets because of the formatting of the worksheet. Then we just need to know what this US account should be and why are people going to pay us thirty five thousand because we did work and earned revenue and we could call this depending on the type of company revenue we could call it income's we could call it sales we could call it fees earned. It just depends on the type of company but it is going to be a revenue type account and Of course it'll be down here in the revenue area I mean it's under the capital chapter on the trial balance.

So when a copy of that Right-Click copy that we're going to paste on the bottom credits traditionally goes on the bottom we are in-cell C6 right click and paste one to three. So I'm going to post this now to basically three different places. I'm going to post it here to the tribe and so we could see a quick easy beginning and try Vallence then we'll post it to the subsidiary ledger. At least the receivable side of it and then we will post the receivable side of it to the general ledger. So let's do that now when I say the receivable is here. So we're here at the receivable of its second account. So we are in I six and say equals and then we're going to point to that thirty five thousand.

What's going to happen? We'll go up here. We will go out of balance by 35000. So the 35 represents customers over 35 and now we are out of bounds by 35. We will then post our revenue in I 14 so our 14 equals are going to point to that 35000 credit. What will happen is the credit will go up in the credit direction because we're doing the same thing to it. We'll be back in balance. Net income is going to go up from the transaction. So where we're recording revenue revenue is being recorded. When we did the work, not necessarily when we got the money because we haven't got any money yet. So now we're going to record that same accounts receivable to the subsidiary ledger here. So we need to record it with the customer. Why?

Because oftentimes when we look at the trough and we're going to say who owes us money or how much do people owe us people it was thirty five thousand The next question we're going to have is well when are we going to get that money and who owes it to us. Let's call those people and to do that we're going to need to know the to your ledger by the accounts receivable by customers using the subsidiary Ledger. So here we have Smith we're just going to record that same debit side to this account here in the city of bedroom's to say equals and that's going to point to that thirty five thousand again.

Now it also we're going to have this stuff in the general ledger so I'm not going to post the entire general ledger out but just to recognize that there is a difference we're talking about something different in the subsidiary Ledger than what we have seen in the general ledger of the general ledger would be posting transactions in order by date or the order of the transaction. So we can post the same thing in the subsidiary and general ledger so we could say that this equals that same thirty five thousand and we see that the thirty five thousand in this chapter is going to be the same information that will be recorded here.

It's just that it'll be recorded slightly differently right here it's only recorded by date right here it's recorded by customer. And Of course at the end of it we have the 35 here 35 is what adds up all the customers that ties out to the islands. All right. Next transaction we're going to scroll over here and we're going to say that we received cash on account from Clarence Smith for work performed in the past. So now Smith paid us this 35000 Well that would be the natural transaction that would happen hopefully sometime in the future we get a check in the mail. Therefore we're going to ask her questions. Is Cash affected? Yeah.

We receive money we got cash cash has a debit balance we need to make it go up. How do we make something go up? We do the same thing to it which in this case would be another debt somewhere to copy the cash. We're going to put that in cell c 8. So going to click and put that in C-8 and how much did we receive. Thirty five thousand. Because that's what we built for 35000. And so we're going to credit the same amount. So there's going to be an equal number of debits and credits and we're going to say well and out of the past 35000 because we did work but we did work in the past. So we're not going to credit the receivable account.

We already did the work in the past. They owe us Of course 35000 that we put right in the receivable. Now they paid us that they no longer owe us that therefore that thirty thousand debit there needs to go down. How do we make something go down? We do the opposite thing to it as what it is that's a debt. Therefore we need to credit it to make it go down. We already knew that because we debited cash. So that's where the credits going to go is going to make receivable go back down to zero. So I want to copy that. Going to paste it in C9 right click and paste one to three values only in C9 recognize what is happening here. We're just getting a better asset cache and we're losing the worst asset the accounts receivable. Now that may not be a word but it sounds good. So the receivables going down cash is going up and no effect on revenue for this transaction. So let's close it out and see what happens.

We're going to go up here to I 5 i 5 equals I want to point to that thirty five thousand. What's going to happen? Cash will go up by 30 thousand because a debit not debit makes the debt go up in a debit direction to six or three thousand then accounts receivable. There's something in it here. I could see it in the form of the borrower Of course. D5 is in there, that's the divide here. In order to post it , I'm going to double click on it. Go to the end of it and say plus and then point to this thirty five thousand here and now we see there's two things in there there's the thirty five debit the thirty five credit ones a positive one the negative ones the debit ones the credit that's going to make it go down to zero again.

So even though we have a zero here we can see what's in there. And I like to use these icons to point to them and we can see OK that makes sense. It went up and went down. And if you want to know where those icons are they are in the formulas tab and they are and the formulas are. And here they are here. So then I can turn them off with this thing here. All right so we're going to also post those out to the subsidiary ledger. And so we're going to say no one owes us any money right now. Therefore we have to reflect that in the subsidiary Ledger meaning Smith doesn't know any money anymore. So we're going to post that same activity at 10.

So this equals the thirty 35,000 thousand and that means Smith no longer owes us that this would be the normal activity within a receivable account Of course it goes up and then hopefully they pay as it goes down. We invoiced them and we got a check in the mail. That's what it should look like if we just look at that in the general ledger. We'll post the same activity to General Ledger. Again we're not going to post all the accounts Of course to the general ledger we would be posting both the general ledger cash and receivable in real life. We're doing the full problem but we're just looking at the receiver of the accounts receivable G.L. account general ledger account and we are on the credit side so we can say this equals that same credits same activity by date.

So we don't know who necessarily bought this 35 by this general ledger account but we can see that it went up when it went down and probably make a safe bet. That's the same client and it may not be. Of course right next to each other in this activity we could have other sales involved. But that's the type of activity we expect to see in the receivable account. Much of the time. So now Of course we have zero here the subsidy Ledger has. And that's what's on the trial balance as well. Next one performs work on account and invoice the client Adams. All right so we're going to do work on accounting. So is cash affected where we did work on account. Is Cash affected and answered No. Because we did it on account and we issued an invoice when we issued an invoice because we did work and therefore we earned revenue and we believe we've received the intangible asset of an IOU called accounts receivable.

So our counsel as an asset has a debit balance just like cash it needs to go up because people owe us more money. How do we make it go up? We do the same thing to it which in this case would be another debit. So we're going to copy the receivables and right click copy that can put that in see 11 right click and paste it one two three. The amount being for 14000 in this case if we debit something.

Accounts Receivable Subsidiary Ledger 700 Part 2

Oven right click and paste it one two three. The amount being for 14000 in this case if we get something 14000 girls are going to credit something 14000 So I'm going to go and sell. The negative for the credit for this worksheet. Twelve thousand no commas or anything entered that will format the cell with the brackets. And then we just need to know what that account should be here. And Of course why are people going to pay 12000. I'm sorry 14000 should be negative 14000. So why are people going to pay 14000 in the future because we did work and earned revenue or income or sales depending on what we do.

We can call it whatever we want but it's in the revenue chapter and it's going to be a revenue type account meaning it has a credit balance and revenue accounts generally only go up. So how are we going to make it go up? We're going to do the same thing to it which Of course is another credit. So we're going to credit the revenue account. We always credit revenue only when a copy that I put on the bottom. See right click and paste it. One two three. So then let's post this out again. We're going to post it to our three locations so it's first posted to our trial balance. So we're going to go into the resealable there's a zero in it.

So we don't want to delete the zero even though it's a zero because I know there's two things in it. There's D5 plus nine and I'm going to double click on it, go to the end of it and so on and then go plus and point to the new receivable 14. That way we can see the activity there when we hit enter week by 14 takes us out of balance by 14. We can then see the activity that is in there like so and then we're going to post the other side to the revenue. Once again something's in it. E6 is in it. So we can double click on it, go to the end of it and then say plus and point to the revenue of the credits of the 14. What's going to happen? It's going to take revenue up by 14%. Put it back in balance.

So revenue which is the credit minus the debits has now gone up to 137. Eight fifty five. All right so now we're going to post the same thing out to the receivable accounts. This was Adam's down here so we're going to be down here in the receivables on the debit side. I'm going to post this same activity. Adam owes us money. So now we can answer the question if we say who owes us money. How much do people owe us? Fourteen thousand says on the trail about who owes us 14000. Well we're going to look at the subsidiary ledger and we can see now that Adams is the one that owes the 14000. We also will have that activity by date on the G.L.

for all accounts. So on the G.L. we can post that same activity it would look like this for the receivable equals the 14000 and enter. And now Of course the receivables are in the general ledger tied to the receivable on the subsidiary Ledger times out to the receivables on the trial balance. So all that activity is there. And once again note that we would have a receivable account for all the trial balance. I mean our general ledger accounts for all the trial balance accounts as well. All right. So let's see what the next one is. We got deep reform work on account and invoice the client Ryan. So the same activity we did work and we invoice the client. So is cash affected.

No, we invoice the client. We haven't got cash yet but we did work. And therefore people it was money the account that people owe us money is represented by the accounts receivable account. It has a debt of balance represented by the fact that it has no brackets in the number and we need to make it go up because people owe us more money. How do we make it go up? We do the same thing to it which in this case would be another debt it's going to copy this one. And to put that on top again the amount being twenty seven thousand if we debit something we're also going to credit something we're going to put a negative 27000 in E-15 and into that will put brackets around it. Then what should that account be? Well, why are there 27,000 people in Paris ? Because we did work and therefore earned revenue again.

So we earned revenue raising revenue we have a credit balance revenue only goes up. We're going to make it go up again by doing the same thing to it which in this case would be another credit which we already knew because we debited the receivables so there's the credit we're going to credit to answer. Let's copy that and put that in the credit side of our journal entry. All right I'll post this out and Of course the two accounts we're focusing on are having a lot of activity in them. But let's pull that out. Again we got 14000 here if we double click on it. We can see what is in there. So Of course this is what's in there and now we're going to go to the end of it after the deal 11 and say plus and point to the 27000 which

Of course will make the receivable go up again by 27000. Put us out of balance.

Down here and then we're going to post the other side of it to the receivable. Double clicking on the receivable goes to the end of it. And plus and then point to the revenants so the other side of that is revenue and the revenue Of course will go up in the credit direction bringing net income up and putting them back in balance here. So there we have that we're going to post this out once again to our subsidiary ledger so we can see your question. How much do people owe us 41000. Well who owes us 41000. Well we're going to go to that our subsidiary Ledger over here and say Well Adam owes us and then we have Ryan who we need to record over here in 89 so nine we're going to say equals that same twenty seven thousand needs to be recorded there and now we have it the 20 I'm 27 by Ryan and that total adds up to Of course 41 which is on the balance.

We will also have this activity by date on the general ledger not as useful in this particular type of account which is why we need the extra ledger of the subsidiary ledger by client. But the activity for all accounts will be represented in the general ledger by date. So we're going to go by date we're going to be selling T 12 to 12 equals the same activity. So I'm just going to post that same debit bringing this 14 up in the debit direction because the same thing makes it go up and there we have that let's take a look at the last one here we're going to say I've received cash on account from atoms. So now Adam is going to pay us this 14 that we built him in the past that's what we expect to happen.

We invoiced them and then we received a check in the mail. That's nice. So then we are going to say well is cash affected. Yes. Cash is affected. We just got the check. Cash is going to go up. Cash has a debit balance. We make something go up by doing the same thing to it. In this case that would be another debit debit and a debit or the same thing making the debit go up copying that right clicking pasting one two three. So that's going to be the fourteen thousand then we're going to credit something Of course 14000 and represent the credit negative for this worksheet. Fourteen thousand. And then we just need to know what account we're going to credit.

Well why do people pay 14000. Because we did work and we did earn revenue but we earned revenue in the past. And people have already recorded that revenue up here. Now when you see the fact that we also recorded up here that receivable that represents the fact that people owe us money that now needs to go down because somebody paid us money that has a debit balance in it. And how do we make something go down. We do the opposite thing to it which in this case would be a credit. And we already knew that we are going to credit it because we debit cash. There's the credit right there that we will credit it for. So what is happening is that receivables will go down. We're losing one asset but we're gaining a better asset that asset being cash going to copy that receivable riposte underneath in Seath 18.

Right click and paste it one two three. OK. And we're going to post this out. So let's post this out. We're going to post cash. Cash has something in it. I'm going to double click on it we're going to go to the end of it and say plus. And so I can see what's in there they're not going to put this 14 in there as well. What's that going to do? Increase cash. Put us out of balance. So there we have that then we're going to record the receivable. So here's the receivable in a six double clicking on Isaac's go into the end of it it's getting kind of long. I see that. But we can see everything that's in there and we're going to go to the and say plus and then point to that 14000.

And then when we hit enter what's going to happen the receivables are going to go down because it has a debt of balance it's going to go down and put it back and balance down here. So now we can see the receivable if we add someone who asked us if our boss asked us for the owner and we're asking Who else's money or how much do people owe us. There Are always 27,000 people. Well who owes us 27000. And Of course we're going to have to look at the subsidiary ledger for that. We need to record this same activity for the subsea Adams down here is the one who paid us the fourteen thousand So we're going to go into the credit side for Adams and we are in sell and 17 equals and we're in a point to that 14000 over here that will bring the 14 down by 14 to zero. So is no longer with the money.

We could see that all the subsidiary ledger accounts now add up to 27000 just what Ryan owes us. That ties out to the balance and Of course this information would be on the general ledger as well. And it would be recorded by date. So we need to record that as well in the general ledger for account receivable. So I mean to say the same activity equals the one the 14000 here bringing the 47 down by the 14th to the 27. So the 27 in the G.L. ties out to the twenty seven in the subsidiary Ledger times out of the 27 in the trial balance. Also note that if we look at the G.L. we can see that the activity being the fact that the same thing makes it go up the opposite thing makes it go down.

So we see that we have the debit side here and are always going to win because it's an asset account and you could think of it as kind of a race that we're saying you know it's the debits against the credits which ones are going to win and how much they are going to win by. Well we already know that debits are going to win because it's an asset account so therefore the credit makes it go down so that 35 minus the credit makes it go down then we're going to say plus the debit makes it go back up to the 14 then plus the debit makes it go up to 47 and then we say minus the credit makes you go down to 27. Either way we can think about it as Of course the debits add up to a total of 76000 minus the credits which add up to 49000. If you subtract those two routes you get 27000.

So that's how the activity will work in the G.L. that same activity is a little bit more difficult to see in the subsidiary ledger because it is Book broken out a bit more detail by customer and Of course we can see the summary of that same activity in the trial balance by just taking a look at what is being included here. So the debit making it go up credit making it go down debit making it go up debit making going up credit making it go down.

Multiple Choice Questions - Accounts Receivable

In this chapter we will take a look at multiple choice questions related to receivables. First question: a promissory note received from a customer is recorded as an equity account the accounts receivable account see always a current asset. D. always a non-current asset or a current or non-current asset rethrows it one more time through the process of elimination. Question is a promissory note received from a customer is recorded as an equity account. So a promissory note. If we receive the promissory note from the customer, it might help by thinking of the journal entry related to that if we receive the promissory note. Typically we might have a sale that we made and we credit sales and then the debit might be the note receivable rather than accounts receivable.

Typically because possibly the dollar amount was larger the longer term that we have that we're going to receive the note receivable for and therefore we want a formal note. So the notes receivable then it's typically going to be some type of asset sale set of accounts receivable we have a note receivable. So the promissory note isn't typically going to deal with equity although the other side is increasing net income and therefore increasing equity. But the note is and so we're going to say that's not it. This is an accounts receivable account. Now we will leave that it is a receivables we might say movements of receivable. But I'll leave that for now.

C says always a current assets type of account. And if we read through the rest of these it says always a non current asset. So note that those two are basically exclusive to each other. So you know if one of those is true than the other you know they kind of cancel each other out and then says a current or non-current asset. So if we look at these three. They're all kind of related. So if we go through this one more time a promissory note receipt from a customer is recorded as either an account receivable account always a current assets always a non-current asset or a current or non-current asset.

Now whenever a question is asked I always want to be careful of that. If it always says that you know all we need is one exception to make that to be untrue. So I'm leaning forward just because of that. And the reason for that we may think that that be the case where the note receivable would always be a non-current would probably be the way most people would think of that because if it were current We may think that it should go into our accounts receivable and not notes receivable. But the definition of a note receivable really isn't that it's over a year. That's the definition of a current asset, a current asset being something that's going to be due typically within the year making it current and the note receivable may be a note receivable not due for more than a year but isn't necessarily so.

So the note receivable could be something longer typically than a normal accounts receivable but still do within a year. So therefore it is really looking good here because the big note we see could be current or it could be non-current just depending on how long the term of the note receivable is and that really eliminates C and D. B says an account receivable and accounts receivable. It's still receivable but it is different. So no conceivable and accounts receivable are similar in nature but not the same in nature. So it's not what it looks like is our best answer.

Once again the question is whether a promissory note received from a customer is recorded as either a current or non-current asset. Next question the quality of receivables is a the reputation of the seller B the speed of collectability see the likelihood of collection d the reputation of the purchaser or e the interest rate. So if we go through this one more time we're going to say the quality of a receivable is the reputation of the seller. Now if we're talking about reputation and we're talking about the receivable, remember what a receivable is, it's going to be something done by a customer.

So we're not really talking about the reputation of the seller in this case. If we're concerned with anything it would be the reputation of the person who needs to pay. Because we're trying to value whether or not the receivable the quality of the receivable is good. So the asset of the receivable represents stuff that is owed to us. It's good. It doesn't deal with the seller's reputation but the customer's speed of collectability. Now that could be a factor in the quality. So we'll keep that as the likelihood of collectability. That too seems like a pretty good factor in terms of determining how valuable the receivables are these days the reputation of the purchaser.

And again if we're looking at reputation we would be considering the purchaser more than the other side of the business and then he says the interest rate on the quality we're not really talking about the interest rate here. And you know some receivables if we're talking about accounts receivable won't even have an interest rate. So we might consider a higher interest rate to be better but that's not really what we're talking about in terms of the quality. With regard to most receivables including accounts receivable which doesn't have an interest rate. So once we got we're left with B C and D.

QUESTION: One more time. The quality of our receivable is the speed of collectability. I see the likelihood of collection or the reputation of the purchaser and I think of all of those the likelihood of collection is really the most concerning factor here. Speed might be better if we get it faster. That might make something you know some receivables more quality than the others and the reputation of the purchaser may have something to do with whether or not it's going to be a collectible or not. But ultimately our major concern is collectability.

So I think C is the best of these answers. Speed is not, you know, the only thing it has that kind of has to do with collectability in some way. And D Also it is not the only thing we're looking at, we're looking at collectability which may not take into account the reputation of the purchaser. So the final answer is the quality of receivables and the likelihood of collection.

Direct Write Off Method

Within the direct write off method chapter of the Book we'll be talking about the direct write off method. This is going to be a method for writing off those accounts receivable accounts that become uncollectible. It's important to note that the direct write off method is not the method preferred by generally accepted accounting principles but is the method that most of us would probably first think of if trying to come up with a method for writing off the accounts receivable therefore being the logical method and one that we should start off with it's going to be a more simplified method doesn't require as much of an estimate as the next method. The one that is going to be preferred for generally accepted accounting principles which is going to be the allowance method.

In this chapter we will be discussing the direct write off method and the direct write off method as it relates to accounts receivable. A quick summary of accounts receivable accounts receivable is a current asset. It's an asset with a debit balance. We are going to be writing off certain amounts for accounts receivable that will become not due or not collectable at some point in the future. There are two ways to do this. One is called the allowance method. The other is the direct write off method. We will be using the direct write off method here. The non-general Accepted Accounting Principles method being this direct write off method. However a method that is typically much easier to use therefore when considering whether or not to use an allowance method or direct write off method we want to consider one.

Do we have to use an allowance method due to the fact that we need to make our financial statements in accordance with generally accepted accounting principles or are we able to choose between having an allowance method or direct write off method. If we choose to have a direct write off method it's probably because we're thinking that the receivables that will be written off are not significant. In other words they're non-material to decision making. So if we had our accounts receivable here that's what people owe us. We want that on the books to represent the fact that we do have an asset. We do have people owing us this money.

However if there is a significant amount that we believe will not be paid to us then we want to note that if we don't we're overstating our assets and we're also distorting our net income on the income side of things. So the deciding factor then is going to be one. Do we have to use an allowance method that will be an accepted accounting principle? If we have to make financial statements in accordance with a strict rule and generally accepted accounting principles then we would typically need an allowance method unless the amount was in material. If we're not required to be recording our books with regard to the allowance method because of generally accepted accounting principles the question then is should we be recording the allowance method. Is it better for making that decision?

Basically again coming down to whether or not it's going to be material to decision making how many of those receivables we believe will not be collectible as we go through the direct write off method. We always want to compare it to the allowance method to see the differences between the two methods. We have this account here, this read account that will not be used as we go through the direct write off method but there to show us what would be there if we were to use an allowance method to compare and contrast as we go through this process. So first we're going to say that a customer CW is not going to pass the accounts receivable of 9000 for whatever reason at this point in time we've decided we're not going to get paid and therefore we're going to have to decrease our accounts receivable and the decrease is going to be a credit to accounts receivable accounts receivable is a debit balance asset account.

We're going to do the opposite thing. To make it go down because we're not going to get paid. Therefore our journal entry will be a credit to accounts receivable that will be the same under the allowance method or the direct write off method. The other side is what will differ under the direct write off method. We will write it off to bad debt expense this is probably what seems most natural at this point in time because it's not getting paid. So we're going to write it off as bad debt expense. What actually happened here. How did that account get on the books in the first place? We debited accounts receivable and we credited revenue when we made the sale.

You would think then that we would decrease revenue at that point in time that we discovered that the sale $9000 worth is not valid. We're not going to get paid that nine thousand dollars but we don't typically reduce revenue one and therefore we're going to make this other account that's going to kind of be like a contra revenue account because we never really earned the revenue bad debt expense. So it's going to be an expense. We're really kind of taking away revenue that we had recorded in the past. Now the problem with this method Of course is that when we record this expense we will be reducing net income at this point in time when really the sale that increased revenue happened in the past.

So it's a timing problem that we have not so good timing in terms of the direct write off method here. Let's see if we post this then we're going to post this to the general ledger account here. Then will record it to the subsidiary ledger so we're going to say that the bad debt is going to go up is the general ledger is the two accounts we're not going to show all the accounts for the general ledger every account year on the trial balance would have Book have a general ledger account showing the detail by date. That means it's going to go up from zero by 9000 to 9000 that's going to be the new balance.

Here's the accounts receivable that started out one million two hundred. The one million 200 was one million two hundred before this. Now we're going to bring it down by 9000 to 1 million 191. There's 1 million 191 now on trial balance after this transaction has happened. We also need to record this to the accounts receivable subsidiary Ledger. So we know that C-w is the individual that didn't pay us. We note that the accounts receivable over here on the trial balance and here on the general ledger show who owes us money. How much is owed to us. The G.L.

gives us detail but only by date the subsidiary Ledger would then give us detail about who owes us this money. We're just going to show the account first C-w here. But in a subsidiary ledger we would be having all the accounts of the customers own money and if summed up then it would add up to the amount on the trial balance. So in this case C-w owes us that nine thousand. We're going to say that they're not going to pay us. We're going to take it out of the subsidiary account and that will bring it down to zero. Now the major problem and difference here between the two methods is that under this method the direct write off method we brought in didn't income down by this nine 9000 we had revenue 378 monsters 9 0 0 0.

We just recorded bringing net income the subtraction of those two to three thousand six sixty nine. Three hundred and sixty nine thousand under the allowance method we would have recorded that through the allowance account that we would have already set up not decreasing net income at that point in time that we determined that something will not be due. But having already done so or estimating what the decrease will be trying to match up the bad debt expense to the revenue that it was actually incurred in rather than waiting and so we determine when something is uncollectable note that we have a lot of control over net income in some ways.

If we're able to then decide when we think something is going to be a bad debt because we can write things off at certain times or wait and not write them off. And that can have a significant influence on the net income. On the other hand if we are forced to basically make an estimate of how much we think of this revenue will be uncollectible then we at least have to give a guess as to what we think a fair number would be that would be uncollectible related to the revenue earned during this time period. Next transaction we're going to say that the company had a payment of 20000 or 30000. In other words of this receivable this one million 91000 the company owes us 30000. But they're going to go bankrupt or something happened. We're only going to get 20,000. We're not going to get the rest.

We can imagine them going bankrupt. We're going to get 20,000 in bankruptcy. 10000. It's something that we're not going to get. We're going to write it off therefore we can say OK cash went up just like a normal payment on account cash is a debit balance. We're going to make it go up by doing the same thing. It's another debit of 20000 then we're going to credit the accounts receivable. The account here Of course saying that they owe us money it's going to go down because they don't owe us money anymore. This is a debit balance account and therefore it goes down with the opposite of a debit or credit.

However we're not going to credit the 20000 but the 30000 The total owed to us so that we totally remove the amount that's owed to us off the books our debits do not equal our credit. Now we need a debit of ten thousand. That then is going to go under the direct write off method to bad debt expense. This is what will differ under the two methods and the direct write off method. It goes to bad debt expense under the allowance method. It would go into the allowance for doubtful accounts. So there's going to be the same type of transaction we had before. Only difference being that we received a partial payment. So don't let that throw you off if you see a partial payment then we're still going to go through our normal transactions we're going to say is cash affected. Yeah.

We're going to increase the cash then just note that you have to take the receivable off but not for the amount received. But for the entire amount because we're not going to get the rest therefore needing to remove the full amount owed by this Cupps customer so we don't show that they still owe us ten thousand. They don't know anything anymore because we gave up on the other 10000. Then we have to decide how we're going to even this thing out. We do so with another debit. If we then post this to our general ledger accounts over here and our subsidiary ledger.

And then we'll take a look at our Indian trial balance. We're going to say that it will go up from 100,000 by the year 20. So we posed that to the G.L. account increasing the goal to 120000. That Of course will now match our trial balance after we post that then we're going to say the accounts receivable of these thirty thousand credits we had 1 million 191 here. It's going down by 30 to 1 million 161. That then matches what will be on the trial balance. Then the bad debt here is the thing that will defer the bad debt changing as we determine that something will not be collectible. Going from 9000 years to 10 years 10 going up by 10 to 19000 that then the amount in the bad debt on the trial balance note once again that the revenue is going and the net income is going down. Bad debt going up is bringing net income down.

That's going to be the major difference between the direct write off method and the allowance method under the allowance method. This gentleman would not be affecting net income. Net income would only be affected when we make an estimate about what the bad debt should be, not based on when it is becoming bad. But based on matching it to the revenue at the same time period. Now we can do that with two different methods. We'll talk about the latter point. But remember that the allowance method should have a better matching principle between the revenue and the bad debt happening in the same time period.

Then we have the accounts receivable subsidiary ledger. Remember that the accounts receivable here represents how much is owed to us but doesn't give us any more detail than that the accounts receivable here gives us detail but only by date of transaction we need that detail by who owes us money that's going to be the accounts receivable subsidiary ledger. We're only going to look at this particular customer here, this customer GTE company but all the customers remember would be included in this subsidiary ledger if we added up all customers. It would then add up to the accountant on the trial balance. And on the general ledger we're going to say we told the same thing this thirty thousand goes here and that's going to bring the balance down to zero. So that's critical.

We know that the company doesn't owe us any more money; they paid us 20 even though the oldest 30. We took the entire 30 off the books not leaving that ten thousand still owed to us because we gave up on it and therefore needed to take the entire authority off the books bringing them down to zero. Next transaction we're going to say received a payment from C-w after writing it off. This is going to be a typical book type transaction not so typical when we have a real life situation because if we wrote off the bad debt we totally gave up on it. So we gave up on the bad debt and then and that doesn't normally happen until we go through a pretty significant collection process.

And then after we gave up on it we're not calling anymore we're not actively trying to collect on it. It then gets paid at some point in the future. How do we deal with that? That's a great book question because it really emphasizes the difference between the two methods and how we are going to kind of reverse this transaction. Now it is going to be the trickiest thing that we have here because typically if we got paid you would think that we would debit cash and then we would credit what we did. We know we wrote it off to bad debt. So you would think OK go ahead roll off the bad debt. I can just credit that debt.

So typically we would go through our questions. Is Cash affected? Yeah. Debit cash. And then the other side can't get that receivable because I wrote it off. Where do we write it off to bad debt. So we could debit cash and credit bad debt. However, we're not going to do that. And this is kind of an exception to the rule of dealing with cash first and that is because if we do that we bypass the accounts receivable and we don't have a record showing us that in the receivable account in the subsidiary ledger for this customer that they actually paid it. What we want to do is put them back in good standing on the receivable account and then write it off as we normally would. Therefore we're going to do this with two transactions and two entries. We're going to put them back on the books.

We're going to say the receivables are going to go back up. We wrote off the receivable, we're reversing the write off and then we're going to put the other side to bad debt expense meaning when we wrote it off we credited the receivable to take it down and under the direct write off method we put the other side to bad debt expense. We're just reversing that now. We're going to put that debit to accounts receivable and the credit to bad debt just reversed right after it happened because it didn't really happen because they actually paid us so we gave up on them. Soon note that this bad debt expense is part of the reversal in part of the difference it would be between the two methods under the allowance method.

This amount would have been written off to the allowance and therefore it would be reversed. Now to the allowance. Once we do that then the second piece is easy because it's our normal transaction we got paid on account the accounts receivable is back in good standing. Therefore we're going to say is cash affected. Yeah. It's a debit or increasing cash with a debit card a debit to cash and then we're decreasing the receivable which we just increased by 9000. So I Can we could simplify this transaction you can look at this and say hey we're duplicating the information. I mean I've got accounts of Siebel here and I've got accounts receivable here and it's just doing the same thing. Being debited once being credited. I could eliminate those too.

We just eliminate these too. We would be left with a debit to the checking account and credit to the bad debt. The problem once again is that we want to see the paper trail in accounts receivable. We want to be able to go to the council, see a subsidiary ledger and say yeah this person paid us. We're willing to do business with them in the future. We can't see that if we don't reverse the transaction and then put it through the subsidiary ledger. Let's take a look at the record in this. Then we're going to say first the accounts receivable is going to go back on the books that we took them off the books here in the subsidiary Ledger back on the books in the receivable increase in the amount to one million. One hundred and seventy here on your side and that's all it's there right now other than others.

It's going to go into bad debt. Bad debt is being reversed here. So here's the bad debt that we wrote off incorrectly. We gave up on it too soon. We are reversing it here at this point in time bringing the 19 down by the nine to the ten thousand. Then we're going to record the second piece which is just a normal transaction for a receipt on account. Receiving money for the accounts receivable for something that we did in the past. So here's the cash going up. Here's the cash going up. And that brings the balance from 120 to 129. And the other side of it is going to be the accounts receivable here. It's going to be the credit. Here's the credit. So note what happened we started before this process in the receivable general ledger at one million.

One sixty one. And then we brought it up, putting them back in good standing and back down to bring us back to that same spot. One on One sixty one thousand we'll see that same process in the subsidiary Ledger the subsidiary ledger for CW. Remember we had 9000 we gave up on them, wrote them off left leaving us at 0 and then ignored those 9000 here we're at zero at this point in time. And then we have the other side of it is going to be a debit to the accounts receivable. So the accounts receivable is going up with this 9000 putting them back on the books. So we took them down to zero. Put them back on the books at nine thousand. Bring it back up to a 9000 balance. That's from this transaction.

And then we're just going to take it right back off the books for the accounts receivable for CW here. So CW another 9000 bringing the balance back down to zero. So if we look at the subsidiary Ledger remember that this would be a subsidiary ledger with every account for every customer. However we're just looking at CWI subsidiary ledger. They had 9000 owed to us. We wrote it off in the past prematurely. We should not have done so because this was still a good customer. They just paid very late apparently. And so we brought it down to zero and then we want to see that we put them back in good standing here so that we can see the paper trail bringing them back up to nine thousand.

And then we record they paid us. If we look at this payment then it still brings us down to zero. But we can look at this page and say well how did we get paid and see that they actually gave us money whereas if we looked at this transaction and we just left it here and we didn't record the other two we would drill down on that transaction and say well they didn't pay us and that would probably stop us from doing business with them in the future. We want to say they're back in good standing and they paid us here therefore we can still do business in the future.

Note the effect here is going to be on the bad debt. The bad debt is now going down and that's going to be a difference between the allowance method and the direct write off method where the allowance account would be the account affected. That would mean no effect to the net income or the income statement accounts at all under the allowance method whereas under the direct write off method Of course that debt is affected. And it would then bring bad debt going down bringing net income up.

Worksheet Direct Write Off Method

In this chapter we will work on an accounts receivable problem related to the direct write off method. The information for the problem will be on the left side. We're going to put the data into the general journal and then post it to the general ledger. The general ledger will then be used to create the trial balance. Note we're only going to use a few accounts here, a shortened amount of accounts just so we can focus on those accounts. We are concentrating on that theme in accounts receivable and the bad debt we're focusing on on those accounts. Now I'm going to include an ad here. The allowance for doubtful accounts just because we want to be able to compare and contrast this method to the allowance method we're not going to use this account. It wouldn't be on the trial balance if we were using the direct write off method.

But again it's a good comparison between this method and the allowance method, the allowance method being the method that would be required under generally accepted accounting principles. However the direct write off method being the method often used for small companies that aren't using that want a more simplified method or companies that have very little in terms of write offs and therefore it will be in material and they can use that direct write off method which is typically an easier method will take less steps and we'll see why. So we also know that we're going to be focusing on the receivables.

Our idea here is that some of those receivables, those sales we've made, the money owed to us will not be paid to us by some customers and therefore we're going to have to deal with how to deal with that. Now we know that this receivable account will be backed up by the accounts receivable general ledger here. So here's the general ledger account but it only gives the supporting data by date and we want to see the supporting data by customer. So therefore we also need an accounts receivable subsidiary ledger and that's going to be down here it's going to give us the customers that US money and the balances per customer.

And then if we add all that up we'll get to that same amount that was on the trial balance as well as the general ledger also giving us that detail that we need and who owes us the money so we can follow up and collect the money owed. So we're going to turn this data on the left side. Let's go through this information. First one is on to 17 says that it was determined that C-w company would not pay off the amount owed of 9000. Now this is going to be the typical type of problem that would be in the case of either direct write off method or the allowance method someone is coming to us and saying that they're not going to pay us or we just can't contact we've been contacting this person forever they've disappeared or this company is no longer in service and we're not going to get paid.

Now we know that nine thousand eight gave us it here. They gave it to her that amount but we can also see that if we went over to the subsidiary Ledger I'm going to the right. I'm going down to the subsidiary ledger here C-w company.

Here's the 9000 owed to us. That's not going to be paid to us. Its part of accounts receivable is part of the total balance here. The one that is one million two hundred. Therefore we're going to have to write down that receivable by 9000. So it's going to be our first component of the journal entry of this receivable of the 1200000 9000 is not going to be paid to us. So we're going to have to give up on the collection of it. It's just not going to happen.

So this is a debit balance indicated by the fact that it does not have brackets. We're going to make it go down by doing the opposite thing to it which is a credit. So I'm going to copy all six right clicks and copies. We're going to put that in C6 right click and paste one two three. I've already indented here you can go to the Home tab alignment and increase indenting or just double click on the cell and hit the spacebar three times and that'll indent it. We need a credit of nine thousand. I'm going to represent a credit with a negative number. So I don't put negative nine thousand and enter then we need a debit up here 9000. I'm going to do that with a little formula and it equals hitting negative. And then select at 9000 and enter. So I'll just take this number and flip the sign.

We could just type in nine thousand. I just like using that formula whenever possible. Now we just need to know what this account will be. And this is going to be the difference between the direct write off method and the allowance method. The allowance method would be selecting the allowance account. Here we would typically have an amount in the allowance that we had pre estimated to be something that needs to be written off based on either the I counted on the prior period or the sales under the direct method. We don't have this account of this count. It's read here because it's not there but this is the comparison we want to make. Instead we're just going to write it off to bad debt when it happens when it becomes uncollectible.

Now why would that be bad. Because we'll see that as we post this it'll decrease net income in this time period. But this 9000 was probably not earned and this year 2017 was probably earned last year. So this is really kind of a violation of the matching principle. If it's a significant amount we should really be trying to put this 9000 bad debt expense to the same time period in which the revenue related to it was earned. And that's the whole point of the allowance method if it's not material. If the 9000 is not material or these write offs typically are small for the business then the direct write off method that we're using now is easier because we actually know what the amount is at the point in time that it becomes uncollectible.

So we're just going to say OK 9000 we gave up on at this point in time we're going to write it off to the bad debt expense at this point in time there's really no estimating going on here it is what it is. So the bad debt expense is an expense account and they all have debit balances. We're going to go up by doing the same thing with another debit. So all right click and copy that bad debt expense going to put that in see 5. Right click and paste one two three. Now we're going to post this. So here's the bad debt expense on our journal entry. Here it is on the trial balance. So it's one of the last accounts in the general ledger. It's in order of assets , liabilities Equity Income Expense same order and the general ledger assets and liabilities, equity and expenses. So we're way over here in the bad debt expense.

We're in a nine a nine. I'm going to say equals and we're going to scroll to the right and we're going to find that bad debt expense and D 5. So there it is indeed D5 and enter. Or you could just type in the 9000 but I highly highly recommend formulas you could also type in equals the. Note that I've added a few more cells here because I think we might need a few more cells. So here's the 9000 if we screwed over to the trial balance then Of course that 9000 will be here as well. That puts us out of balance and it brings net income and broad net income down that calculated by this 3 7 8 thousand minus the nine thousand net income is decreasing. And again that's really the point of contention between the two methods between the allowance and direct write off method.

The argument being for the allowance method the preferred method for generally accepted accounting principles that the 9000 should be decreasing not this period is net income but the prior periods. Net income. And in order to do that you would have to make an estimate on the prior period net income of how much you believe would be uncollectible based on past performance. So the other side's going to go to accounts receivable here it is on the journal entry here it is on the trial balance and it's going to be the second account. So it's the second account here as well. So here is the second account we want to be on the credit side. So we are on the credit side here 16 and so 16 16. We will say equals and then point to that 9000.

I'll bring the 1200000 down by 9000 to 1 million. 91 Of course we also see that 1 million 191 here that puts this back in balance as well. Now this information shows us who owes how much money is owed to us if we want more detail on that. We see more detail here by date of when transactions happened. And if we want to know who owes us money however we need another ledger we call the subsidiary Ledger down here. So we need to record that same information in that same journal entry. We can take it from the journal entry or from the G.L. here in the subsidiary Ledger. So we here in TI 31 weigh down here in 2:31 we're going to say equals.

And I'm just going to take the same information from that G.L. that 9000. This is basically like another G-0. It's just formatted rather than just by date by customer first and then date. And so if we add all the customers up then add up to 1 million. One 91 that ties out to what's on the accounts receivable. General Ledger which also ties out to what's on the trial balance next transaction. We're going to stay on for 12. The company made a partial payment and went bankrupt. It was determined that we will not receive the balance. So this time this company is going bankrupt and they said hey we can pay you and when the bankruptcy is probably 20000 and they're not going to be paying us 10000.

In other words let's go look at how much the energy company owes us on the subsidy ledger. It's going to scroll the right way and say Gee company they went bankrupt. That's not good. They owe us thirty thousand. We're going to get as much as we can of that apparently 20000. So we're going to have to write down this 30000 by the entire amount. We're never going to get it back. We're going to get cash of 20000 and then we'll have a difference that will have to be recorded somewhere. So let's think that through again up here we're going to say here's a council sealable they're paying us off 10000 or 20000.

So the first thing we might take off is cash. And so yeah we've got $20000 cash and a debit balance account. We need to make it go up so we're going to do the same thing to it. Another debit so we can start with that. I'm going to copy the cash count in L5 right click and copy. We're going to put that in C-8 right click and paste one two three. The amount will be 20000. Then typically if someone pays us for an account for something they oh yes it's DEQ accounts receivable. So we're going to credit the accounts receivable because we didn't make the sale today. They paid us on account. So count Sibyls he has a debit balance we need to make it go down.

So we'll do the opposite thing to our credit when it copies accounts receivable, put that in C9 right click and paste one two three. I'll go ahead and end by going to the home tab alignment increase in Dantin. You can double click on here and hit the spacebar three times as well. The tricky part here is that we're not going to get credit for 20000 because if we did sell it would still show that they owed us 10000. Given the fact that they owed us for this transaction 30000 but we're never going to get the other 10000. So we can't just leave it there. We have to take it down to zero. So we're going to credit it for a negative credit of 30000 and then we're gonna have a difference Of course of 10000 to make our transaction in balance.

We have 10 20000 here debits and 30000 credits. So we're going to need another debit. So going to be here in 10 DTN and we could just put the ten thousand here but I like to put a formula here. So we're going do that with a little formula. So and so that equals negative. And then as you end the sum function the most common function will double click that some function highlight from the 20000 down to the 30000 and enter. So sum up those sales. It will highlight those, it'll add them up and flip the sign. It would be a negative $10000 deposit of 10000. And note that I'm going to put the debit out of order. I'm not going to put it on top because this is how I think it's easy to think through this transaction.

It's easiest to think " oh we're going to do something with the cash the other side gets from their accounts receivable but we have to take the whole thing out and then we have a difference here. If you want to shuffle that around or if you need a multiple choice question the two debits will probably go on top in that format if you want to go they will figure things out in practice then whatever order makes the most sense may trump the idea of having the debits on top all the time. So now we're going to say that that 10000 Where does that go to. Well if it were the allowance method it would go to the allowance account here which we would already have an estimate for but under the direct write off method as we did here we are going to write it off directly to bad debt expense at the point in time we determine it becomes uncollectible reducing net income at this point in time that it became uncollectible that being the contentious topic because really the revenue it was earned not in the year 2000.

For this year whatever year this is it was earned in the prior year and therefore it's not a violation of the match in principle. So if it's a small amount if it's in material it's not a big deal but if it's a large amount if it's significant to decision making we shouldn't be using the direct write off method for that reason we should be using the allowance method. So we're going to say bad debt as a debit balance. We're going to make it go up by doing the same thing with another debit. So we're going to copy the bad debt right click and copy. We're going to put that in Cetin right click and paste one to three so there's going to be our transaction we're going to post this out now. So here's the cash count here in our general journal. Here it is on the trial balance. The first account is going to be the first count on the general ledger then as well.

We're going to be here in 0 9 so we are in 0 9. We're going to say equals and just point to that 20000 bringing in that 10 or 100000 up by 20000 to 120000. That amount Of course appearing now on the trial balance putting us out of balance by 20000 then we'll record the accounts receivable side the 30000. So here the 30000 here. Here it is on the trial balance second account second account then as well on the general ledger. Are we to go down here to up the 17 so I mean the 17 and we will say equals and point to that thirty thousand. It's going to bring that debit balance at one point 191 down by a thousand to one no one.

Sixty one thousand. And then the last one is going to go to the bad debt expense which is way down here it's going to be the second to last the count on the trial balance going to be in the same order on the general ledger assets ingrained liabilities in orange. I think we just got one down here. It's right there in that we've got the capital revenue and expenses. So we want to be here in 88 and we are in a 10 and we will say equals scroll all the way to the left. I'm just using the scroll bar left or the arrows scrolling with the arrows. And we're going to point to that 10000 and DTN we are indeed 10 and enter. So here's our balance that went from nine thousand Baghdad extends up by the 10000 to the 19000 that amount then will also be found on the trial balance.

Scrolling back to the balance there's the 10000 here on there it is on that general journal. But the 19000 that was on the general ledger is now here on the trial balance. OK so the next thing we need to do Of course is that we reduce the accounts receivable by 30000 this 30000 we need to do the same thing to the subsidiary ledger which is the same stuff with the same information. However rather than being an order by just date it is an order by customer first and then date. So if we scroll down here to look for the customer it was a customer I believe because it was at 30000 0. So we need to bring this down. They don't think it was anything anymore; they only pay us $20.

They really kind of were 10 but we gave up on it. They went bankrupt. We're never going to get it. So here we're just going to say an I mean p. 31 where and so p. 31 will say equals. And then scroll back up and point to that 30000 Panter. That'll bring the 30000 down by 30000 to zero. If we look at our total accounts then they all add up to 1 million 161 for all customers that will Of course be the same amount on the accounts receivable general ledger and on the trial balance next transaction we're going to say it is on 7 to receive payment from C-w after we had assumed the debt uncollectible and had written it off. Now this is going to be really common in these types of problems.

A direct write off or an allowance method problem because it really gives us an example of these methods and what the differences are between the methods. In practice it probably doesn't happen, it's not going to happen all the time or very very rarely because we're going to do everything we can to collect on the receivable. So we don't write the receivable off until we've done everything we can do to collect on it. So for us to have written the receivable off and then a customer to walk in the door and say hey here's that nine thousand I owed you. You know like five years ago that you've been trying to collect on forever. That's right. And you gave up on it. I'm no longer getting any mail on it. So.

So someone that's the scenario here someone owed us money we made a sale 9000. We try to collect on it forever. We couldn't get it. We couldn't get any money. We totally gave up, we stopped collection action completely and just said that we're going to give up. It's not worth our time to keep on going after this. And then C-w comes in and actually pays us at a later point in time. That's that's the scenario. So under this scenario you would think this is one kind of violation of what our normal rule is and that is is cash affected and we're going to say yeah we've got $9000 and we're going to increase if we increase cash by 9000 and then we could credit the other side to what we took the amount off by which was the bad debt account meaning. OK. Don't do this.

But we could say OK copy checking account don't do this again. This is just an example and page that one two three and copy the bad debt and that would be the credit and that would make sense because we wrote the accounts receivable off to bad debt and now they paid us. So the bad debt needs to go down. And we got the cash. So that would make sense. But what happens there is we know the subsidiary Ledger would never be adjusted. We know it would never go through accounts receivable showing that they owed us money. What we want is a paper trail and accounts receivable. I want to look at a subsidiary ledger and say Oh that is his.

His account was paid not that it wasn't paid even though it was paid late. We want to be able to see that. So we can't just do this kind of shortcut method which would work but it doesn't show us the detail we want to see in the subsidiary Ledger. So what we're going to do instead is reverse what we did up here. Here's the journal entry we did to write off this person and this was a mistake in essence because the person actually or the company came back and actually came through late very late. But one actually paid us so we want to put them back in good standing and then do the normal transaction of writing it off.

So if someone says that we gave up on something and then they paid us we're just going to reverse what happened before. So accountancy was going to go back up. So we'll debit accounts receivable. So when I copy they count Siebel and else's right click and copy we're going to put that in see. Well right click and paste one two three and then we're going to reverse the bad debt expense. So here's the bad debt expense. Here it is on the trial balance. We're going to credit it in order to reverse this transaction, this kind of mistake we made. So in all 11 we're going to right click and copy bad debt expenses. We're going to put that in see 13. Right click and paste one two three.

I'm going to then not go into the home tab alignment increase in Denton or you can just double click spacebar three times and then we're going to put the amount which is only nine thousand debit credit. I'm going to do that with that little formula which will be negative of that 9000. So that'll put us back in good standing and that'll put that receivable back in. Correct this kind of error. We did, we gave up, we didn't have faith in this person, this company and we should have held out a little bit longer. Another really late and then now we're going to do the normal transaction. We would do it if the customers were back in good standing which is cash affected.

Yeah they paid us nine thousand cash and a debit balance. We're going to make it go up by doing the same thing to it's another debit so I'm going to copy L5 right click and copy. I'm going to skip a line, make another transaction, see 15 reichlich and paste one two three. The amount will be nine thousand and then we're going to credit 9000 again. I would do that with our little formula negative of that 9000 and enter. And this is just going to be our normal transaction as if you know bad debt was never a part of it. Meaning they paid us off on account of the Odo's money for a transaction sale that happened in the past at tables. A debit balance we need to make goes down because they no longer owe us that $9000.

So we're going to copy the account Siebel in all six right click and copy. We're going to put that in see 16. Right click and paste one two three going to go ahead and indent that by going to the home tab alignment increases indenting. So all we did here was reverse what happened and then do our normal transaction when someone pays us. And so let's post that out now. So we've got the accounts receivable first. That's our second account on our trial balance. Second account on the general ledger here it is an oh we're 18 because we want to be on the debit side here of 18 and we are here we're going to say equals and we're going to point to that 9000 and enter so that brings the balance back up to 1 million 170000 matches what's on the trial balance. I'm also going to record that on the subsidiary Ledger.

So if we go down to the subsidiary ledger we see the nine thousand here we need to put it back on the books it was on the books. We took it off the books for CW. Now we're going to put it back on the books. I'm back in good standing in the company. Equals when I scroll back up and just pick up that same nine thousand. So now we're kind of back to the same place we were as if we didn't write them off so we're leaving an audit trail for us to see what we did and why we did it and then we're going to scroll back over and we're going to say right now bad debt is here. It's going to be way down here and on the trial balance.

Second to last count second to last count van as well on the general ledger. So we've got assets, liabilities , Equity Income and Expense. We're going to be over here with bad debt. We want to be on the credit side. So we are in a b 11 a B 11. We're going to say equals. Scroll to the left. Scroll to the left and we will find that bad debt expense right there. We want the credit side in IE 13 and entered. So that brings the nineteen thousand down to 10000. If we scroll back over to the trial balance that 10000 should also be on the trial balance right there. That puts us back in balance.

Now we need to record the second of the two journal entries for this transaction checking account. We now have cash. Now we can record the cash to our normal transaction for the receipts on accounts from the customer checking account as our first account. Of course it needs to go up. So we're going to debit it's going to be the first account on the general ledger. Here it is on oh 10 oh 10 we're going to say equals point to that 9000 bringing a balance of 120 up by nine thousand to one hundred twenty nine thousand. Then we're going to record the accounts receivable side Of course that same amount here on the trade balance. And we're out of balance by 9000 then the accounts receivable side is your second account on the trial balance.

Therefore a second account on the general ledger as well. We're going to go to the credit side. P 19 19 equals pointing to that 9000 and enters bringing the bounce back down. So just look at the repetition here. We started here at 1 9 161. We put it on. We brought it up by 9000 and then brought it back down. Seems pointless to do that other than it gives us an audit trail. In other words we could have got to the same point by removing this and this and just having this journal entry deboning and checking and crediting the bad debt expense. However that doesn't give us an audit trail so that's why we're doing the detail.

Same thing down here in the subsidiary Ledger why we want the detail. We recorded it here bringing the balance to one million 161 that matches the trial balance. That puts it back in balance. We also want the details on the subsidiary Ledger. So if we scroll back down we're in C-w company we're going to bring the 9000 back down again very repetitively. We had 9000 here. We wrote it off. We put it back on the books and we wrote it off again because they paid us. And the point is that this would show us that this account this customer no good not someone we want to do business with because it looks like they never paid us but by just putting it back on the books and then taking it off with an indication that they did pay us we can see that they paid us and and we would more likely do business with them in the future. So we're going to put that same amount in t 33 equals scroll back up and just post that same 9000 here.

And that brings it back down to zero. So they don't owe us any money anymore. And if we add everything up we're at 1 million 161 for all the customers in the subsidiary ledger that match what's on the trial balance that matches what's on. Well that Matchroom was on the general ledger matching what's on the trial balance as well. Next transaction if we scroll back over we're on a 20 says determined that the company and the company would not pay the amount owed. So P and D-B now they didn't give us the amounts at this time. So now we have to go over here and say a subsidiary ledger for PPI and so this one and this one.

So I could just highlight this and I'm holding down control and that and Excel will highlight it or add it for 14:7 or you know I should be able to do that in my head with my project where I could do that over again. So it's obvious a 6 of them was that 8000 and that's going to be 14:7. So 14:7 is what we're gonna have to write off. It's going to have to reduce the receivable by these two amounts and I'm going to go ahead and highlight these two so I can say these two are the ones we're taking off the books and it's going to be for that 14:7 So let's calculate that one more time. So it's the eight thousand plus the six 14:7.

So if we scroll back over here it's the same same idea and now that we have 2 customers doesn't change anything. Accounts receivable as far as the journal entry goes. It's going down by some of those two 14:7. So we're going to assume that the accounts table has a debit balance. We're going to make it go down by doing the opposite thing to get a credit so I get a copy of the council sealable right click and copy scroll down and put it on the bottom so on and see 19. Right click and paste one two three indents. Going into the home tab alignment increases indent. You could double click and click the spacebar three times as well and the amounts are going to be here. I'm going to put this at 14:7. I'm going to put a credit by a negative 1 4 7 0 0 0. Then we're going to have a debit for the same amount. We're going to do that with a little formula or I will.

I would practice formulas any time and every time. That's what I do. It's got to be negative of this number. There we have it. Now we're going to need the debit and this once again will be what the difference is between the allowance method and direct write up. Would you use this account which is not being used at all here because we're using the direct write off method. This is just a demonstration to have it there and we instead are going to be writing it directly off to the bad debt expense which will increase the expense decreasing the net income.

At this point in time that being the point of contention we're decreasing net income now even though the revenue was earned in the past and under the matching principle we would rather match the expense to the revenue earned. Only way to do that is with an estimate. That's why we would have the allowance method. So if it's immaterial however this is an easier method to use the direct write off method. So we're going to do this. This is a debt of balance. We're going to go up by doing the same thing to it another day that we're going to copy all 11 by right clicking and copy scroll back down where to put that in see 18 reichlich is 1 2 3. So here's the amount: it's 14:7. What is it to see and DTN?

Well we have put that here. It's going to be our second to last account on the trial balance and therefore also the second to last account on the general ledger. So we've got the assets, the liabilities, the equity and the bad debt. We're way over here in a 12. We are in 12 bad debt expense debit 12. We will say equals we're going to scroll to the left. We're going to scroll down and we're going to go to that 14 7 in da 18 and enter. And that'll bring the balance from 10000 by the 14th. 1724 thousand seven hundred. It's going back over to the trial balance. Year that same amount. Twenty four thousand seven hundred. Here we are Of course out of balance by 14:7 until we record the other side. Here are the accounts receivable there's that 14 7.

If we scroll back up, that's the second account on the trial balance. Therefore the second account on the general ledger we're going to be here on the debit side on the credits that are going to be on the credit side or I'm calling the and we're going to go down to the 20. So we're in he went and we're going to say equals and to point to that 14:7 bring the balance from one million one sixty one thousand down by 14:7 to 1 million 146 thousand three hundred that amount also found on the trial balance. Next thing we need to do is report the same information on the subsidiary. You notice the detail here. We've got detail that shows us people it was one point forty six thousand three hundred. We need more detail.

The general ledger gives us more detail but only by date of occurrence. What we need to know is who owes the money. Therefore we're going to scroll back down and we get to put that same information down here. Now I know it's a little tricky. I can't really use a formula here . I mean I pretty much have to hard code this information because we combined the two transactions up here. So this is one area where we're just going to have to basically say negative 6 7 0 0 and over here here's the 8000 we're going to bring that down by 8000 negative 8000. And obviously the 8000 if I clicked there and I hold down control and click here that's 14:7.

So there's the 14:7 that we had to break out between the company and the company bringing that to balance down to zero. If we sum up all of it then all the customers add up to 1 million 46 3. We have to then rely on this. So I mean to know that we're still in balance we have to hard code this number every scroll back up. We have that same amount on the account suitable general ledger. And Of course the same amount on the trial balance. Now that's going to be it for the direct write off method if we were talking about the allowance method then we would have to now make our estimate in order to estimate the allowance method that's going to be the other difference between the two methods here meaning we wrote off the bad debt expense when they happened in this time period and we earned revenue as it happened during this time.

We're not focused on the revenue transactions here. Note that we were not recording transactions related to the sales here. We're just focusing on the transactions related to accounts receivable and accounts becoming not due. But if we earned three hundred seventy eight thousand. The point here is that we're writing off this 24/7. And that's really related to probably sales that happened last year not sales that happened this year. So we're kind of riding this expense off to do the wrong period. We have sales this year but this 24000 7 doesn't relate to this 370000 that we had this year under the direct write off method because they're really sales that we didn't have, they didn't become bad or not collectable until this year. So that means that the sale was actually made and recorded in revenue last year.

And that's going to be the issue between the two methods under the allowance method. We would if we would have written everything off to the allowance account up here where we had already made an estimate based on the revenue or based on the accounts receivable from the prior period and then we would have to now make another estimate for. And the idea there would be that we're trying to make an estimate based on the revenue earned at this time period and match the bad debt. What we think is going to be uncollectible for the sales that happened this time period it was going to be the differences between our Some a brief description of the differences between the two methods just note that under the direct write off method this twenty four thousand seven hundred is bringing down net income at a point in time that we determined that the accounts would be uncollectible.

Multiple Choice Questions - Accounts Receivable

In this chapter we will take a look at multiple choice questions related to receivables. First question: the materiality constraint A does not allow the use of the direct write off method B requires the use of the allowance Method C requires use of direct write off method that permits the use of direct write off method. When bad debt expenses are relatively small or e requires that expenses be reported in the same period as sales they helped produce. So we'll go through this again and go through the process of eliminating the materiality constraint A does not allow the use of the direct write off method.

Now if we don't know what the materiality constraint materiality extreme constraint is we may think that the direct write off method is a good answer because the direct write off method is not the preferred method. Now if we go through some of these we might be able to use them to have some process of elimination. So the Says requires use of the allowance method. So aces did not allow the use of the direct write off method and Beezus required the use of the allowance method. Now those are basically you know there's only two methods typically to write off the accountancy. Either we use the direct write off method or the allowance method.

So if A says we are not allowed to use the direct write off method and B says we are required to use the allowance method that can't both be right. And so those almost eliminate each other from the answers here C says requires the use of the direct write off method so that one just intuitively doesn't make sense really because the allowance method is typically the one that we would think is the preferred method. So if there's going to be any one that is required you would think it would be the allowance method that would be required so I don't think so. Sounds good. DS says permits the use of the direct write off method when bad debt expenses are relatively small and so that gives a qualification here we get. We might be able to use the direct route method and then Eiza requires that the expenses be reported in the same period as the sales they helped produce and that actually sounds kind of good too. Right.

I mean that I've heard that somewhere what type of principle is that so let's read through this one more time. See if we can just use the process of elimination as if we don't really know what materiality is and then see if we can define it. So the materiality constraint A does not allow the use of the direct write off method or B requires the use of the allowance method which are both of those cannot be right. And they seem to be you know if one is true then the other seems like it should be true. So I'm going to say that those both can't be true. And that's basically telling us that it's not requiring the allowance method.

And then he says permits the use of the direct write off method when bad debt expenses are relatively small. That sounds kind of reasonable because that would mean that we usually would need to have to use the allowance method unless something happens less the direct write offs are pretty small. So that sounds pretty good. And then it says the expenses should be reported in the same period as the sales they helped produce. And that sounds really good. That sounds familiar to me but that's an accrual principle that's a standard accrual principle. One of the main to the matching principle and it's not really dealing with the materiality constraint here directly. So that's although it probably rings a bell. It's not the one we're looking at here. So does the one we want.

So materiality constraint means that you know if something is small enough that it doesn't affect decision making processes then we can use that non-preferred method which is the direct write off method. So the direct write off method does not apply the match in principle as well but it's easier typically. And if the difference is in material because of the dollar amount then it would be permitted to use. Given this materiality constraint. So once again the materiality constraint permits the use of direct write off meth head when bad debt expenses are relatively small.

Next question and accounts receivable subsidiary Ledger is important for all reasons except a. It shows how much each customer has purchased on credit. It shows how much payment history per customer sees. It shows how much each customer owes D. It helps to generate invoices and it tells us when customers plan to pay. Let's go through this again with the process of elimination and accounts receivable subsidiary Letcher is important for all the reasons. Except now when we think about a Accounts Receivable subsidiary ledger we first probably want to define that as we go through these questions and see which ones would apply or not the subsidiary Ledger is going to be supporting backing up the amount on the general ledger or on the trial balance or on the balance sheet.

Now the general ledger supports that information. But given the detail by date what we want to do is give the details to the customer and that's what we're doing here we're trying to give the details to the customers so that we know who owes us the money. So Avon says it shows how much each customer has purchased on credit. That's typically what we're doing. That's what the subsidiary Letcher is therefore. So it's not that one that's what it does for sure. He says it shows how much payment history per customer should be payment history per customer and it does show the payment history because it shows how much they bought and the payments that they made. So he says it shows how much each customer owes.

And again it does show how much each customer owes because it's going to show the purchases, the payments and how much is still owed by the customers. And that says it helps to generate invoices which shows how much the customers are so it helps us to collect on the invoice and or to generate them so yellow is good. And then he says it tells us when the customer plans to pay. So of all this it doesn't really tell us even how it has the term of when the payment is due but the customer Of course could pay any time if it's due 30 days from now the customer could pay us any time within the 30 days. Hopefully they will pay us by the end of the term. At the end of 30 days hopefully sooner than that we'd like to get the money sooner.

But I don't really it doesn't really know when the customer can, you know, be in the customer's head and we don't know that. So I think this is the correct answer. So the question and answer one more time is an accounts receivable subsidiary. Pleasure is important for all reasons except it tells us when the customer plans to pay.

Allowance Method

Within the 11th method chapter of the Book we'll be discussing the allowance method. The allowance method is a method for dealing with bad debt expense and the valuation of accounts receivable and is the preferred method for generally accepted accounting principles for dealing with accounts receivable valuation and bad debt expense. The reason it's preferred is it's going to be a better match in principle than the direct write off method. In other words it's going to be able to match up the revenue and the expense related to it in terms of the bad debt as well as give a better evaluation on the balance sheet for how much would actually be collectible for accounts receivable giving the accounts receivable amount and then the amount we think is uncollectable which would give a more conservative estimate.

If we subtract two out of how much the receivable actually is which would be preferable from a conservative type of standpoint for the readers of the financial statements. The problem with the allowance method is that it's a little bit more complex to do and it does require us to make some estimates in order to come up with what we believe to be the valuation of the accounts receivable account at any given time as well as the valuation of the bad debt expense to write off in a given period related to the revenue that has been earned.

Allowance Method Accounts Receivable

Hello when it's chapter we're going to take a look at the allowance method which is Of course related to the accounts receivable account. We will be able to define the allowance method of record transactions related to recording bad debt records and the receivable account that has been determined to be uncollectible and record every single count that has been collected after being determined that it was uncollectable. So we're going to take a look at some different transactions, the most common transactions when dealing with the allowance method and see what those look like and why we used the allowance method.

We're going to work through the problem. So what we're going to have here is we've got our accounting of the equation Of course we have our trial balance. I do suggest working problems to take a look at a child balance because it can give you the context in which to work problems. So here's what we have: we've got the assets in green. The liabilities are going to be orange, the light blue of the capital account and the equity chapter. And then we have the income statement the darker blue which is going to be the revenue and the expenses we can see in this example we have net income.

The net income is going to be cheaper as a revenue minus expenses. We don't have any expenses at this time we're just going to note this revenue number so that when we work through the problem we can see what the effect is on net income. Note that we're representing debits with positive numbers are not bracketed numbers and credits with bracketed numbers. That allows us to have fewer columns and use this quick worksheet to calculate the balancing of the debits and credits by having the debits minus the credits equals zero. And that's what we have here. We are going to be focusing on the receivable chapter Of course and we're going to post transactions to this trial to see the adjustment in relation to the trial balance.

Then we'll also look at the accounts related to the receivable accounts so oftentimes we'll take a look at the general ledger. There's going to be a general ledger account Of course related to all types of accounts, all accounts on the balance. We'll have a general ledger account which will be in order by date. We're going to look at the to general ledger accounts that are going to be working with in this problem being accounts receivable and the allowance accounts those We're going to look at Of course and just keep in mind that there's going to be other general ledger accounts for all of the accounts on the trial balance then we're going to take a look at the accounts receivable subsidiary Letcher.

So remember that the subsidiary Ledger is going to give the same detail that's basically in the general ledger. However instead of just breaking up by date it's going to break it out by a customer who owes the company money. So remember the questions that will happen in relation to the receivable. We're going to ask who knows Do people with money that people owe is one million two hundred who owes us money for that we go to the receivable account so we just have the generic name. These are our customers G company D Company G Geo's us 30 BIOSes 8 CDO zero Katie three thousand OSes for C-w OSes nine pearls of 6:07 and all other vendors.

Note that this thing our customers all of our customers know that this thing could be very long this subsidiary Ledger could be very long and we could have a professional account suitable for employees just tracking this information which would be dealing with this report a lot. All the other customers add up to 1 million 1:39 3 and that means that if we add all those up it adds up to 1 million. So note that the receivables subsidiary Ledger ties out to the general ledger ties out to the trial balance now the new account we have here will be the allowance account here.

So now we have an allowance account note that it's still green. It's an asset account but it has brackets meaning it's a credit balance account. What's a contra asset account? It's an asset account that has a debt credit balance which is contrary to the norm which is normally a debit balance of asset accounts. So the question many times when I teach a cruel accounting to new students they often think that the way we recognize revenue is overstating revenue under an equal basis because when we do work on account we're going to increase revenue and we increase the assets by increasing debit and receivables and credit in revenue. And if we haven't received the money there could be a valid argument to say well yeah we did the work and you can say we earned it but it could very well be that we never get the money.

And if we're recognizing revenue at the point of sale before we get the money then isn't it true that we're probably going to be overstating revenue by those revenues that we're not going to receive in cash. And isn't it true that the accounts receivable is going to be overstated by the amount that we're not going to get your reporting this asset of one million two hundred on the books. Pretty large asset. Are you sure you're going to get all that? Aren't we overstating?

And isn't there a generally accepted accounting principle that basically said that we want to be error on the conservative side meaning when we talk about conservatives it's conservatism in this case we don't mean political conservatism we mean that we'd rather err on the side of looking kind of worse meaning assets being understated and liabilities be overstated rather than the other way around. Because from an accepted accounting principle these statements are being geared towards outside users being stockholders and creditors and out we don't want to overstate our position to them.

So you can see from a regulatory body they would rather us err on the side of understating the receivable and it would seem that the accrual method does the exact opposite. And if not till this point that we can kind of talk about how the looks at that kind of principles deals with that and the way they deal with that as they say that we need to account for that we need to say hey you know what we have people with one million two hundred but we believe that in this case 40000 thousand is going to be uncollectible.

How do we know that we're going to talk a bit more about that towards the end but the general idea of a general principle will be that we need to tell our readers that we believe that certain amount is going to be uncollectible So if it's going to be significant if the amount is significant the generally accepted accounting principles requires us to use the allowance method rather than the direct write off method the allowance method is this method we're looking at here which says that we're going to have to report the amount of the receivable that we think is going to be collectible.

So under the direct write off method by contrast what would happen is for example if this individual C-w company could not pay C-w company went bankrupt or whatever we determined that this company is not going to pay us when they come to us and tell us OK we're not going to pass we we're going to look at their accounts receivable and say all right yeah they always 9000. We need to make that go down. So the receivable accounts are going to go down. When that happens under either method we use we know we've got to take it out of the receivable because we have now determined we're not going to receive it therefore we're going to credit the receivable we issued that debits go.

And if you think about it what really happened if we're not going to get paid by a client or customer It means that we overstated revenue at some point in the past in the past we overstated revenue because we increased revenue by say sale that's not really going to happen and really it's not really a sale. We're never going to get paid for it. So you would think that the debit would go to revenue which would reduce revenue because we overstated revenue. There's a couple of problems with that however. One is that we don't like to decrease revenue directly. Remember that revenue basically always goes up and we almost never debit revenue.

So and so therefore we make another accounting that other accounts are going to be called bad debt expense. So the expense is going to go up which brings down net income. So under the direct write off method that's what would happen we would take it out of the out the receivable and we would record the expense when it is determined that the client's not going to pay us and we wouldn't have this allowance account at all we wouldn't have it here and that would be a fairly simple method. That's the easiest method to do if the receivables are in material and in decision making then we can't use that method. But if the receivables are material there's another problem here and that is that note that if we write off this 9000 that we we wrote into revenue last year it was part of revenue last year and we're writing the expense related to it or the reduction in net income this year then we're violating the matching principle bit because we're reducing it in relation to this income. But the 9000 isn't included in this income and is not included in this 379 378 because it was earned.

We recorded it in income last period and we already closed that out to the capital retained earnings accounts. So that means that that's the problem. So under the accrual method what we want to do is match the expense with the revenue. So we want to look at the same time period and say okay

I'm going to. I'm going to say that this amount is going to be uncollectible in relation to this revenue and that's going to be an estimate. So we had to make an estimate and do that. We'll talk more about how that estimate will work later. But just know that at the end of last period we made an estimate and we said okay of the 1 million 2 that is outstanding. We believe that 40000 is not going to be collectible.

And now when someone comes to us and says that we're not going to pay the 9000 then instead of debiting the expense at that point in time we're just going to debit the allowance. So it would look like this. So under the allowance method when someone a customer is determined that they will not pay us then we're going to reduce the receivable with a credit. The debit will go to the allowance account. What will that look like in terms of the trial balance? Well we can see here that the receivables are going to be credited. So that's going to go down. So obviously that has to go down and all we're going to do on the other side is we're just going to debit the allowance. The allowance has a credit balance.

We're going to debit it doing the opposite thing to it which will make it go down. Notice that the book value of the receivables the net value is going to be unchanged because it was before one million to minus 40. That's the net value. And now receivables went down and so did the allowance so therefore now it's the one million 9 91 minus the 30 31. So notice there is no effect on net income down here and that is because we basically already wrote off this 9000 included in the 40000 last time period. When we created the allowance account, we'll do that again at the end of this chapter. So you can see if we go through our series of questions and we're going to ask what people always do with money. Yeah the travel agent says that people 1 million 191 well who will have some money.

Well if we look at the jail account it doesn't tell us that if we look at the jail account it just tells us by date that we had one million two and it went down by nine. If we look at the G.L. account for the allowance we can see that that's basically telling us that this wasn't enough that was not paid. And we had to write it off even though we were not paid for it. And then we're going to have to look at the subsidiary ledger which is an order by customers. So if we look at the customer in this case we're going to say that C-w is the one that we are writing off. So this nine here is also recorded here and it's also recorded here so this is the same information that is now recorded in terms of customers.

And then if you take that off now CW owes us 0 and we add up all the customers then it adds up to 1 million 191. So those are the people that it was money that ties out to the general ledger that ties out to the receivable account here and note that we have 31000 that we do not believe is collectible. We cannot apply that 31 to any of the actual customers because it's just an estimate. We don't know who's not going to pay as we just believe that certain folks aren't going to pay off based on prior experience.

So now we have a company that made a partial payment and went bankrupt. It is determined that we will not receive the balance. So we're going to receive 20000 of cash and then we're not going to receive the other 10. So if we look at it here we can see that the company owes us 30000. They're going to go bankrupt and within the bankruptcy assuming they paid off who they could which they paid off us 20 and then they're not going to pay the rest because they went bankrupt. So that is what's happened if we go through our series of questions then and we can say well is cash affected in this case it is. We got 20,000.

So we're going to increase cash. It's going to go up in the debit direction by 20%. Normally when we get paid the normal credit will go to in this case receivables because that's why they paid us they paid us to pay off the receivable. So the receivable has a debit balance. We're going to make you go down by credit in it. However we're not going to be accredited by that 20. We need to be accredited by the entire amount owed which is 30. And the reason for that is because if we only credited 20 then we would show that he owes us 10 still. And they don't or they're not going to pay us. So we've got to write that off.

So therefore we don't have a difference and we're going to need another debit. Where will that debit go? That is going to be the uncollectable portion which we're going to put into the allowance method. Remember under the direct write off method that debit would go to the bad debt expense at the time it was uncollectable or determined to be uncollectible under the allowance method. We already had this 31000 . We already estimated that that 10000 wasn't going to be collectible. We just didn't know who was not going to collect it. We already wrote it off in the prior period to match it to the income that was generated in the prior period.

And now we're just going to take it to the allowance that a journal entry would look like this. We have the debit to cash going up by the 20000 we're going to credit the receivable for the entire 30. And then the difference is going to the allowance to debit here. We can see that the 20 plus to 10 equals to 30 that debits equal the credits. Also note that I put it in this order because this is the order that when I think through the journal entry that's the order that works best for me to think through it. However if you're going to post this to something that's going to grade you on having that debits on top you might want to put the two debits on top if it helps you to audit or something like that and go back to the information and look at it.

Then I would record it in whatever way helps you to think through the process. All right so we're going to record that in terms of the trial it would look something like this. The cash is going to be debited So it's going from one hundred plus to 20 it's going to go up we're doing the same thing to it. So we're debit in a debit account increasing it the receivable is going to go down. So we had the debit here. We are crediting it doing the opposite to bring in the receivable down by the 30. And then that difference is going to go to the allowance and notice the allowance is a contra account meaning it's an asset with a credit balance where debit in it doing the opposite thing to it bringing it down. So then if we think of our questions, do people owe us money?

Yeah people it was 1 million 161 who owes us money. Well if we look at the general ledger it tells us details but it only tells us the activity by date. So we had people hold as one million two. Then we had those 9000 that went down by and then we had the 30 that it went down by. Normally that would be from payments in this case it went down because we were not paid and we were or we weren't paid on all that we got we got 20 out of the 30 on this one. But some of them were due to writing it down. We also have the allowance here showing this activity. Here's where the 10 is being posted to the allowance.

Here's Of course with a 30 is posted to the general ledger. Now if we want to know who owes us money we would have to go to the subsidiary Ledger. So in this case. Note that this 30000 is being recorded in Jee's accounts and they otos 30. Now they paid us 10 and we wrote off. I mean they paid us 20 and we wrote up the other 10 because we determined it was not going to be collectible that's backed down to zero. If we add up all customers then it will add up to 1 million 161. That ties out to the general ledger that ties out to the trial balance of that we still have this estimate of 21 that will be not collectible.

So the reason it went from the prior balance and when we started this which was 40 and now is going down is because we now know who's not going to pay us. So this was the estimate and we didn't know who wasn't going to pay us. Now we have determined that these amounts are uncollectible and we're writing it off against that 40000 and then applying it out to the correct customers which are now determined to be uncollectible. All right next item received payment from C-w after we had assumed the bad debt uncollectible had been written off. So in this case what we're saying is that this is an unusual case but it's good to look at because it kind of shows us what would happen if someone came in the door and said Here I am, I'm going to pay you now. And we had totally written them off in the past because we didn't think we were going to get paid from them.

So in this case you remember that the CW company otos 9000 we determined we're not going to get paid so we wrote off the 9000 to the allowance account here. So we wrote them off and now they came into Dorn's, which I know showed you where you haven't returned our calls and whatnot. But here I am and I'm going to pay you the night out. That's great. So how would we record that? I'm going to tell you the way not to do it first and I'm going to tell you why it doesn't work that way. So one way that it would you know it kind of works but it's not the way we're going to do it is that we can think it through our transactions and say well is cash affected. Yeah we're going to debit cash because we got cash from the clients and we would normal credit receivable.

However we cannot credit the receivable now because we already wrote the receivable off. Where did we write the receivable off too. We wrote it off to the allowance account. So therefore since we already wrote We can see that 9000 was written off to the allowance account. Why don't we just debit cash and credit the allowance account which would cancel out this 9000 that we wrote off here that would work.

And that works in terms of journal entries. However it doesn't really work in the system because if we then analyze the receivable account it looks like this payment was not paid. It looks like the customer is kind of like a deadbeat with him. So if they came to us again we don't have an audit trail in their subsidiary Ledger showing that they actually paid us. It looks like they never paid us.

So what we want to do is record this activity in the subsidiary ledger and have an audit trail on it. Therefore instead of doing that we're going to kind of break the rule of thinking about cash first. And in this case we're going to say well let's reverse what we did last time. As of today we're not going to we're not going to go back in time and do it. We're going to say as of today we're going to reverse the prior journal entry putting this customer back in good standings on the subsidiary ledger and then we'll do the normal transaction which would be to debit cash and credit receivable. So that would look like this. So we're going to reverse what we did last time which was to write off the receivable we're going to put the receivable back on the books by debiting the 9000 to put the receivable back in good standing here and then we're going to credit the accounts accounts. So we've reversed what we did last time. Now we're in our normal circumstance. Now we're back to the norm.

And now we can then debit the cash like we normally would when we get money from the clients and credit the receivable reduced in the receivable. So it would look like. If the cash is going, the receivable is going to go up by 9000 and then the allowance is going to be credited by 9000 and then we're going to debit the checking account by 9 and credit the receivable by 9. Note the net difference in the receivable is zero. It went up and down. Therefore in terms of journal entries we could simplify the journal entry a lot by just debit in cash and credit in the allowance. You'll note in essence that's what we did here. That's what happened.

But why don't we do that? Well let's look at what happened on the general ledger and that is that the receivable went back up here. We debited the receivable here and then we credited the receivable so we put it back in good standing. And then we took it off in kind of a normal process on the allowance account. We can see that we reversed the allowance account here and then on the subsidiary Ledger what happened for C-w is note that we put the 9000 back on the books as being owed to us. And then we wrote it. We wrote it off here.

So the reason for that is if we look here then the audit trail will basically show us that yeah we wrote it off but then we put them back in good standing. And then this 9000 if we you know if we checked the audit trail on that from the subsidiary Ledger it will show a payment whereas if we didn't do these two transactions and we just looked at this item and we checked the audit trail it would show that there was no payment and we wrote it off. So that audit trail is pretty much the reason why we would do this reversing process instead of just having a simple journal entry that would just be half as long. All right.

So then we determined that the company and the company would not pay us the amount owed. So two more companies we've determined maybe at the end of the period at the end of the year or so that they're not going to pay us. We're going to probably analyze every single count periodically and see that companies will not pay us and if we look at the company here we're going to write them off so that 6:7 is going to have to go down and the company is going to have to go down. That's the receivable accounts. So those are the amounts it will go down by. Therefore the receivables are going to have to go down by that. And that's going to be a credit.

And then what are we going to do once again we're going to debit the allowance account so that it would look like this we're going to debit the allowance account for the 14:7 and credit the receivable. And once again that adds up to the two clients is the company of the company and the company the amount that they owed. And therefore we're going to debit the receivable. I mean credit the receivable. So the receivables are going to go down and a debit balance is going to do the opposite thing to make it go down. And then we are going to debit the allowance account making it go down. Note that once again no change in the net receivable because the net receivable here was a debit of the receivable of 1 million 161 minus the credit of the allowance that would be the net receivable. And then they both went down.

Therefore the new net receivable is now one million 1:46 3 minus the 15 3. So if we look at the activity then the questions being do people with money that people over 1 million 1:46 3 will who owes us the money. That just tells us by date what has happened. So what has happened it went it went down by nine it went down by 30 it went back up by now and it went down by nine and then we have this 14 went down by that the allowance shows us the activity for the accounts that were uncollectable then the subsidiary Ledger breaks it down by customer or client.

So here's what happened. There's that 8000 here as well as the BB&T the 6:07. That's what adds up to this 14:7. So we had to break that out between the two customers that don't pay us if we add up all the receivables. Then in the subsidiary Ledger it adds up to 1 million 146. Three times out to the general ledger that ties out to the trial balance and we still have this estimate of 15:3 that we determined was uncollectable. So now we're going to say it's at the end of the period if it's at the end of the period now and we're done with the year and we need to then determine what the allowance account should be at the end of the time period. There's a couple of ways we can do this if we think about this.

What we're saying here is that the revenue account here of three three seventy eight thousand if we made all those sales on account we need to think about the amount that will be uncollectible. So part of those sales are going to be uncollectible and what we want to do is write off that uncollectable portion this period. We don't want to close out the books and then write it off next period because then we'll write off the bad debt expense to the next period. We want to match up the uncollectible accounts to this period. Now we don't know who's not going to pay us. That's the problem. We know that we made a bunch of sales.

We don't know who's not going to pass but we can make an estimate of that and under generally accepted accounting principles we have to because if we don't then we're going to be overstating the revenue or the net income that we have earned in this time period and we'll be overstating the assets. So we have to make some kind of estimate and that's controversial because any time you make an estimate that you know it's just an estimate and you can be off on an estimate it's not exact. But in order to fix the matching problem in order to present our financial statements in the most fair way and not overstate them, an estimate is better than not having an estimate.

So how can we make an estimate one we could look at the revenue side here and we could say well if we made all these sales on account then based on past experience we could take some percentage of the revenue and say that based on past experience we have learned that this percentage is uncollectable therefore we can write off the bad debt expense debiting the expense increase and the expense for that percentage portion of the revenue. The other way we know that we can do it which I'm going to show here which I think is probably to me it's more exact to do because it seems like you can come up to a better estimate in this way to actually look at the balance sheet account and that would be the receivable account here. And then try to find a way to break down what portion of the receivables are going to be uncollectible.

And so that's oftentimes you're going to look at something like an aging account in order to do that. So if we have this one million 1:46 three if we break that out that window million 1:46 3 in terms of an account Siebel agene which could look something like this a lot of software will have this and stuff like Quickbooks or something can generate this record and we have something that's 30 days past due. We can up to you know what we might say that 2 percent is uncollectible if it's between 30 and 60 past to 4 percent perhaps 60 90 10 percent perhaps and over 90 maybe there's a very high chance that it's going to be uncollectible.

And this way we can break it down by how old the debt is which is usually a fairly good indicator if it's old if the thing is older and we've been calling people forever and then and they haven't gotten back to us then at some point we can say that there's a higher likelihood or probability that you know we're not going to get paid on that one. So where do we come up with these percentages? We would have to get those based on past experience.

And again that's something that is a problem the book would have to give you in real life. We would have to do some careful analysis in terms of how we would come up with that. But if we multiply that out then we're going to say this time we would come up with these numbers and that would say that OK. Of the 1 million 146 3 we think based on this estimate that 50000 437 will be uncollectible therefore we still have 15 300 in the allowance account here and that's because we basically overestimated last time we thought that we weren't going to get I think it was 40 at the to begin and yet was 40 here last time.

And we're still left with 15:3 at the end meaning that we didn't write off as many not many people came and said they were not going to be collectible as we thought. Therefore in order to get this 15:3 up to the 50 we would do a subtraction problem. And the difference being one thirty seven is what we would need in order to bring that amount up to the estimate of 50000. So if we posted this if we took the fifteen thousand minus the 15 three we come up with the 35 win 37. So now if we post this out then we're crediting the 35 1:37 to the allowance. So that's going to take the 15:3 up by 35 1:37 to the 50000 3:47 which matches the 50000 3:47 here.

Then the other side is finally going to go to the bad debt expense. So now we're going to debit the bad debt expense by 35%. And that's going to bring it up to 35. And then if we look at what the effect is on net income we're going to say of this revenue here 35% of it we believe is going to be uncollectible meaning we're never going to get paid on that. And we make that estimate kind of like an adjusting entry as of the end of the time period. So that as of the date when we create the financial statements we're showing a net income of 3:42. Eight sixty three instead of three seventy eight. So we're recording the fact that we're representing the fact of these sales.

We believe this amount is going to be uncollectible on the balance sheet side we're also saying yeah we have revenue we have receivables of one point 146 three. However we believe based on past experience that 50000 4:37 will be uncollectible. We want to disclose that to the readers. We want to be as fair as possible and not be overstating our value. However it's also just an estimate and we could collect more than we could collect less. That's our best guess. So we are now able to define the allowance method for transactions related to recording bad debt recording receivable accounts that have been determined to be uncollectible recording receivable accounts that have been collected after being determined to be uncollectible.

Allowance Method 900 Part 1 Accounting Financial

Hello, during this chapter we will be working on a problem concentrating on accounts receivable and allowance for doubtful accounts and be working on the allowance method for writing off accounts receivable. So we're going to have the activity over here. These will be the transactions that we're going to record. We're going to record them in the blue area here in the general journal and then we also have the trial balance over here. We're going to see the effect on the trial balance. Note the format of the trial balances we will have and the assets Of course will be in green. Then we have the liability accounts, the equity accounts and then the income statement revenue and expenses.

We have a very limited amount of counts accounts so that we can just concentrate basically on the writing off of the accounts receivable but also be able to see the effect on a trial balance in context. We also have the assets here in the accounting equation equaling the liabilities and the equity Of course and we can see that we are in balance down here by saying that the debits of the assets and minus the liabilities add up to zero. Therefore the debits equal the credit. So note that there is only one column here. But we're saying that debit to mine is the credit to equal zero. That green zero means we're in balance. Net income as of now is just three seventy eight thousand. Then we have the general ledger over here.

We will post our activity to the general ledger which Of course is in the same order as the trial balance assets in green. And then the liability in orange and then the equity in the light blue and then the income statement in the darker blue then we have this information down here which will be the accounts receivable subsidiary Ledger. So this is going to be similar to the general ledger up here but by contrast instead of recording this information just by date as it will be done in the general ledger we're going to record it by a customer down here. So we're going to need to know that in order to be able to account for customers that cannot pay. And so these are going to be the customers in names.

And if we add up all the accounts by customer then it should sum up here to this one million two and that time out to the receivables here. And that ties out to the receivables here at the end of this problem we're also going to take a look at an Asian account and this will come into play later on. So we'll take a look at that towards the end. All right so let's take a look at our first transaction which is going to be up to 17 which says determined that C-w company would not pay the amount owed. So we're saying that one of our clients is not going to be able to pay us. We've determined that their account will be uncollectible. So under the allowance method then how are we going to record that.

How are we going to adjust for that? Now note that we can see this down here in our ledger if we go down to our subsidiary ledger. I hear C-w owes us this 9000. That's the individual that is not going to pay us or the company in this case. So we're gonna have to write that off. So the question is is cash affected in this case. No, we're not going to get cash. That's the problem. And so with the account that is affected the receivable is saying that receivable there includes 9000 from C-w and it will not be paid. So that needs to go down. We need to go down even though we haven't got paid for it because we don't believe we're ever going to get paid at this time. So we need to take it off the books so that it has a debit balance.

We're going to do the opposite thing to it then which in this case would be a credit. So I want to copy the receivable right clicking and copy it in l 6 but our cars are in C-Six and we're going to paste it here in a Right-Click. Paste it one two three just two values not the format of the cell values only. Then we're going into the credit column. We are going to be recognizing credits in this worksheet with a negative. So I type in negative 9000 and when we select enter it's going to put brackets around it because of the formatting of the Excel worksheet like so. And it also includes Of course the comma here. To put it in a number format then we're going to also have a debit for the same amount for 9000 because we need an equal number of debits and credits. And the only question then is what account should we debit.

And normally Of course we would get cash in this situation and we would be debit in cash but we didn't get any cash. So under the direct write off under the allowance method we are going to debit the allowance for doubtful accounts. So notice what we will not be doing at this time. And under the direct write off method we would be expensing it as bad debt expense at the time it was written off. Now why are we doing this? The idea being that we want to try to match the expense with the revenue. And so that means that in the period that we generated the revenue we would like to write off the amount of those revenues that we think are uncollectible in the same time period in order to do that we're going to have to do an estimate which we'll do at the end of this problem and we'll estimate the bad debt for the time period.

All at one point in time but when we write off the debt when it becomes uncollectible that's probably going to happen at a later date. And so you'll note that if we wrote off the expense now then it wouldn't be matching up with the revenue that helped to generate it. So we're going to use an estimate to try to match that up under the allowance method. So what we have here under the allowance account then is this 40000 that represents the amount that we believe will be uncollectible. So if we think about the receivables then we now have a contra account related to the receivables so the receivables 1 million two of the 1 million do we think that 40000 have been estimated to be uncollectible. Now we're going to put that in a second account for someone to reason as cumulative depreciation as a quarter asset account.

It's a contrast of an account meaning it's an asset account with a credit balance. You could see that with the brackets. So normal as accounts have a debit balance. This is an asset account but it has a credit balance. Why does it have a credit balance? Because basically it's kind of like the second half of the receivable account. This is the receivable account. It's an asset and part of that we kind of broke it in half again the tea into you know like a seven and an organ. And this is kind of of like the credit half of the t account that we think are going to be uncollectible.

Now we're going to put it in a different account for a couple of reasons. One we don't know who is not going to pay us. We just made an estimate based on past experience that 1 million to 40000 will be uncollectible. That's just an estimate that we've made based on past experience and we can't write it off to a particular person or a particular customer. For example if I scroll over here down to the accounts receivable these are the people that owe us. We don't know which one is not going to pay us but we do know from past experience that someone's not going to pass and therefore we're going to estimate that and put that into the allowance account. We're also telling our readers hey it's just an estimate. People with 1 million too.

But we want to be straight up front that based on past experience 40000 not going to be paid. Therefore the 192 minus 4 is 1 million 160. That's the net receivables at this point in time. Now when someone does not pay has them going to say hey we already estimated that we already made this account saying that these people aren't going to pay us over that forty thousand nine of it now has now come to pass. Now we know who's not going to pay us and we can take it out of the allowance meaning we're going to reduce the allowance and reduce the receivable.

So basically the allowance has to 40 in it and we are going to debit it making it go down some of that account. Now put that on top in C5 Right-Click and page 23. And obviously it might be easier to think about the allowance by first doing the receivable and then we know that we're going have to do the opposite to the other account. Notice there will be no net effect on the net receivables meaning this minus this will be the same because the receivables are going to go down and the allowance that contra account is going to go down by the same amount nine thousand making the balance the same.

So let's post this out and see what happens to make this a little bit smaller down here on the taskbar to bring it down to like late 80s probably get it I'm going to scroll over here so we can see more information. And let's post this out. So we're going to go to the allowance now. It's in the same order here. The third account here is the allowance on the general ledger 3rd account and we have the debits going to be on the debit side of the line item and cell C 9 I mean 9. So as 9 we're going to like equals and then point to this 9000 over here. So what's going to happen when we hit enter. Well that's a credit.

This is a debit. Those are opposites. The 40000 is going to go down by 9000 to 31000. That Of course puts us out of balance here. We see the 31000 here and we're out of balance here and here until we post the other side to accounts receivable. So here's the counter people were posting. That's the second account on the trial balance and that's the second account on the general ledger. We're posting it to the general ledger. We're going to be in the credit column. So we are in a column in that cell P 16 or so piece 16 equals then we're just going to point to that 9000 what's going to happen once we hit enter. Well this is a debit that's a credit it's going to make it go down we're doing the opposite thing to it.

The receivable goes down to 1 million one 91. That's the same number here in m. 6. And note that we now have affected the receivable account. We're also going to have to see what happens by customers so what we think about when we think through the receivable. We often think of how much money people owe us. Well people owe us 1 million 191 and we estimate that the 31 will not be paid. Next question is who owes us that money. The GPL doesn't give us that information necessarily because it's only in order by date. So we're going to have to scroll down here to the subsidiary ledger and we're going to that individual that we think is not going to pay us.

Here's the individual or the company. So we're going to put the same information that we have here in the jail down here. But you know, it's a bit more complex in nature that I'm going to have to do it by customer, not just by date. So in-cell TI 31 we're going to select equals and then point to that 9000. We're going to post that same information down here. So there we have it. And then it goes down to zero so we no longer do or that individual no longer owes us the company no longer owes us because we have written it off. And if we add up all the companies that owe us it ties out to 1 million 191 which is the same amount on the receivable which is the same amount up here in the trial balance. All right, let's see what happens next.

We have on for 12 the company paid a partial payment and went bankrupt it is determined that we will not receive the balance. So the company paid us the 20000 and then we're assuming we're not going to get the balance. The difference of 10000. So the questions we're going to go through are cash affected. Yes we got money. We've got 20,000. So cash is going to go up. Cash is a debit balance. We're going to go up by doing the same thing to it which in this case would be another debit from a right click going to copy the cash going to put that on top right next to the date because of debits traditionally go on top right click paste it one two three. That debit will be for cash received of twenty thousand dollars or 20000. I'm going to make a little bit larger on the taskbar down here to make this a little bit larger. I want to scroll back over so we can see that a bit more clearly.

So there's the 20000 we got in cash. Now Of course we got paid cash and who paid us the cash the customer and they owed us the cash and we're not going to credit revenue Of course because we already credited revenue in the past. What we're going to do is say people OTAs 20000 represented by the receivable that receivable now needs to go down by the fact that they paid us. So I'm going to put that in there now. Now there are going to be more than two accounts affected but this would be the normal transaction if someone paid us the money for a receivable. Receivables have a debit balance that needs to go down because they no longer owe money.

So when a copy that and going to put that underneath. Right click and paste it one two three and it's going to be a credit. However it's not going to be a credit for 20000 because they owed us 30000 if we look at the amount of money that was owed to us down here on the subsidiary ledger for G for G 30000. Now we're going to say that they only paid us 20 but they're not going to give us the difference therefore we can't just write it down 20000 cars and we'll still show that they were 10. And if we never believe that we are going to see that we got to just give that up we're not going to, we're not going to get it because they went bankrupt. So we're going have to take it off the books for the entire 30000.

So that means that credit then will be for 30000 so I don't put our cursor in IE 9 negative thirty thousand. So there's the credit. Now Of course the debits do not equal the credits when going to need one more account. So the other account is going to be 10000 because we need 20 plus 10 to get to the 30 I'm going to use or negative some function I'll call this the plug function and this type of work to put this in there. So instead of selecting equals and unswept negative as you m and then some of these up on some of that up. But I wanted to flip the science on so that being a negative 10 which is what some function will be this will be a positive and therefore the debits minus the credits will then equal zero in this case.

So that's what we're going to put. We're going to need to put some other account there in order to put this in balance. Also note that this I'm putting the debit on the bottom and on it under a perfect world we'd have two debits on top and formatting it so that we have a debit and credit debit and that's not as perfectly proper. But if it's helping you to build the journal entry to think through it in a way that doesn't have all the debits on top then I would prefer to do that. If it's something that will help you think through it and if it's something that you go back to you and you have a better audit trail meaning I can look at the journal entry and see what happened.

Then I would break with the rule of having the debits on top and the credits on bottom but just keep that in mind that traditionally we have the debits on top and the credit credits on bottom. I'm just thinking through it in this way. And I think that's worth doing. So we are then going to see what account we need to put this into. We're not going to get the cash therefore we're going to debit them.

Allowance Method 900 Part 2 Accounting Financial

We are then going to see what account we need to put this into. We're not going to get the cash therefore we're going to debit the allowance for doubtful accounts. So again this is the allowance method meaning we're not going to write it off to bad debt expense. When someone tells us that they went bankrupt. Why? Because we've already come up with an estimate of what we think is related to this receivable that will be uncollectible. We didn't know who was going to be uncollectible but based on past experience we said we were pretty sure that some of these receivables are not going to be collectible.

And we've already accounted for that and made an estimate and tried to match that estimate with the same time period in which the revenue was generated. Now we know part of that that didn't is not going to pay us and that's going to be this company here. So we're going to say take it out of the allowance and reduce the receivable. There'll be no net effect on the receivable because we already adjusted for this estimate. So I want to copy this. We're going to put this down here in cetane right click and paste it one two three. All right so let's post this out and see what happens. I'm going to go to the task and bring it down to about 80. Then we'll scroll over here and post this. So Cash first account cash is here.

Cash is our top count on the trial balance and cast the first count on the general ledger. This is called posting. We are in cell 0 9 when it's like equals and then point to the 20000 what's going to happen when hundreds are going to go up by 20 201 put us out of balance by the 20 and we see the 120 and the trial balance then we're going to post the receivables second account. Here's the receivable Here's the receivable second account on the general ledger so the receivable will be right here. We're going to have credit. So we are in the 17 equals going to point to that thirty thousand. What's going to happen?

The receivables are going to go down from 1 million one 91 to 1 million 1 61. We see that receivable here we see that we are now out of balance by the 10 that we now need to report to and record to allowance for doubtful accounts. So here is an allowance for down for accounts on our third account. It's going to be the third account in the general ledger. So we are now in S 10 sequels. I'm going to point to that 10000. So the 30000 is a credit that 10000 over here is a debit. Those are opposites. Therefore the credit is going to go down to 21.

That'll put us back in balance here with either 21 there. Note also that we affected the receivable account. And whenever we think about the receivables we often are going to ask the boss is going to ask us how much money do people owe us. Well people owe us one million 161 according to the trial balance. Well who owes us the money and when are we going to get paid in order to do that we cannot just go to the general ledger we have to go into the subsidiary Ledger down here and here's all the people that own us and companies that owe us and we will then be saying that this company no longer owes us the money because they paid us 20.

But we're also writing off the other piece because they went bankrupt of 10 therefore that 30 needs to go down to zero. All we're doing is recording the same information up here in the general ledger down here with a bit more detail that detail being by customer. So in-cell p. 31 we're gonna say equals pointed to thirty thousand. That's going to bring the company balance down to zero. So they no longer owe us money if we add up all of the accounts in the subsidy ledger for accounts receivable adds up to 1 million 161.

That ties out to the general ledger that ties out to the trial balance of what happened to the net receivables. No change because the 1 million 161 minus the 21 is that one million 140 actually there was a change by the amount that was received in cash. So the change was the 10000. There was no change from the amount that was taken out of the allowance account. All right. So that's all we have. Next we are now on is going to make us a little bit larger going to bring it back up to 100 percent down here on the taskbar and then when I scroll over so we can see the question and we are now on 7 2 which says that received payment from C-w after we had assumed that the debt uncollectible and had written it off.

So now what's happening that we wrote off that C-w company wasn't going to pay us and then we came back and all of a sudden they walked in the door and paid us and we were amazed by that doesn't usually happen with we without that they were we're not going to pay as they hadn't paid us for a long time. We wrote them off. So how are we going to account for that? And just so we can see this activity obviously if we scroll down here to the subsidiary ledger we see they owe us money. We took them down to zero meaning.

We assumed that they were not going to pay us even though we didn't get the cash. Our books now show that they don't owe us any money because we gave up on collecting from them. Now they came in and paid us. So how are we going to account for this? It's a little bit different than we might think because the first thing I've always asked us to think about is cash. And Of course in this case it is a fact that we got cash but we really want to reverse the transaction we did last time first and let me try to explain why if if we just debit cash then we're not going to record the fact of the audit trail down here showing that this company is is good that they were good on their transaction.

Our subsidiary Ledger should show that they paid us the cash and so we want to basically reverse our last transaction to basically put them back into the receivable and then do our normal transaction which would be to debit cash and credit receivable. So in order to help our audit trail for the most part we're going to make this a little bit longer of a transaction than it otherwise would be. So let me show you how that works. We have the journal entry up here. This is the journal entry we did to write them off. We want to put them back in the receivable and then take them off again to give us that audit trail.

So basically we reduced the receivable. We're going to put the receivables back on the books so we credited the receivable reducing the receivable we're going to debit the receivable now to put them back on the books. I'm going to copy this and paste this in. See 12 reichlich paste it one two three. We're going to debit the 9000 and then we're going to credit the allowance for doubtful accounts. We're going to reverse this transaction showing that we wrote them off that this client did not pay us. So I want to copy that and put the cursor in see 13 right click paste it one two three and that'll be the negative 9000.

It's going to post this and then will record the second half of this transaction and bring it down to 80 again. We're going to scroll over here and we're going to post the receivable. That's the debit. That's the second account on the trial balance. That's the second account on the general ledger. We're going to go to the debit half because we are now debiting these accounts and we are in Sale. Oh 18 equals. Then point to the debit of 9000 and that's going to bring that balance back up by 9000 to 1 million 170. So we wrote it off. We put it back in the book. We can see the activity now.

We're going to do a post on the allowance. Now that's a credit and that's the third account on the trial balance it's a third account on the general ledger. Here is the allowance we're going to put it in the next open area so we are in t 11. So with 11 we'll say equals and go to that 9000. So now that 21000 is going to go up in the credit direction because the credit and credit makes credit go up and back to 30000 here.

So there's our transaction we're also going to have to post this 9000 activity in the receivable down by a customer. So if we go by a customer down here and we see CW and we can post that same 9000 going to put them back on the books.

So we are in S 32 equals that 9000 bringing the balance back up from 0 to 9000. So now we basically put them back on the books here. They now own us the money and now we're going to write it off again. So now we're going to write it off again but we're going to show this time that they actually paid us within the transaction. So if we go back to the auditorium and look at what happened we will show that that was payment through this process so we can see now that the total here of all the people at all is money in the subsidy Ledger adds up to $1 in 170 times out to the one line 170 year times out of the 1 9 170 on the trial balance. So going to bring it back up to 100.

Scroll back over here and now we're going to record the normal transaction that happens when someone pays us and they owe us money. So now we can think through the questions. Is Cash affected? Yeah we got cash because they owed us money. So we're going to debit the cash. Copy that paste on top. I'm not going to set a new date. I'm going to skip a line however and put it down here. Right click paste it. One two three and we're going to put the 9000 in and then we're going to credit something for 9000 and we're going to do our normal transaction why did they pass. Because we did work but we did it in the past and they count showing that they owed us money is the receivable. So here we are going to credit the receivable.

Now reducing it again. So we're going to copy that and we're going to paste it one two three here. OK so a couple of things to note that once this full transaction these four transactions are these four accounts note that once again I broke it out into two accounts to simplify it. If I would go back to this transaction and if we see it in two accounts rather than one account with two debits on top and two credits it might be a little less. Two followed it probably would be easier to fall to have two accounts. So that's why I would break it out in that format. Also note that you might be saying well why don't we.

We're doing too much work here we could have just debited cash and then credit the allowance right there. And instead of doing this idea and having four accounts because all we're doing is putting it in the receivable and then taking it out of those saveable. Why are we doing that when we could have just gotten to the same point by just debit in cash and then credit in the allowance for Delphi accounts. And the reason is basically the audit trail we want to show on the audit trail that hey we put him back on the books they're back in good standing. And then we have our normal transaction taking place here. So that's why it's going to be looking like this. All right so now we're going to post this second journal entry. I'm going to bring this down a bit back down the 80 on the taskbar going to scroll back over here and we will post out the checking accounts checking account Of course is the first count on the trial balance.

First count on the general ledger we are in cell 0 10. So equals and we're going to point to the D 15 and that makes the cash go up to 1:29 that we're going to post the receivable half of it so here's the receivable Here's the receivables checking account balance checking account on a general letter. We're going to be down here in the 19th 19 equals. I'm going to point to the 9000 that debit will go down. So we're going to do that. And there it goes down to 1 million 161. We're going to post that same activity in the receivable accounts in the subsidiary ledger for the receivables. So scroll down here and look at the subsidiary ledger.

We're going back to C-w we just put the 9000 back on there and now we're going to take it off again. So we are now in sales 33 equals. And when I post that same 9 and there it is. So they originally gave us 9000 . We wrote it off thinking we weren't going to get paid. Then we put it back on the books so that we can see the audit trail and write it off. But this time the journal entry would look like a normal journal entry meaning we got paid for it and we put them back in good standing. In that way and now Of course the company no longer owes us the money. If we go down to the subsidiary ledger and look at all of the subsidy ledger accounts that add up to 1 million 161 on the subsidiary ledger for receivables that ties out to the general ledger for receivables and that side out to the trial balance for receivables.

All right, let's make this larger again we're going back up to 100 percent on the taskbar scrolling back over the next activity on 820 over here saying that we determined that the company and the company would not pay the amount owed. All right so we have two more companies that were terminated that we are not going to receive the funds from.

So we're basically saying that the receivable related to those two companies is not going to be paid. Therefore cash is not affected because we're not going to get the money for it and we're going to have to take this receivable down. So if Siebel has a debit balance and that we need to make it go down, how do we make something go down? We do the opposite thing too as what it is that's a debit or credit.

So I'm going to copy that receivable and put it on the bottom in see 19. Here's the date I'm going to put it on the bottom because it traditionally goes on the bottom right click and pastes it one two three. Now notice they didn't give us the amount. Here we don't have the amount but we can find that on the subsidiary Ledger. So the company and bidi companies of the company and the company and I have to remember that the company the company and so we're going to be down here. And so the company owes us 6:7 BD owes us eight thousand. So the total in the receivables 6:07 up last 3000 means that we're not going to get 14 7.

So that's the amount that we're going to have to put over here that will not be receivable from these two companies. So we're going to go back over here. And I'm going to put a negative in the credit side negative 14:7 That's how much we're going to have to take out over the receivable in order to account for the fact that we do not believe that these two companies will pay us have a debit something for that same amount to have an equal number of debits and credits. What will the debit not be ? We didn't get any cash which is unfortunate but we had planned that that would happen by setting up the allowance account and saying that we understand that of those 1 million 161.

Part of that will not be collected and we have already made an estimate that we currently have 30000 in there. So what is going to happen is we now know who's not going to pay us and therefore we're going to reduce the receivable directly by the amount that's not going to be paid. And we're just going to take it out of the allowance. There'll be no net effect on the net receivables of the allowance of minus. I mean that I see or minus the allowance of 1 1 million 131. So the debit will be the allowance account going to copy that can you put that in see right click paste it 1 2 3. We're going to make this smaller again going back down at 80 on the taskbar scrolling over so we can see the information here we got the allowance. That's the second or third account on the trial balance third account on the general ledger. We are on the debit side so we are at 12. So within 12 and say equals pointed to.

Allowance Method 900 Part 3 Accounting Financial

The allowance that's the second or third account on the trial balance third account on the general ledger we are in the debit side so we are in as 12. So within 12 and say equals point to the 14 7 that's going to bring the balance of 30 down because that's a credit and we're debit in it which are opposites brings it down 15 free. Then we have the receivable account here. The receivable count is the second account on the balance. We are going to be the second account on the general ledger. We are going to credit the receivables so we are in CLP 20 equals and then point to that 14:7 that's going to bring the receivable balance down to 1 million 146 free if we do something to the receivable balance here.

We're also going to have to do that to the subsidiary ledger and so we're going to scroll down the subsidiary ledger and we determined that the two companies that will be affected on this is P and B. Now note that I usually have a formula here to try out what's going to happen but in this case it's because we have the two areas we kind of have to just hardcoded the number in here and that is because were this 14 Of course 14:7 is accounting for this 6 7 and this 8000 that need to go down. So I'm going to hard code this in cell x 37 negative 6 7 bringing the balance down to zero. And then I sold a B 31 negative 8000.

And Of course if we are going to hold down control and highlight those two cells and Excel will add that up, that's

14:7, that's 14:7. If we scroll down here we can see that if we add up all of them all the customers they owe us 1 million 1:46 3 in accounts receivable subsidiary ledger which ties out to the accounts receivable general ledger here which ties out to the accounts receivable on the trial balance. All right we got one more transaction to make this a bit larger on the taskbar back up to 100 percent scrolling over we're now on 12 thirty one says See analysis of receivable agene adjust the allowance account accordingly. All right. So now we're at the end of the time period and what we're going to do is we're going to say of the current revenue that we have made in this case we have 378.

How much of that do we think will be uncollectible and there are two ways to think about this we could think about the revenue and try to multiply that by the amount of revenue that was sold on account that we think will be uncollectible and a lot of places that I have seen have looked more on the balance and we can also look at the balance sheet and say hey well these are the receivables we have right now. Let's look at how old those receivables are and come up with some type of estimate in terms of how much of those receivables will be uncollectible.

And then by adjusting the allowance account to match the account that we will be uncollectible we will write off the bad debt expense that it will take to get to that amount. So note that what we already have here we've got 15-30 that we think are going to be uncollectible because basically we overestimated the amount that would be uncollectible from the prior period. We thought that we started out with the allowance account thinking that we were going to not receive 40000 for this time period and we still have a 15:3 that we thought we were not going to receive. That we are still good.

We haven't written that off yet and so therefore once we come up with how much of this we do not believe we're going to be receiving. We will then record this or adjust this to that number. So let's show what I mean. This is kind of the idea of where we might come up with this number and what that number should be. So if we had an AG note that what we have here is 1 million 1:46 3 in the receivable. If we broke that out to some type of aging meaning we're trying to find out how much of the receivables are still do how much or over 30 days between 30 and 60 60 90 over 90. Now if we looked and broke out the data in this format then and type out the total the total receivables then tout to the amount on the track about 1 million 146 free then we could come up with some kind of estimate and we would say well if it's still kind of current then we think that 2 percent will not be correct to be collected.

The longer it stays outstanding then the higher the percentage that we believe will not be collected. So we're going to say for ten ninety five you might be asking where you came up with these numbers. And those would come up with past experience. Past experience would tell us that. How much of the account would be uncollectible then we can come up with an estimate and say okay well if we add these up we're going to say that of the receivables of 1 million 1:46 3 based on this estimate. We think that 50000 4:37 will be uncollectible. So we think that the receivable account and the uncollectible account should be 50000 4:37 And if we scroll over here and see what we have in it right now we have 15:3 of accreditations. So 15:3 of credit we want to beef up 50000 4:37.

Therefore I'm going to subtract that minus 15 free. We're going to need another 35 1:37 in order to get this 15:3 up to the amount that we believe is going to be uncollectible based on our aging calculation that we just look at for the receivable account and so that 35 1:37 is what we're going to have to increase this receivable account to buy. So this allowance account has a credit balance in it. We're going to make it go up so we can do the same thing to it which in this case would be a credit. So I got a copy of the receivable allowance . I'm going to put that on the bottom. Here's the date we're going to put it on the bottom.

Paste it one two three. And the calculation that we have here. Thirty five one thirty seven. For that credit negative thirty five point thirty seven. And then we're gonna have to debit the same amount. So 35 137. And then Of course what the debit will be and the debit is not going to be to the receivable because we don't know who's not going to pay us yet but we do. We're estimating how much of this receivable will not be paid. Notice that if we took it out of the receivable we'd have to basically go to the subsidiary ledger and try to estimate who is not to be paid in order for the time. We don't know what we're doing if we're going to expense that amount right now because that amount should be coming out of the current revenue. So the idea is we're backing into the amount of this revenue that we believe is going to be uncollectible.

We don't know who's going to pay us but we know from past experience that this amount probably will not be paid and we need to disclose this to our readers. It would be unfair for us to tell our readers that we have receivables of this amount when we know from past experience that it's really lower than that. We're not going to get that much money. It would be unfair to our readers to tell them that we made this much money when we know that that revenue is too high. Really. Because some of the payments will never be received. So we need to take that down. So the amount will be too bad. You also might be thinking why don't we debit revenue to take the revenue down because the revenue is overstated.

That's what we're really saying. We're saying hey we made a sale but we didn't really make a sale because we're not going to get paid on it. So why don't we reduce revenue? And the same idea we never reduce revenue really revenue generally only goes up. We make up this other account that's basically taking down the revenue or matching the expense of people that will not pay. So we're going to copy this and paste this down here in C-21 right click and paste it one two three and then I can make this a little bit smaller and the taskbar back down to 80 so we can post this out and see if it does what we expect it to do.

What do we expect it to do? What do we expect from this account here? The allowance account here to go from 15-40 to our estimate that we came up here to 50000 4:37. All right. That's what we want to do is let's be pulseless out. So we will then first go to the bad debt. Bad debt is here. It's way down here on our trial balance therefore it's going to be in the dark blue area way over here. It's at 9 so we can barely see it. But we are in the dead half of it and who is going to select the schools and then point to that 35 1:37 when we hit enter it's going to increase the bad debt expense we'll see it increase here and we'll also see the net income go down.

So here it puts us out of balance and the net income went down. Meaning net income as the credit of revenue minus that expense took it down because we reduced it by the amount of revenue that we don't think we're going to get that 35 1:37 then we're going to post the other side to the allowance account so the allowances here the allowances here on the balance the allowances here on the general ledger are here on the general ledger we are in so t 13 and we're going to select equals and then point to that 35 137 what's going to happen. This is a credit.

This is a credit going up in the credit direct from 15 free to 50000 4:37 that we can see here as well. And that ties out to our estimate here. So when I scroll back over here so there are activities so now we think that we are going to have receivables of 140 1 million 146 300 but 50000 347 of those are going to be uncollectible. How do we know? Just an estimate. We had an estimate from the prior period but we need to make that estimate because it would be best for our reader to understand that based on past experience we don't think we're going to collect that much money. We're going to have to reduce that the net receives all this minus This is

1 million ninety five 863. Also on the revenue side although we made sales of seventy eight thousand We believe that those sales on account 35 137 will not be collectible based on past experience. We need to report that to our reader and show the net income reduced from this 378 by 35 137 to a net income of 3:42 863.

Multiple Choice Questions - Accounts Receivable

In this chapter we will take a look at multiple choice questions related to receivables. First question. Calculating the allowance for doubtful accounts by examining the accounts receivable account is the sales Agena method the the percentage of accounts receivable method see the accounts payable aging method d the percentage of sales method or e. Not a valid method. Well read that again and go through the process of elimination calculating the allowance for doubtful accounts by examining the accounts receivable account is a the sales aging method. Now if we go through this we might first want to just think about this question and what we're talking about calculating the allowance for deadfall accounts.

We're talking about the contra asset account when we think about the receivables. How much of those receivables do we think is uncollectable? There's a couple of methods we can use. One is the receivables method where we try to value the receivables to determine how much of them will not be collectible now. Ace says the sales agent method and that is concentrating not on the receivable But on the revenue on the sales side on the income statement side. So it's not a.

Says the percentage of accounts receivable method. It sounds kind of razored But we're dealing with it with the accounts receivable side in order to determine how much of them are uncollectible see says the accounts payable agent method.

We're not going to use the payable. So that's kind of deceiving because it's payable and it sounds kind of like the accounts receivable aging method. So it's not the percentage of the sales method. And once again that's concentrating on the sales side. We could concentrate on the sales side but here it says we're concentrating on the receivables side.

So that's not it and it's not a valid method and it seems to be a valid means we have to either concentrate on the receivables or the sales. Either of them are valid to do so be Looks like the correct answer. Once again calculating the allowance for doubtful accounts by examining the accounts receivable account is the percentage of accounts receivable method. Now note they could get more detail just in terms of the receivable depending on who we're talking to how how detailed we can get in terms of receivables method meaning we could just take a percentage of the receivable total as a whole which probably would not be as accurate if we took a percentage of an aging type method if we broke it out into an AGM account and then took the percentage there. So if we took that more detailed method you could think of it as three different methods but in essence we're either focusing on them on the balance sheet on accounts receivable to figure out the allowance amount or on the income statement on sales.

Next question calculating the allowance for devil accounts based on credit sales is a sales agent method the percentage of accounts receivable method see the accounts receivable aging method D. Percent of sales method or e. Not a valid method. Once again we'll look at the process of elimination going through these a second time calculating the allowance for deficit accounts based on credit sales is. So once again we're looking at the allowance for doubtful accounts. But this time concentrating on not the receivable size to do so but the sales side the income statement side. So because of those two sides of the transaction remember once again I'm here to have it to bad debt expense an income statement account and the other is going to be the allowance for Delfin accounts a asset account in contrast.

So the sales aging method. Now that is focusing on the income statement, the sales side. So we'll leave that for now. He says the percentage of accounts receivable method that's going to focus on the receivables and we're focusing on the other side of it we're focusing on the sales side. So I'm going to say that's not it. She says the accounts receivable aging method and again that's focusing in on the receivables we're looking at the income statement side. So it's not say the percentage of sales of the method. So that is focusing on the sales.

So it looks like it's the right side we're looking at. I'll keep that for now. He says it's not a valid method and it's going to be valid. We could focus on the sales or on the receivables. So we're left with HMD once again calculating the allowance for deadfall accounts based on credit sales. It is either a or D either the sale of aging method the sales 18 method or the percentage of sales method. Now the first one might sound familiar with this aging method but that's typically what we age is the receivables when we're age in the receivable side of things. So we don't really do that same thing typically for the sales side of things. On the sales side of things we would typically take the percentage of the sales or the percentage of the credit sales.

So believe me is the more correct answer here. So the answer to calculating the allowance for doubtful accounts based on credit sales is the percentage of the sales method. Next question, next question. The matching principle requires that expenses be expensed in any time period as long as they reduce net income. The use of the direct write off method sees expenses to be recorded when cash is paid and the income to be recognized when earning me the use of the allowance method.

So we'll go through the process of elimination now. The matching principle requires expensive expenses be expensed in any time period as long as there is reduced net income. Now just intuitively that just doesn't seem to make it we can just expense anything anytime we want in any time period. That doesn't really make sense to you and we have to restrict that somehow some way. And that's what the matching principle does. It says we can't just expense everything at any time period we want even though expenses will always decrease net income. That's what expenses do. And then he says we're going to eliminate that one. So Pompeys says the use of the direct write off method.

Now I know even if we don't know what the matching principle is we probably should at this point if we're looking at the accounting method and the direct write off method should know that we want to be able to just know that the book of the methodology the preferred method for is going to be the allowance method. So it's not likely that an accounting method is going to require the use of the direct write off method, the preferred method. So I'm going to say that's probably not going to be it. And then she says the expense to be recorded when cash is paid. Now that it is talking about the cash basis rather than a cruel basis and the matching principle is one of the major two accrual principles and it doesn't say that we have record expenses when cash is paid. But when the expenses incurred at the same time period as revenue is generated.

So it's not a C D that says income be recorded when earned and you might look at that and say that sounds kind of reasonable. Remember that's a key accrual principle. Income is recorded when earned. I'll leave that for now. He says the use of the allowance method. So that sounds pretty good because typically the answer is often in this area of the questions related to receivables will be the allowance method being the one we want to use. So we're left with D and E. So let's read through this one more time. The matching principle requires the income be recorded when earned or e the use of the allowance method.

So the matching principle isn't D because D has to do with the revenue recognition principle. The other of the two major principles has to do with the revenue side not really the expense side the matching principle has to do with timing on the expense side. So that's why it's not really deep. And note that since we're talking about receivables here that's why we might be in a situation we would assume that we're applying these principles to the the allowance method the direct write off method and the use of the allowance method would be the correct answer because it it applies the matching principle by trying to match up the bad debt expense that will be incurred with the related income that was used to generate it in the same time period. So it's the most correct answer. The match in principle requires the use of the allowance method.

Managerial Accounting

In this chapter, we will introduce the topic of managerial accounting. When considering managerial accounting, we can compare it to the other major form of accounting, which is financial accounting. There will be overlap between managerial accounting and financial accounting, but the major difference when we consider managerial accounting is that our main focus is for management. Our main focus is for management's use. Management's goal is to make decision making for the company. So managerial accounting is geared towards decision making processes, making reports for management. If we contrast that to financial accounting. Financial accounting is the creation of the financial statements. Ultimately, we're entering data.

We're going to create the financial statements, the balance sheet, the income statement, the statement of equity, and we could use that by management. However, the primary goal in the way it is constructed is actually for external users. So when we make the financial statements, when we think about financial accounting, everything that we put together is really geared towards the eyes and the objectives and the goals of external users. People like investors, people like creditors. They're not designed necessarily or ultimately solely for the primary purpose being the management.

Usually when we think about this, we think, hey, wait a second. The financial statements are basically all of the financial data. So wouldn't the manager wouldn't management need to be using the same income statement, balance sheet statement of equity when making decisions as would the external users? And the answer is yes. The management will be using that information. The financial data that we're putting together will be used for managerial accounting as well. But the managerial accounting isn't restricted in the same way as we are with the financial statement reports, because the financial statement reports are really geared to and there's going to be restrictions on in terms of regulatory regulatory restrictions so that the financial statements are proper and for the best use of is the goal for external users.

So although there is going to be the same financial data for managerial accounting, we can do other things with it. Outside of just the norm of the financial statements. We can customize them. In other words, make custom reports for management, for decision making processes. So everything that's going to flow forward in terms of what's the difference between managerial accounting and financial accounting, will gear back to this answer. It seems fundamental, it seems basic, but everything stems from this, and that is that managerial accounting is for management, it's for internal users as opposed to external users.

It's for the decision making processes for that management to make decisions about future decisions as opposed to external users to make sure that they have the information they know they need typically for investment decisions or credit type decisions. So given that, given that managerial accounting is for management, let's think of some of the differences. And it's always useful to think about the differences in contrasting the financial accounting versus managerial accounting. So who are the users for financial accounting and managerial accounting? The users are going to be external for financial accounting. Managerial accounting is going to be internal.

And again, that's the major focus, the financial accounting, although we use the same information, the information is designed and put together in such a way and regulated to be put in together in such a way so that external users can trust it, be able to know exactly what's going to be expected from it, and be able to use those external users, being investors, creditors and the managerial accounting. We're talking about internal users. So we don't have that same problem of the internal users trying to, you know, print reports that might be deceptive to themselves or anything like that. And therefore, management can print their internal reports in more of a free way.

How, however, they want to create their reports or put the numbers in order to make the best decisions. So most of the differences between these two types of accounting will fall into alignment with this major difference here. Who are we focused on, internal users or external users? Then we have the reason for the accounting. The external decision making in terms of financial accounting is what we're putting this together for. So we're looking for external users, investors, and creditors. They want to make investment decisions. Should they put their money into the business, Should they invest in the stock? Should a bank loan money to the organization, those things they need in order to make those decisions? They need some financial statements that they can rely on, numbers they can rely on.

And those numbers need to be based on what they want to know. Big picture. Typically the full company. How is the company doing as a whole? Managerial accounting is going to be focused on managerial planning type decisions. So that means that the whole purpose is to really take that information and put it into a plan for the future. Now, note that there is overlap, Of course, because if I'm thinking about investing in a company, I might do my own kind of projections and try to think about what they are going to do in the future? Do they have a good plan? Is it going to be a good plan? However, really the investors are trying to see where our company stands at this point in time.

It might not be getting so much into the nitty gritty as managerial accounting may do to take these numbers and use them to make more detailed projections, especially about a piecemeal piece by piece, unit by unit, area by area, department by department of the company. And then we got flexibility. Financial accounting is going to be limited by regulations and generally accepted accounting principles in the US. Typically, there's going to be limitations. And the reason for that is because these external users need to know what they're getting. They need some form of standardization so that they can compare this company's financials to other companies.

Financials, and therefore financial accounting is going to be much more standardized. It's got to be in order to build trust with the public. If we're trying to get investments from the public, then we have to be in alignment with standards that the public can expect so that they can read what we're giving to them and be able to compare and contrast what's being given with other companies. So when we think about the financial statements, then we know exactly what to expect. For the most part, because it's regulated. We have a standardized format and we have to have that standardized format in order to make these comparisons, in order to make trade and investment and transactions as easy as possible.

Managerial accounting, however, is not limited in the same way. Why? Because we're not giving these reports to anybody outside the company. They're internal reports. They're US inner workings trying to make the internal decisions. So we might be making reports about a small group, a small unit. We might be making reports about some type of product or something like that. One product out of many. In order to make those types of decisions, we could format the reports in any way we want because we're not giving them to external users who are then relying on them to make decisions.

So we have a lot more flexibility for that reason for managerial accounting to run reports, to make reports to think about what we can do in order to make the best decisions and what kind of data we need in order to do that. The availability of the data. Financial accounting is typically going to be if it's a publicly traded company in particular, it's going to go through an audit. We're not going to have the data possibly quarterly or yearly. We have to wait through that audit process to take place for them to really be finalized to have those financial statements. So it could be a very set process on when we're going to get those numbers.

And the numbers might not be finalized, Of course, for a little bit of time after, you know, after the period has ended. Whereas managerial accounting and that, Of course, deals with regulations, we have to go through the regulations. We have to make sure that everything is set up in accordance with rules and regulations, especially if it's a publicly traded company. Do these financial statements align with generally accepted accounting principles and whatnot? That process is going to take time for financial accounting, and it's very regulated for managerial accounting. We don't have that same kind of regulation.

We have limits, Of course, but those limits are typically going to be what can we do? So for managerial accounting, the question is often a cost benefit analysis. You know, we could get this more information. The question is, is it worth it for us to get more information? There's always a balancing question of is it worth us to put in the time to get more detailed information or is the better decision that we can probably make with that more detailed information not worth the added cost? That's typically the type of decision making restraints that we have on managerial accounting as opposed to the types of regulatory restraints.

So if we want to put numbers together, if we want to put reports together, if we want to analyze whatever we want to analyze internally, no problem, except that it costs money to do so. And we want to make a cost benefit analysis to decide whether or not the time spent is worth the effort, as opposed to conforming to regulations as is typically going to be what we're going to do with financial accounting. The time focus for the financial accounting is typically going to be passed. We're looking into the past. In other words, we're looking at historical data. Now, Of course, investors are going to be looking. To project into the future as well.

But all the financial statement preparation is geared towards what happened in the past from our side, from putting the stuff together from a company side, we're trying to just say, Hey, what happened? And put it together as accurately as possible? And then the investors could make future projections based on that. Managerial accounting. When we put this information together, it usually has a future focus. So we're trying to focus on future decision making. So when we put together reports, internal reports, whatever we need to do from an internal standpoint, we're typically thinking about what we can do for the future in this place so that we can increase production.

If we look at the information focus, it's going to be on the entire organization for financial accounting. We're looking for information that's going to affect the entire organization, and that's by design. The financial statements are there for the entire organization because investors and creditors are typically worried about the entire organization. They're not really looking into the details. They're not looking at segments of the organization. Some will. And but for the most part, the reporting is going to give a whole as a whole, what do things look like as an entire on a managerial accounting? We're typically going to go more into detail.

We're going to look at the department by department. We're going to look at product by product and try to make those decisions. So typically, financial accounting is looking at the big picture. How do we stand overall? Whereas managerial accounting is going to go down into more of the nitty gritty and try to figure out what we can do from a piece by piece standpoint to improve operations. Nature of information. Financial accounting is going to be purely monetary. So remember that, Of course, the balance sheet is going to have things like equipment on it and this stuff and stuff. That's not money in and of itself.

Equipment is. It could be a forklift or something. But when we put it on the financial statement, we report it in terms of dollars. Everything is reported in terms of dollars. And Of course, that same information will be used in managerial accounting. But it's not the only type of information we recognize that that's only one set of information. If we can put numbers to something, we typically will, because that makes things a lot easier to compare and contrast if we have numbers to them. But oftentimes we may not have numbers. The numbers may not be representing monetary amounts. We might be having to compare other types of things, time or other types of things, and we could have other things that are completely non numeric that we're comparing.

We might have to actually compare different types of data, actually just reviews or something like that and try to make managerial decision making processes based on that. So again, we typically will break things down to a monetary basis if possible, break things down to a numeric basis if possible, because that's better for making comparisons or easier to make comparisons. But we're also going to use any type of data that we can to increase decision making processes.

Cost Classifications

The cost classifications chapter of the Book will talk about different ways that costs can be classified in managerial accounting. Cost classifications are going to be important within managerial accounting because we often want to group costs in different formats depending on the types of information we want to get for the decisions that we are making. For example we may want to classify the costs by behavior. We also might want to classify costs by the function that the costs are used for. We'll use these terms of cost classifications within a job costs system. As we track the costs related to inventory through the process from raw materials to work in process and finally to the finished product to finished goods inventory and then through the sale to cost of goods sold.

In this chapter, we will take a look at cost classifications. There's a few different ways that we can classify costs, and they all have their pros and cons, their benefits to classification in different ways. We're going to classify costs here by behavior. Now, you may think, what does that mean? Do costs have behavior? And we can say, well, yeah, costs do have behavior in that they act in certain ways in relation to other activities. We're going to classify the two types of costs here being fixed costs and variable costs. This type of classification is not included in financial accounting. So if you're going from financial accounting to managerial accounting, this is going to be a new concept. And the reason we're going to have cost classifications by behavior is that it really helps with projections.

So we have to have this because when we're looking into the future, what's really going to be helpful if we can determine how costs act so that we can make projections based on different levels of production. So we have fixed costs. Fixed costs mean that as production level rises, the cost remains fixed. So, for example, if we have the activity down here, we'll say this is production. If we're making units of something, as we make more units of something, the cost total remains the same. Remember here that we're talking about total cost, not cost per unit. We're starting here with total cost. So, for example, if we're saying that the rent is going to be $1,000 a month, then it really doesn't matter how many units we make.

If we're producing things in a warehouse and we make one unit in that warehouse, then it still costs $1,000. If we are producing in that warehouse and we make, say, 100 things, the rent still is $1,000. If we keep producing in that warehouse and we maximize the production of the warehouse, let's say it's 5000 things, well then units of production, whatever we make, then it's still going to cost us $1,000. No matter what we do, the rent is going to be the same. And so if you look at that in terms of the fixed costs, you're going to say, well, it's going to be what it is no matter what. So when making projections, then we can think of, okay, how many units do we have to produce in order to pay off the rent, pay off the fixed cost? So the other types of behavior that we're going to have, the major second group that we're going to have and we're going to try to basically break everything out into these two groups, even though it's not possible or not all costs fit nicely into these two groups.

We would really like it if they did because that would simplify the world here. And we're going to try to do so so that we can make accurate projections. And so the other type is variable costs, and variable costs are going to go up with each new unit of production. So, for example, if we're making guitars and this is the cost of wood, the total cost of wood and this is the activity, how many guitars we're going to make. Well, if we make one guitar, then it's going to cost. Or if we make one guitar here, it's going to cost so much. And then if we make two guitars, well, the activity went up and the cost is going to go up in proportion. It's going to be a straight line because the cost is going to go up with the same number of units. Let's say the cost is for wood that's going to go in the guitar.

If we make three guitars, well then the cost of wood is going to go up in proportion to the number of guitars that we're making. So, wood or direct material that goes into the cost of production is going to go up your wood at a constant rate. And as opposed to something that is fixed such as the rent, if we know those two things, then it's really useful for us to then make projections into the future because now we can say, okay, how many guitars do we need to make in order to get to this level of cost? And Of course we'll add into this pretty soon. We'll add into it the amount of revenue per guitar we're going to get.

And if we take the revenue minus the variable costs, then we can say, okay, how much are we making over the variable costs to see how many units we then need to have in order to clear the rent price? And that's how we start to kind of think about these things. What do we need to produce in order to clear our costs? It's a lot easier to make those types of production projections if we can break all costs up by behavior between fixed costs and variable costs. Now, some costs will line up in these two very easily, and it won't be a problem. If we're talking about wood in the guitar, then that's probably pretty straightforward.

If we're talking about the rent, that's pretty straightforward, but we're going to have some things that aren't quite as easy to go into these two components they may have. Some combination between fixed costs and variable costs. And what we really want to do is break them out between those two for our projection purposes. And we'll talk about different methods that we can do. That's going to be one of our goals in managerial accounting is to break everything out between fixed costs and variable costs that allows us to make nice projections into the future. Another way that we can classify costs is by function.

What does that cost do? Why are we incurring this cost? So we can have direct costs and indirect costs. Direct costs are going to be costs that are traceable to a cost object. So if we're in a production cycle, then direct costs would be things like direct materials and direct labor. These are things that we can trace to a particular unit of inventory that we are producing. So direct materials, we know exactly if we're making guitars, for example, we can trace the wood in the guitar to a particular guitar that we are producing and allocate the cost of that wood to that piece of inventory, to that guitar. If we're talking about direct labor, same thing. If someone's putting together a guitar, we can allocate the cost of the labor that's being put together to a particular piece of inventory, a particular guitar.

On the other hand, indirect costs are things that we can't trace, are not traceable to a cost object. So examples of that are going to be maintenance costs for, for multiple departments or things like glue or things that we can't put to a particular guitar. If we're making one guitar, then we can't really have these indirect costs allocated specifically to that guitar. It's going to be indirect. So if we talk about maintenance for multiple departments, then possibly the maintenance is going to be for the entire warehouse. And we can't apply the maintenance, for example, to one particular guitar because we don't know how much to apply to a particular guitar. The production process needs maintenance within the warehouse, but we can't assign it directly to a particular guitar and we can take that concept to different departments as well.

If we pay for maintenance for multiple departments, then the maintenance is there for multiple departments, but it's difficult to allocate to a particular department and we're going to have to figure out some type of way to allocate these indirect costs. That's going to be one of the challenges we have. If we have maintenance for multiple departments or multiple units of inventory, how then can we take this information and allocate it to a particular unit, a particular unit which we don't really know? We have a similar problem. If we're talking about small materials like glue or something for a guitar, it might be possible for us to classify glue as a direct material that we can then allocate specifically to a particular guitar that was used.

It was used in. However, doing so would typically not be cost effective. So if we're talking about something like glue or something like that, then we might have to use some other type of allocation method. We don't know exactly which piece of unit of inventory it was used on. So it's indirect. So we have to find some way. Then our challenge will be to take these indirect costs, these costs that we know need to be allocated in some way in order for us to properly value our inventory and try to allocate them in some way, even though we don't know directly where they apply. And that'll typically be the concept of overhead.

So anything, for example, in a factory that we work on will be, well, if we can't apply it to directly direct materials or labor, it's probably going to be an indirect cost, something that's going to go into overhead that we're then going to have to figure out how can we allocate this to our units of inventory to properly allocate the inventory. So if we're talking about depreciation on a warehouse, then that depreciation is part of the cost of making stuff, making the guitars. But how do we allocate it to any particular guitar? We're going to have to figure out how we can make those types of allocations. There's a supervisor in the warehouse that's supervising all the guitars we make.

How do we know how much time we should put that supervisor's time on a particular job? We'll have to figure out how we can make those allocations. So that's going to be one of the challenges we'll have as we work through the manufacturing process, as we allocate costs.

Product Costs & Period Costs

In this chapter, we will take a look at product costs and period costs. When considering a manufacturing company, we can break out the costs to those costs that are used to create the product, to create the inventory, the inventory that we will eventually sell, and those that will not. The product costs are going to include costs of direct labor, direct material and overhead. So we just want to memorize these types of things as the three main categories we will be using when we manufacture inventory, when we make the asset of inventory, when we make the stuff that we're going to sell, That stuff is not just stuff, meaning not just direct materials.

In other words, the creation of something like a guitar that we intend to sell is not composed of just the materials in the guitar, the woods, the strings and whatnot, but is substantially composed of other things such as labor and overhead. So these are the three things that make up the cost of the guitar that we're going to sell, make up the cost of whatever product it is that we sell. The direct materials are pretty straightforward. This is going to be the material that goes directly into the units of inventory that we're creating. So if we're creating guitars, if we're making guitars, the wood is clearly a direct material that we can assign specifically to inventory and more specifically to whatever batch of inventory, whatever unit of guitar that we are making.

Direct labor is very similar in that we are applying Labor directly to a unit of production. So if we're making guitars and we have a custom guitar, let's say, and an individual producing that guitar, then the labor that's being put in will be included in that guitar. And again, it's a little bit less conceptual to think about that the labor is being included in the guitar. It's not physically in the guitar. It's something that's intangible within the guitar. But when we think about the cost of the guitar, it's far more than just the wood that's in the guitar. The cost is primarily the labor that's going to be in the guitar. The thing that converts that wood into something useful, a guitar.

So that's going to be the direct labor that we can apply directly. And then we have this bucket of overhead, the most confusing bucket, the bucket we're going to have to do something about something with and those are going to be things that we cannot apply directly to a specific unit. So if we're in a specific area. So for example, if we're making guitars and we're applying costs directly to a guitar, if we make custom guitars, then things that we can't apply directly might be things like glue because it's so small that we don't want to apply it directly. Would take too much time for us to apply the glue to the guitar. So to track the amount of glue we use and whatnot.

So what we'll do is we'll put it into overhead and then we'll find some type of cost allocation to then allocate it out. And that's going to include anything that we can't allocate directly. So if we think about things like overhead in the factory, anything within the factory that we use that we cannot apply directly, pretty much anything other than direct materials or direct labor, things like the depreciation of the factory. We're going to have to apply that out to the guitars. We need the factory to make the guitars. If we weren't making guitars, we wouldn't have the factory and therefore wouldn't be depreciating it. And so the cost of that depreciation should be allocated to the guitars, but we want to allocate it specifically to units of guitars.

If we're using a job cost system, things like a supervisor salary, we don't know who the supervisor was supervising at any given time or how much time was spent supervising one job versus another job. And therefore we're going to have to allocate that production supervisor to overhead and then figure out some type of allocation method. So the utilities on the factory, same way, the maintenance on the factory. So we're going to have this is going to be the most challenging of our segments here. So we know it's part of production that's not a problem. Anything on the factory's part of production.

But it becomes challenging to know if we're in a job cost or process cost, what job or what process should this overhead go to? And then we're going to have period costs. Now the period costs are typically you can think of them as things that are not going to be part of the production, part of the inventory. These costs up here, direct labor, direct materials and overhead are going to be costs. The production costs are going to be costs that we're going to use to create the product and therefore they're going to be capitalized when we use them. And this will seem a little unusual if you're used to looking at a service company, because when we do something like pay wages, for example, we're not used to we're pretty much used to just saying it's going to be a wage expense. And here we're going to put it as part of the inventory asset.

When we use materials, we might think of it as a materials expense. We're going to capitalize it as an asset when we do things such as overhead depreciation and things like that. We're used to saying depreciation, expense and expense, but here we're going to capitalize it because it's part of the product that we're going to make. When are we going to expense it? When we sell the product. The period costs, on the other hand, are going to be costs that are not related to the production of the product, and they're going to act more typically, as we would think when we're dealing with like a service type company, they're going to be costs for a particular time period and they're typically broken out between two items selling and administrative.

And they act like we would think, for a service type company. So if we're talking about the executive salary, anything that's not in the warehouse, anything that's not in the production area, which will be very distinct in like a book problem, we'd have to separate that and separate what's in production and what's not. If we're talking about the corporate office that's not in production, anything in there will probably act very similar to a service company, meaning if we pay the salary of administrative staff or the accounting staff, then that's going to be done during the period because the cost was incurred during that period. We paid people in order to do the job during that time period.

The matching principle would then allow us to expense it at the point in time that basically the wages happened. For the most part, the utilities on the executive office, unlike the utilities, on the production, on the factory, which would go into overhead if it was utilities bill on the office, the executive office, we would expense it like we would typically think if we're talking about depreciation, if it was depreciation on the executive office, we would depreciate the expense. If it was in the factory, we would include it in the inventory in some way.

So these selling and administrative expenses are typically going to act a little bit more like we would think if we're used to having dealt with companies that aren't production companies that don't deal with making inventory, companies that either buy or sell inventory or companies that are service companies, as you would imagine, most of our time here is going to be up here in the in the production cost to make the product one, because that's the most interesting part, because that's where we have to all the activities happening within a manufacturing company that we have to track all this stuff. And two, because that's going to be something that's different from other types of industries. Therefore, that's where we want to focus our time.

If we look at some examples of the type of classifications we've had so far, we had variable cost versus fixed cost, direct or indirect cost and product or period costs. So if we think let's look at some examples and think about where they would go in these cost allocations. And again, when we first learn this stuff, some people probably learn a few of these allocations better than others. It's important for us to know all of them. So the variable cost versus fixed cost, the behavior that we're going to have between the cost, the direct or indirect, can we apply the cost out to a particular unit or a particular function and a product cost or period cost really is dealing with are we dealing with the inventory stuff that and that's making the inventory or are we dealing with non inventory stuff, which is basically admin, administrative and selling? So let's take a look at why we're going to make guitars up here.

So if we have wood and this is a wood guitar you can see here. So if it's a wood guitar, we would say it's typically going to be variable because every time we make a new guitar, we're going to have to have a fixed number of increases in wood cost, you would think. And so that's going to be a variable cost as opposed to fixed. It's going to be direct typically because if we're making custom guitars, we would know exactly which guitar that wood goes to. We would be able to assign the guitar out directly and the product or period.

It's going to be clearly a product cost because the wood is going to be for the production of the guitar. If we have direct wages, someone actually making the guitar, we're paying someone to make the guitar. It once again will be variable because if we make two guitars, we would expect the wages to go up at some variable rate. If we have direct or indirect, we're going to say it's direct because that person, we can apply their cost directly to whatever guitars they work on and then the product or period. It's clearly a product cost because we're working on the production, the cost of those wages.

And again, that's something different because then when we actually record the journal entry and we say instead of wages expense, we're going to debit the guitar, we're going to debit work in process inventory of some kind. We'll talk more about that later. Then that's going to be unusual at first because a lot of times when we go through. Just memorizing transactions. We think of wages as an expense just automatically without knowing the rule so much or applying the rule. Same with utilities. We're going to have utilities, not utilities expense the debit, but go into some type of asset for the inventory.

That's going to feel unusual if we've just memorized the rule saying that utilities are always utilities expense debit and we credit cash. So these things, it makes sense right here. But as we record the journal entries, we'll have to really think about it probably in order and possibly unlearn some rules of advertising that's going to be typically fixed. Oftentimes it's going to be fixed advertising. Is it going to be direct or indirect? It's going to be indirect. Now, these are going to be things advertising isn't dealing with production, so it's not within the production.

So when we think about direct or indirect, oftentimes we're thinking about the production process. Is this something that we can assign directly to a particular guitar, for example, or or is it something that I don't know which guitar was worked on? If it's selling an admin, it may not. Sometimes you might think, well, that's not applicable, that's not as applicable because we're not really even dealing with production at all. This is going to be as we see a period of costs. So here you could put like an A or not not as applicable or indirect and it's going to be a period cost, meaning it's not part of the production process.

It's going to be something that we pay for selling and admin. And then we have the manager's salary. So the manager 's salary is fixed. We're going to say it's going to be because they get paid salary and not wages. As we produce guitars, it's going to be indirect. If they're managing the warehouse, then again, we don't even know which guitar they're actually managing there. So we're going to have to apply their costs out to the guitars in some format and we're going to say it's a product cost because we're going to say they're managing the warehouse.

So this is going to be a fixed cost as opposed to what we would think the workers of the guitar would probably be variable. We're going to say this was an hourly salary. It's indirect even though they're in the warehouse because we don't know which guitar they're working on. We don't know who they're supervising, but we're going to have to allocate that somehow. And it's going to be a product cost because they are in the warehouse. So we're going to have to allocate it out somehow.

Admin equipment, depreciation. So if we're talking about the depression depreciation for the administrative office, like the fax machines or something like the copy machines or something like that, where depreciation in the administrative office, not the factory, we're going to say it's fixed depreciation. We know exactly what it's going to be, it's going to be indirect or not applicable because it's not in the production, it's not in the warehouse, it's not going to the making of the product. And then it's going to be a period cost because it's in the admin, it's in the administrative office and therefore it's not part of production. So it's not going to be in the production area. And then we have factory depreciation, factory depreciation on this type.

It's both depreciation here. But notice if it's in the factory, it's still going to be fixed because we know exactly what the depreciation will be. You know, it's a set amount. It's still going to be indirect, not because it's not in the factory this time, however, it is in the factory, meaning it should go into the production of our guitars, but we don't know which guitar it's going to go to. We made all the guitars in the factory. So how if we have a job cost system, how do we apply it to a job? It's a process cost system. How do we apply it to a process? And so it's going to be a product cost. So it does apply to the product, but it is indirect because I don't know which product exactly.

It goes to something like glue that we use to make the guitar together. It's going to be variable because it changes with the number of units of guitar. We're going to need more glue with more guitars. It's going to be indirect, however, because we don't really know how much glue we used on one particular guitar, so we don't know. We can estimate it and that's what we'll have to do. But we don't know exactly what that estimate should be. And then it's going to be a product cost. So it's going to be part of the production process. So the idea here on glue is it's going to be pretty small compared to something like the wood.

So if you compare the glue and the wood up here, then we're going to say, well, the wood is variable, but it's direct because I can I can assign you know, I probably had to assign the wood that I that I took out to a particular job, whereas the glue down here is, is variable, but it's not direct because I probably didn't have to go assign out to get the glue. I just went and got the glue. I didn't have to get any kind of documentation telling me how much glue I'm going to get to put on a particular. Their job, it wouldn't be worth our time to track that. And therefore it's going to be an indirect cost that we're just going to have to take that glue, whatever we paid for the glue overall and allocate it using some kind of allocation method sales Commission.

So commission on the sales, it's variable, which is unusual for a period cost. So this is a period cost that would be variable. It's going to be indirect or not applicable because it's not part of the production process and it's going to be a period cost. So this is one of those costs which are a little bit confusing because most period costs are oftentimes fixed. So most salaries are fixed in the corporate office. We don't typically have a lot of variable costs with the sales except for the commission here. And when we do our different types of allocations, that's going to kind of how we deal with that? We're going to have to deal with that when we think of something like projections, we're going to have to break this out to a variable cost.

And in that format, it'll probably be grouped more with some of the production costs because we're trying to break out variable versus fixed. Oftentimes when we're looking at productions, when projections that are so sales commissions are variable, it's indirect or not applicable and it's a period cost because it doesn't deal with the production process.

Prime Costs & Conversion Costs

In this chapter we will take a look at prime costs and conversion costs. When considering prime costs and conversion costs we are looking at the cost of production we're looking at production costs as opposed to period costs. When considering production costs we always think about direct materials, direct labor and overhead. They should always come to mind when we think about production any time we think about inventory whether we make it or whether it be made someplace else. Its costs include the direct materials direct labor overhead. We are talking about a manufacturing company that is going to apply these three items at this point in time because we are the individuals of the company that is manufacturing the products. Remember it's not just the materials within the product.

That's one component but the other component is going to be the labor that we're going to put into it. The cost of the labor and the wages we pay are not going to be a period expense but part of the cost of inventory to be capitalized will be put on the balance sheet until we sell the inventory put on the balance sheet as in as a piece of the inventory as an asset and then the overhead. Anything dealing with the factory anything that deals with the factory will be part of the inventory if we have depreciation on the factory if we have if we have maintenance on the factory if we've got supervisors within the factory that are paid salary all that stuff is going to be in the inventory in some way they're going to be part of the product. So any time we think of inventory we have direct materials, direct labor and overhead.

Now when we consider these in terms of prime costs and conversion costs there's a bit of an overlap here because the prime costs represent what is going to be directly within the product. Therefore the prime costs include the direct materials and the direct labor. Now the direct labor we can't really see within the product Of course like the direct materials but it's so closely associated with the product it's so essential to the production that we're going to call those the prime costs. Now that's going to differentiate from conversion costs although there are some overlaps. The conversion costs are the costs that we're going to have. That will be used to convert the raw material to the finished goods. The cost means that we're doing something, we're doing something to the raw material.

So for example our guitar, the direct material would be something like the wood, the conversion would be anything we do to that in order to make it into a guitar. So conversion costs are then going to include direct labor and the overhead because the direct labor is going to be part of us processing it and the overhead is going to be included. Anything that's in the factory because Of course we need that factory in order to convert. So anything like a depreciation on the factory the supervisors salary on the factory the small tools that we use the glue that we're going to use all that stuff is part of the conversion process part of the things that we're doing to adding onto that piece of wood in order to convert it from just a piece of wood to the end product to the guitar.

Now this is going to be an added category that we can start to get confused with something like direct versus indirect costs. It's a bit different of a concept. We need to keep these separated so the prime costs and the conversion costs we're often going to use more when we use that process cost system that we'll talk about a job cost versus the process costs system. But it's different from the direct cost and the indirect costs. Remember that our direct costs are going to be those that are direct materials and direct labor are both direct costs which happens to be the two prime costs as well but for different reasons these two are going to be direct costs because we can we can apply those activities to a particular unit if we have a job cost system we can apply those two activities to a particular guitar we know which guitars were worked on and can therefore apply these these costs to that guitar.

Whereas the overhead was indirect because we didn't know which in a job cost system we wouldn't know which guitar to apply all the stuff in overhead too we have to find some way to do that. So if you compare that to the prime costs are utilizing the same factors as as indirect costs but for different reasons the prime cause meaning that they're going to be prime the prime factors of production is the primary expenditures the ones that are going to be most associated with the manufacturing of the inventory. So those two are similar. The difference Of course is the conversion cost does not light is not at all the same as the indirect cost. The indirect costs are just going to be the overhead because we can't apply them if you think of a job cost system. We can't apply them to the job.

That's why they're indirect, that's why they're overhead from a conversion standpoint. The conversion means anything that we're doing to the inventory to convert it so that's why it's going to include direct labor. So here's where the overlap is. This direct labor becomes a bit confusing because it's both a prime cost and a conversion cost. And when we consider that and compare and contrast it to direct versus indirect costs indirect costs happen to have the same two components but for different reasons the conversion is not the same as the indirect cost because the conversion represents us converting this information which will include this direct labor as well as the overhead.

Discussion Question - Job Cost System

In this discussion, we will discuss the discussion question of describing what a job cost sheet is and how it is used. If we see an essay question like this, we're looking at a job cost sheet and that could give us an indication that we are using a job cost system. So on May 1st, if we don't know exactly where to start, start off with what a job cost system is, when it might be used, and then we can go into the job cost sheets and how the job cost sheets relate to the job cost system. So a job cost system is typically a system one of two that's going to be used for production processes, although it could also be used for service companies as well.

Usually in cases where we're going to have some type of customization, where the things that we're producing, the jobs we're working on will be different. And therefore we need to track costs between the inventory or the jobs in a separate way so that we can track those costs that will differ from job to job because those jobs are going to be different in nature. There's going to be some type of customization typically, so we can think of a construction company or we can think of anything we make that's going to be customized if we have the custom guitars or custom jewelry, anything that's going to be customized could be used.

A job cost system could be used in. So within the job cost system, then we have the job sheets. So what is a job sheet? It's going to be the supporting document. It's kind of like a subsidiary ledger. If you take all the sheets together, you can think of them as a supporting documentation, kind of like a subsidiary ledger to the accounts on the trial balance or the balance sheet for inventory, including the inventory that's not yet completed work in process and the inventory that is completed finished goods, those two numbers on the balance sheet are just going to be one number for say, work in process. We're going to have one number representing work in process and that's going to include a lot of stuff.

The work in process account includes direct labor and will include labor material and overhead, and it includes those for multiple jobs. And so we need more detail than what is going to be on the balance sheet or the or the trial balance. That detail. Some of it can be found on the general ledger as can be found with any kind of account, but that only gives us details by date of when things happened and we need more detail than that. That's what we use the job sheets for. The job sheets will give us details by job. So it's going to break up this number by job for both work in process and finished goods, depending on if the job is open or closed, completed or not completed.

And for each individual job, we'll then see how much of the direct labor goes to it, how much of the work in process and how much overhead is applied to each individual job. So we'll get the details of each individual job that we are working on and we'll also be able to sum up the jobs, all the jobs that are not yet completed. That should add up to what is on the trial balance under work in process or the balance sheet and all the jobs that have been completed but have not yet been shipped, haven't gone out to the customers yet, should be if we sum up all those jobs, the number that's on the balance sheet for finished inventory that is not yet gone out, has not been transferred yet to cost of goods sold.

The content of any individual job cost sheet is usually going to tell us who the customer is. We're going to have the very important information of the job number. That's how we're going to track the jobs typically, and we're going to have any customer information on the job cost sheet, and then it will break up the costs of the job. And those costs will typically include direct materials, direct labor and overhead per job will sum those up. Those will give us the total cost for the job. The job cost sheet could look somewhat like an invoice. We might see it like a construction company or some type of service business.

It's not the same thing. The job cost sheet is tracking the cost, but we could use that cost information Of course, then to fill out and make an invoice with it. We might be very transparent in our invoice and say, Hey look, this is how much it cost us and we have a mark up. That's going to be typical for a construction type of company or possibly many customized projects where we actually say, Hey, here's how much the materials cost, here's how much the overhead is, here's how much labor cost, and here's how much our markup is. This is basically our profit margin, and that could be one way to create the invoice. So it's just important to keep those two things separate. The job sheets are not the same as an invoice, but the invoice may look similar because we may base our invoice in part on the items on the job sheet.

Manufacturer's Financial Statements

Within the manufacturer's financial statements chapter of the. We'll talk about financial statements related to a manufacturing company as we do so we're comparing and contrasting it to other types of companies including a service company one that doesn't have inventory or a merchandising company one that purchases and then sells inventory. The manufacturer Of course will be producing inventory. So we'll take a look at the differences. Focusing on what will be different from a manufacturing company.

That being typically things that are going to be within the production process tracking the costs through the inventory process through the raw materials to us working on the raw materials to those materials being completed finished goods and finally to us selling those finished goods inventory and recording the costs on the income statement in the form of cost of goods sold.

Manufacturer's Balance Sheet

In this chapter, we will take a look at prime costs and conversion costs. When considering prime costs and conversion costs. We are looking at the cost of production. We're looking at production costs as opposed to period costs. When considering production costs, we always think about direct materials, direct labor and overhead. This should always come to mind when we think about production. Any time we think about inventory, whether we make it or whether it be made someplace else, its costs include the direct materials, direct labor overhead.

We are talking about a manufacturing company that is going to apply these three items at this point in time because we are the individuals or the company that is manufacturing the product. So remember, it's not just the materials within the product. That's one component, but the other component is going to be the labor that we're going to put into it. The cost of the labor, the wages we pay are not going to be a period expense, but be part of the cost of inventory to be capitalized, to be put on the balance sheet until we sell the inventory. But on the balance sheet as a piece of the inventory as an asset and then the overhead, anything dealing with the factory, anything that deals with the factory will be part of the inventory.

If we have depreciation on the factory, if we have maintenance on the factory, if we've got supervisors within the factory that are paid salary, all that stuff is going to be in the inventory in some way. They're going to be part of the product. So any time we think of inventory, we have direct materials, direct labor and overhead. Now when we consider these in terms of prime costs and conversion costs, there's a bit of an overlap here because the prime costs represent what is going to be directly within the product. Therefore, the prime costs include the direct materials and the direct labor. Now the direct labor, we can't really see within the product, Of course, like the direct materials, but it's so closely associated with the product, so essential to the production that we're going to call those the prime costs.

Now that's going to differentiate from conversion costs, although there are some overlaps, the conversion costs are the costs that we're going to have that will be used to convert the raw material to the finished goods, the cost. That means that we're doing something, we're doing something to the raw material. So in the example of a guitar, the direct material would be something like the wood, the conversion would be anything we do to that in order to make it into a guitar. So conversion costs are then going to include direct labor and the overhead because direct labor is going to be part of us processing it and the overhead is going to be included. Anything that's in the factory because Of course we need that factory in order to convert.

So anything like the depreciation on the factory, the supervisor salary on the factory, the small tools that we use, the glue that we're going to use, all that stuff is part of the conversion process, part of the things that we're doing to adding on to that piece of wood in order to convert it from just a piece of wood to the end product to the guitar. Now this is going to be an added category that we can start to get confused with something like direct versus an indirect cost. It's a bit different of a concept. We need to keep these separated.

So the prime cost and the conversion costs were often going to be used more when we use a process cost system and we'll talk about a job cost versus a process cost system, but it's different from the direct cost and the indirect cost. Remember that our direct costs are going to be those that are direct materials and direct labor are both direct costs, which happens to be the two prime costs as well, but for different reasons. These two are going to be direct costs because we can apply those activities to a particular unit. If we have a job cost system, we can apply those two activities to a particular guitar.

We know which guitars were worked on and can therefore apply these costs to that guitar, whereas the overhead was indirect because we didn't know which in a job cost system we wouldn't know which guitar to apply all the stuff in overhead to. We have to find some way to do that. So if you compare the two, the prime costs are utilizing the same factors as the direct costs, but for different reasons. The prime cost means that they're going to be prime, the prime factors of production are the primary expenditures, the ones that are going to be most associated with the manufacturing of the inventory.

So those two are similar. The difference, Of course, is the conversion cost is not equivalent or is not at all the same as the indirect cost. The indirect costs are just going to be the overhead because we can't apply them. If you think of a job cost system, we can't apply them to the job. That's why they're indirect. That's why they're overhead. From a conversion standpoint, the conversion means anything that we're doing to the inventory to convert it. So. That's why it's going to include direct labor. So here's where the overlap is. This direct labor becomes a bit confusing because it's both a prime cost and a conversion cost.

And when we consider that and compare and contrast it to direct versus indirect prime costs and direct costs happen to have the same two components, but for different reasons. The conversion is not the same as the indirect cost because the conversion represents us converting this information, which will include this direct labor as well as the overhead.

Manufacturer's Income Statement

In this chapter, we will take a look at some of the components of a manufacturer's income statement comparing and contrasting where a manufacturer's income statement may differ from a surface company or a merchandiser where a manufacturer, a company that makes the inventory could differ from a service company that has no inventory, or a merchandiser who just purchases and sells inventory rather than making the inventory. Part of that will be the calculation of the cost of goods sold. So clearly, one of the differences we're going to have from a manufacturer to a service company will be related to inventory.

And the major difference between the inventory accounts on the income statement is the cost of the inventory, the expense related to the inventory at the point of sale, that being the cost of goods sold. Therefore, a service company is often going to have just a single step income statement where we group up revenue and then we group up all of the expenses and we subtract out to get the net income for a merchandiser that has inventory and a manufacturer that makes inventory, we're also going to have the cost of goods sold. The cost of goods sold will be very similar, but it will have some differences that we want to note from a merchandiser company to a manufacturing company.

Very important formula. We want to just memorize this formula. We'll be using this formula in many different ways. So the merchandiser company, if we thought about the merchandiser company first and then convert and say, okay, what do we need to change to go to a manufacturing company to calculate the cost of goods sold for a merchandiser? A company that just purchases and sells inventory doesn't make the inventory. The cost of goods sold calculation would be the beginning inventory. What was inventory at the start of the period, the start of the month or the year? And then we're going to add to it purchases.

We know what the purchases are because we actually paid for the inventory that we bought, and therefore there's no real estimation in terms of the purchases that's going to give us the cost of goods available for sale. That's what we could have sold during the time period. If it's a month, we could have sold this many units. How many did we sell to do that? And this is kind of a periodic calculation. And again, we can use the cost of goods calculation, whether we use a periodic system or a perpetual system oftentimes.

But note, when the format of it is kind of more of a periodic type of format because we're saying this is the cost of goods available for sale, and then we're going to subtract out ending inventory, which we can imagine we got through a physical count, we count the inventory at the end as we would in a periodic inventory system. And therefore, if this is the inventory we had available for sale, the inventory we could have sold and this is the inventory that we have not yet sold, The difference between those two is what we have sold on a cost basis, and that's going to be the cost of goods sold. That's going to be the expense.

That's what will be reported on the income statement as an expense, the most important expense for a merchandiser or a manufacturer, the cost of the inventory that we are selling. Now, if we look at a manufacturer, we can say, okay, how can we convert this in order to deal with a manufacturer rather than a merchandiser? We're going to have that same beginning inventory. And then rather than having purchases, however, we're going to add to it the cost of goods manufactured.

So we didn't purchase these goods. Obviously we did purchase the materials, but we're going to have the cost of goods manufactured, which is going to include what we made in terms of not just materials, but what we made in terms of the work that we put in the direct labor and the overhead that's going to be put in there. Now, this number, you might be saying, well, where are we going to get that number? We're going to have to figure that out through our production process. And once we do that, however, this is the number that we're going to use and it's not going to be purchased. So that's where the big difference is.

You can see that they're basically similar in that purchases are obviously the activity that we had happen through our merchandiser company and the manufacturer. What had happened is that we not only purchased materials, but we made them into inventory. So that's the cost of goods manufactured that then will give us the cost of goods available for sale, and then we're going to do the same, subtracting out the ending finished goods inventory. So what has been completed in the finished goods and that will give us our cost of goods sold. So you can see the two formulas are going to be very similar. Now note that you can use this formula not just for the calculation of cost of goods sold.

I mean, if there's a book question, especially multiple choice questions will often maneuver things. A. Round so that we'll have to solve for different types of items here. So and that's one way that a multiple choice question can be used in order to, to, to test conceptual components. And so note that any of these components of the formula a multiple choice question could ask for meaning the multiple choice question could give us beginning inventory and not be asking for beginning inventory and give us the rest of the data. What we do not want to do is try to memorize a formula to get to the beginning inventory, because all we're doing is adjusting the algebra.

What we want to do is write down this formula and say that, okay, we have the cost of goods sold and we can back into the beginning inventory. The same would be true for if they gave us all this information, but not the cost of goods manufactured. We're not going to rewrite another formula to figure out what the cost of goods manufactured is. We're going to use this formula and just use algebra to say, okay, this is the unknown. Now I know everything else, this is the unknown. So any question that's going to be related to any of these items could be ending inventory, Of course, as well. You want to just be able to write down this formula and then apply out whatever you need. And also note, Of course, that this is a subtotal, this is a subcategory.

So sometimes you can actually if you want to simplify your algebra, then you can eliminate this item, say beginning inventory plus cost of goods sold minus ending inventory gives us cost of goods available for sale. And then if you do that, then they can ask for the other components, they can eliminate any one of these and ask you for that. And what you want to do is just write down this formula, okay, and say this is the unknown. I don't know that one. So now I'm going to do what I have to do to make that number right. If I know this number, then I can do what I have to do to make that number what it needs to be.

If we look at an example here, we're going to say if the beginning inventory happened to be 14,000, we're going to add to it the cost of goods manufactured. What we made, we're going to say 200,000 here. That gives us what's available, 214,000. Now, Of course, note that we're talking about dollars when this is the cost of what we made here. So we're not talking about units. We're going to have to convert that into dollars. And that's a bit more confusing than we might first think to do. But then we have the cost of available for sale, cost of goods available for sale, and then we're going to subtract out what's still in the ending inventory, which we can get from typically a physical account.

Now again, this physical account is in dollars, so we have $12,000 worth. The physical account would be in units which we would have to then convert it someway to dollars. If this is the number of dollars worth of inventory we had available for sale in the month and this is how much it has not yet been sold. The difference between the two then is going to be what had been sold, which we're going to say is the cost of goods sold.

This then is what will be reported on the income statement reducing gross sales by the cost of goods sold to get to gross profit and ultimately to the net income. This is going to be our most important expense on the income statement if we are a manufacturer because it's going to be the highest cost. Typically the things that we make if we make stuff is going to be the highest cost of what we do and therefore we're going to break it out separately most of the time and have the sales minus the cost of goods sold, giving us that subcategory of gross profit on the income statement.

Multiple Choice Questions – Job Cost System

In this chapter, we will take a look at multiple choice questions related to a job cost system. First question job costing system characteristics include all but a product diversity be high production volume, see heterogeneity, d customized inventory and E higher cost of inventory. So we'll go through this again, see if we can use the process of elimination. So we have a job costing system. Characteristics include all but either a product diversity. So if we think about that product diversity, we might not know exactly what they're trying to get at with product diversity.

I'm going to keep that for now. We're looking for the exception here of high production volume. So again, high product, we might say, well, that kind of depends. I mean, maybe some job cost systems have higher production volumes than others. So it kind of depends on what we're comparing to here. So we'll keep that for now. We'll see, say heterogeneity or heterogeneity. So what that means is different, meaning they're going to have different types of characteristics within the inventory and we might see this contrasted to homogeneity, which is going to be meaning the same.

And the reason I'm going to use those two words is because sometimes textbooks will use those words. It basically just means that there's going to be products that are going to be much the same and products that are going to be much different in nature. So hetero is going to be different in nature, and that's typically going to be the case for a job cost system because we're going to have different types of inventory. And when we think about a job cost system, you'll note that this problem is a kind of contrasting or implied contrast against the other system, which is a process cost system.

So we kind of have to keep that in mind in order to see this. We can see that there's going to be diversity in a job cost system. Some job cost systems might have more heterogeneity than others, but in some less. But when compared to other systems like a process cost system, there's going to be more difference in the types of inventory. So I'm going to say that that's going to be a characteristic D says customized inventory. And again, we might think we'll customize compared to what we might have a job cost system that's more or less customized. But in comparison to a process cost system, it's going to be more customized. And that's really kind of how we have to think about these things.

And then E says higher cost of inventory and typically we typically will, because these characteristics all follow from the concept that we will have more differentiation in product products. And if they're more customized products, then Of course we are going to have higher prices for them. That's the point in comparison to a process cost system where our goal is to lower prices and costs by making everything all the same. So this one is going to typically have higher prices. So we're left with A and B, let's go through this again. Job costing system characteristics include all but a product diversity and high production volume.

So if we go as we go through this again, product diversity is basically the same as heterogeneity, right? They're going to be meaning there's a difference in products. So if we take a look at a C and D, they all basically mean the same thing, right? A, you know, product diversity means there's going to be different types of products. And customization basically means there's going to be different types of products that we're making. Heterogeneity means there's different types of products and all that differentiation that we're talking about in these three different ways.

So these three, in other words, could cancel each other out if we were to look at this in terms of just test taking skills, we can probably say, well, those pretty much all look the same. They can't all be right. Those must be gone. And then the higher cost of inventory follows from the fact that they're all different in nature because that'll be different than if they were all same in nature, which would make it easy to produce and therefore cheaper. So we're left with a high production volume and that makes sense because we can't have a high production. We'll probably and again, we're comparing this to a process cost system.

We're going to have a lower production volume because of all this diversity in production. So all of our products are different in nature. So when compared to a process cost system, then we're not going to be able to make as many of them. We're going to customize them, make fewer of them, hopefully charge more for them. So final answer: Job costing system characteristics include all but B high production volume. Next question. The production. In activities for a customized product is A accounts receivable. B, a job. C, a unit of production. D finished goods or. E a process. Let's go through this again. The production activity for a customized product is a. Accounts receivable. And now that one just doesn't sound right at all.

You know, a production activity doesn't sound like accounts receivable, so I'm going to cross out B says a job. And that's plausible because we're talking about a job cost system, the production activities for a customized product. So I'll keep that for now. C says a unit of production that's, you know, that's possible. A unit of production. I'll keep that for now. D says finished goods, the production activities for a customized product, it may not be finished goods because it could be either type of inventory work in process or finished goods as we go.

So I'm not going to say it's probably not that finished goods is going to be the unit of all the goods finished, but it's not really breaking out which units were having which units are owed to who, which is going to be grouped up in finished goods. It's not the supporting documentation. And then E says a process. And again, you could think of that, that it would be part of a process. I'll keep that for now. Let's go through it again. The production activity for a customized product is now when we think of a customized product, we're thinking about a job cost system, probably not a process cost system.

So I think we can eliminate E here and then it's between a job and a unit of production. Now, these two, these two are kind of like the same thing, right? A unit of production is one thing we're working on, it sounds like, but it's more specifically termed typically a job. So a job I think is most likely the answer here is that we're looking for the unit of production being the job. So the final answer. The production activities for a customized product is B, a job.

Discussion Question - Job Cost System

In this discussion, we will discuss the discussion of how materials flow through a job cost system. So if we see a discussion question or an essay question like this, we can first think that we are considering, Of course, a job cost system. So we might want to start off with just what is a job cost system, and maybe that could pick up some points in an essay type question, then get into the materials within a job cost system and talk about what's going to be the Book of materials, what are materials going to do through a job cost system.

So a job cost system is going to be some type of manufacturing system, typically a system used for manufacturing or for service companies, but for which there's going to be some type of customization in the jobs that we have. Typically, construction companies, any type of customization in terms of producing custom jewelry production or any type of customization. So that all the products, all the services and products are not standardized. And therefore we need to track the cost of them specifically to the job so we know exactly what's happening in terms of cost relative to each job. So that's going to be the job cost system. Now the materials, Of course, are going to be one of the major components of products.

If we produce inventory within a job cost system, it's not the only component. It's only one of the major three categories we typically think of, including materials, direct materials, direct labor and overhead. So whenever we think of inventory, we think of those three things. But clearly materials are going to be one of those core components. So what's going to be the Book of materials in a job cost system where we make stuff? It's not that we buy stuff and sell stuff. We buy stuff, then make it into other stuff and then sell it. So we're going to buy materials, make it into the inventory and then sell it. And in essence, that's what's going to happen to the materials. But we probably want to get a little bit more detail than that. So Of course, we're basically going to buy the materials, we're going to make the materials into things and then sell it.

So to get a little bit more detailed, we would say first we would purchase the materials, possibly putting it into our warehouse. So if we're making guitars, we're going to purchase the wood for the guitars, we're going to put that into our warehouse, we're going to track the materials as we would in a similar way that we would have for inventory in a merchandising company. We're going to track the purchase of that and we're going to track the use of it. Now, Of course, we're not selling that. It's part of inventory, but we're not selling the materials because it's just raw materials. We need to convert it to inventory.

So instead of tracking the inventory when it's sold, as we would with a merchandiser and tracking the inventory in that way, using possibly a flow assumption like first in, first out, last in, first out, Of course, the raw materials will leave the warehouse, but they're going to go into production. So they're going to go into production once they do that. And this could be done with forms, too. We might have a requisition form that would record the requisition of materials that would be needed in the factory from the warehouse. And then the materials would, Of course, move from the warehouse to the factory where we would start production. Once we do this, once we start working on the materials, we're going to move them on the ledger from raw materials to the work in process account.

And as we do that, anything that's in the work in process account needs to be supported by kind of like a subsidiary ledger by the job cost sheets. So we will also record on the job cost sheets where these materials are going to be, which jobs they're going to be included in. Now, if it's indirect materials, we don't know which job to apply it to, then we're going to move those on our books, not to a job cost sheet because we don't know where it goes, but to factory overhead. So then the next step, Of course, is we're going to work on those materials, We're going to add direct labor, we're going to add overhead to it to finish the direct materials.

And once those direct materials are finished, we will then move them to a journal entry. We're going to move them out of the production process in our factory to wherever we store the finished goods so that they're ready for sale, possibly going to a store or whatever our sales process will be, and then they'll be in finished goods. So the journal entry there is going to be taking it out of work in process and going into the finished goods. Now if you consider the job sheets, then Of course what we have to do is indicate the fact that these jobs are now complete. And when we think about the job sheets that support the work in process, they're no longer going to be including the ones that. Are now finished and have now been moved to finished goods.

The finished goods. Then the number is going to be supported by the job cost sheets as well. So we're going to have the job cost sheets for the finished goods that have been completed. Then Of course, the last step once they're in the finished goods is we'll have a sale. So we're going to have a sale at some point. And then just like in a merchandising company, we're going to sell the inventory. Now, when you think of the sale, it's a little bit confusing because we've always been thinking about this whole process.

We've been thinking about the cost and not so much the sales price, which is the thing that we usually focus on all the time, the sales price. So here we've been tracking the cost all the way through. So when we sell something, you might start thinking, Well, where does sales fit into this here? And remember, there's two things that happen on a perpetual system. We have the sales entry and the cost of goods sold. You can think of them as one entry, but it's easier to think of them as two entries that happen at the same time.

So. So we usually debit accounts receivable or cash credit sales. That's going to be the one half that's not really directly applied to our inventory. However, the number isn't because we'll have to figure that out. We could base it on our costs that we have tracked, but it's not necessarily derived directly from exactly what we have from the cost. The the inventory then is what we've been tracking the other side of the journal entry, which is to decrease inventory, taking it out of finished goods inventory and then put it into or debit credit inventory, debit cost of goods sold, the expense related to us selling the inventory, an income statement account it finally going to the temporary accounts to the income statement accounts us finally expensing At this point the costs related to the inventory, which include the costs related to the materials at the beginning of the process. So way back when, when we bought the materials, they're finally being expensed not in the form of materials expense, but in the form of cost of goods sold, that cost of goods sold, including not just the materials, but everything that goes into production, including materials and direct labor and overhead.

Cost Flows For a Manufacturing Company

Within the cost flows for a manufacturing company chapter of the corps we will discuss cost flows for a manufacturing company that produces inventory focusing therefore on the cost of inventory the flow of costs as it goes through the materials that are purchased to us working on the materials to the finished goods. Finally to us selling those and the cost then go into the income statement in the form of cost of goods sold will focus in here on more of a broad sense not looking at a job cost system in particular but being able to look at just what happened in terms of inventory flows in general there are two major systems that will we could use for a manufacturing company.

Those being a job cost system. The one we're focused most on this Book and a process cost system. We want to get some idea of both of those. So we'll have to compare and contrast them a little bit in the next chapter because in order to understand either one of them it's easiest to do that by comparing and contrasting to the other. Either one of them however will have similar issues in terms of tracking the production of inventory. Meaning we're going to have the raw materials that we're going to need to convert in some way to the finished goods before we can sell them and record them at an expense at the time of sale in the form of cost of goods so as.

Manufacturing Activities Flow

In this chapter, we will take a look at the manufacturing activities flow. We'll take a look at the costs of the manufacturing process and how they flow through the manufacturing process, how we will track and organize these costs as we go. Remember that the major difference between the cost of goods sold calculation for a merchandiser, a company that purchases and sells inventory and a manufacturer, one that makes the inventory is going to be that a merchandiser has these purchases item where they just going to purchase the inventory and the manufacturer is going to have the cost of goods manufactured.

So this number then becomes the number that we need to determine how we are going to get to this number. If we talk about a merchandiser, it's very easy for us to know what the purchases are because that's what we purchased. That's pretty straightforward for the manufacturer. However, the cost of the goods we manufacture is going to include more than just what we purchased, more than just raw materials. It's going to include things such as direct labor and overhead. So we'll take a look at this in three broad categories. Well, we'll have the materials, we'll have the production, and then we'll eventually be selling the materials we're making.

Remember that the process here is, Of course, the production of inventory, the ultimate goal to be selling it. So most of this that we're thinking about is all kind of balance sheet stuff until we get to the end when we sell it, which is going to be similar to a merchandising company where once we're at the end, we sell it, moving it from the balance sheet to the income statement in the form of cost of goods sold. So first we have the materials that we think of and the materials we can think of. We'll run through a similar process as when we just buy and sell inventory from a merchandising company, meaning we're going to have the materials that's already in the warehouse.

The materials that we have from last month are still there. This month we're going to include those materials that we purchase. So we're going to add purchases to those materials and then we're going to subtract from them ending materials. What is still there? We're going to count the materials. Those will be the ending materials and that will give us the materials used. Now, this calculation should look pretty similar to our cost of goods sold. You want to be able to understand this calculation because it's the same kind of thing for a cost of goods sold for a merchandising company and similar to the cost of goods sold for a manufacturer as well.

We have the beginning inventory materials we could have. We could have a subcategory if we wanted to say, materials available for use. And then we're going to subtract out the ending materials to give us the materials used. So this is going to be our purchase. And you can think of this just as us purchasing the materials that we have and going through this process to determine the materials that we're going to use within production. Now, once that happens, we're going to say, okay, that's going to go to our production area here. This number here is going to be part of production. This is what we used to produce, but it's not the only thing that we had in production because in production we also had the beginning work in process.

When we think about production, we're thinking about what's in process, work in process. Whip Whip is often used here, so we're going to say, well, we already had some stuff that was in process. Now, in this month, according to this calculation, we included more materials here based on this calculation to the work in process. And so we're going to add that in, but we're also going to add direct labor and the overhead. And these are the two areas that are often overlooked within the production process, because when we think of goods and services, we often think of just the stuff it's made out of. It's made out of plastic, it's made out of the guitars, made out of wood.

But Of course the major components that comprise the cost of it are labor and overhead. So we have to include that in the production process. And these two items are the confusing things to most people because they're going to differ when we record them here as to when we had a service company or a company that just buys and sells inventory because some things like utilities on the warehouse, some things like depreciation, we're not going to expense them as we had in the past. We're going to include them in the cost of production. We're going to include them in the cost of inventory.

And that's going to then we're going to subtract out the ending work in process, what's still there, what's not completed yet. So we're going to count what's still in the process and not yet done, and that'll give us the cost of goods manufactured. So again, these two calculations you can see of them are similar. They're similar in nature, meaning we had beginning work in process and then not purchases, but the materials used and all the labor. These three items being what we added to it, what we made from it. We didn't buy it, we made it.

We transferred over this and then we added the labor and the overhead. Those are all costs that we put into it. We could have then begun. We could then have a subcategory if we chose to, which would be work in process available and then and then subtract out the ending work in process. So it's similar to the formulas that we have here. This time our bottom line number goes to the cost of goods manufactured, not to be confused with the cost of goods sold, the cost of goods manufactured is what we made during this time period. Cost of goods sold is going to be what we actually sold during this time period.

Cost of goods manufactured will be used in the calculation for cost of goods sold, however, which would be the beginning inventory. I'm sorry, beginning the finished goods inventory. So now we're looking at the goods that are done now, the finished goods inventory, and then we're going to add to it the cost of goods manufactured instead of as we would for a merchandiser, a company that just purchases and sells inventory where this would be purchased. So this is the differing number here between those two that's going to give us the goods available for sale. Just a subcategory. This is what we could have sold during the time period. This is our calculation of the cost of goods sold that we saw prior.

And then that's going to give us our ending finished goods, and then we're going to subtract from that our ending finished goods inventory, which we could get from a physical account to finally get the cost of goods sold. Now notice we have the sales item here. The only area here that's going to be on the income statement is the cost of goods sold. And it's not a sale item. We don't know what we sold it for or if we would. But this flow doesn't track the sales price. The sales price has nothing to do directly with the cost of the goods sold. We might use the cost to derive the sales price.

But remember, we're tracking the cost. So when we sell something, we're going to if it's a perpetual system, we're going to debit cash or debit accounts receivable. Credit sales revenue sales will be recorded. That's the part that's not here. We're also going to debit the cost of goods sold, the expense and reduce inventory. And that's in credit inventory. And that's what we are tracking here. This is going to be the cost of goods sold, the expense portion of the sales we make when we make a sale, we have the related expense of cost of goods sold.

Note that this expense, this one time that we're finally hitting the income statement, consists of all this activity that we've done. The direct materials are included in it, the direct labor is included in it, the overhead is included in it. All that stuff that we've been tracking this whole time and haven't been putting on the income statement at all, we've just been putting it on the balance sheet as just lumping it in together as part of inventory is finally being expensed all together as we sell it in the form of cost of goods sold.

Just In Time (JIT) Manufacturing

In this chapter, we will take a look at the manufacturing concept of a just in time inventory system. The concept of a just in time inventory system is going to be that we're going to start to put together the inventory after we get the order. In other words, we're going to get an order from the customer and then start to put together the inventory. For example, if we're a Dell Computer and we're putting together computers, we're going to get the order for the computer before we start to assemble it. There are pros and cons to a just in time system. One of the pros is it's often considered to be more customer focused because we can allow for the customer to give us a bit more customization if we're going to create and put together the computer after it has been ordered.

It's also helpful that we may not have to have as much cost in just inventory being stored if we're able to just create these computers as we go. We don't have we don't need as much warehouse space. We don't need to just be storing computers. We don't need to deal with the risk of those computers that have already been assembled to go down in value and no longer be desirable in the market. We can just build them as we go. So the concept is we're going to get the customer order and then we're going to schedule production at that point in time. Notice this has to happen pretty quickly.

We need to because we want to get the computer out pretty quickly. So all these components of production then are going to have to happen smoothly and that's going to be one of the downfalls. Of course, if there's any problems with any of these processes along the way to the production of the computer, then we don't we don't have any warehouse in order to just go and pick up a computer. So that's going to be one of the risks that we have. Then we're going to get the materials just in time for production. We're going to go ahead and get the materials.

That means we have to have a good relationship with our suppliers and make sure that we can get everything we need at the point in time of order. And as long as these things are all secure, then the just in time system can help the benefits will outweigh the cost. Then we want to complete it just in time for assembly. So we're going to complete the parts so that we can assemble it and then we're going to complete products just in time to ship. So notice all these things are basically happening very quickly after the customer has made an order and all these links along the way for it to work well, need to have good communication with our suppliers.

We need to be able to assemble everything in a systematic process and have everything done fairly quickly. If that's the case, then we have the benefit of being able to have a more customer centric design so that we can have some more flexibility in the types of products we're going to put together. And that's generally going to be beneficial and what customers are looking for oftentimes these days.

Multiple Choice Questions – Job Cost System

In this chapter we will take a look at multiple choice questions related to a job because first question which industry would use a job cost system a cracker's production B candy production C soda production d soap production or E. custom jewelry. Let's go through this again using the process of elimination. Which industry would use a job cost system. Now when you think about a job cost system really what we're thinking of is comparing and contrasting between a job cost and process cost system. And when the main thing between those two systems typically is going to be is there diversification in the types of things that we're making through is probably going to do the job cost system if there isn't if they're all totally the same then we're probably going to try to use a process cost system and that and thereby lower the cost of the job cost is going to apply to specific inventory because they're different.

And that process costs can apply to the process because all the inventory is the same. So if we're taken if we have crackers that we're making then that seems like they're all the same. So we're probably not going to use those sort of like custom crackers that were made right another. And then candy production again unless it's going to be really custom customized like a type of shop then probably not if we're talking about a normal candy Taffy's and stuff it's probably that they're all the same and we're working on making them you know as cheap as possible. So the production you know is the same type of thing and all the Sotos are pretty much the same.

We're not going to apply to a job of soda again unless we're doing some type of customization, some kind of strange. So not mass production. And then soap again the same kind of thing we would think there soap I would think that you know most of it would be the same unless we're doing some kind of specialty type of thing and that leaves us with custom jewelry and basically anything that says custom in it is probably going to be the answer. And this type of question if we're looking for a job cost versus process cost and that's really always the case when we're comparing and contrasting what we're working with a job cost system we're really pretty much contrasting it to a process cost system.

Next question which industry would use a job order: a costing system, a taffy candy production, oil refinement, see cement, custom surfboards, paperclips. Let's go through this again using the process of elimination. Which industries would use a job order costing system. And again if you're thinking about this you're pretty much contrasting it in your head whenever we think there's two types of cost systems typically a job caused in a process cause we would typically use a job costs when there's differentiation in the types of inventory we are making as opposed to a process cost where everything is all the same and therefore we apply the cost by process rather than by individual job.

So if we think through that we're going to say a taffy candy production and if we're talking about just normal like you know the mass production. It's all done by one machine. All the taffy is exactly the same. Typically or that the goal of it and therefore that's probably a process cost rather than AGEOD cost. So it's probably not that oil refinement. That's pretty much like one of the most classic kinds of examples of a process cost system because again our goal is to make everything really standardized. We want the end product to be as standard as possible. No differentiation. And you know in the end product generally we want consistency to cement the cement production.

And that would be the same kind of thing. We don't really want differentiation in the cement. We want it all to be the same we want in one production process so I would think that would be a process cost says Custom surfboards and that is customized. So that means there's going to be differentiation. Anything that says Custom is pretty much probably going to be a job cost system. So we're going out to say yeah that's probably a job cost. And then he says paperclips and I would assume that all paperclips are going to be made pretty systematically. They all want to be the same type of paperclip and therefore would be using a process cost rather than a job cost.

So that leaves us with the final answer which industry would use a job that is costing System D customers for. Next question. Production of customized products or services for each customer use is either a customer production system or job order production. See just in time production the first in first out production and process production. Let's go through this again using the process of elimination production over customized products or services for each customer using a customer protection system. I mean that sounds kind of reasonable and it sounds right I'll keep it for now. B says job order production and that's it.

That's the kind of system we're working on these questions so I'll give that one for now. C says a just in time production system. And you know that it's possible that we could be using it just in time. I'll keep that one for now. DS says first in first out production that you know that might be the way that we kind of track the orders. But usually first of all deals with a merchandising company. How do we track the cost of the merchandising company going in and out so it doesn't usually apply to the job costing system except for like the materials portion only. So I don't think it's that and then you said process production and that might be like a process cost system and it's probably not that because we're doing some customization.

So I don't think it's a process call system. So let's go through it again. Production of customized products or services for each customer uses either a custom customer protection system, a job order production or just in time production of those three I would think would be because we're basically working on a job order production type of problems here now. A. I don't think it's going to be the answer because it sounds nice but I don't think it's an actual term that we're really using typically in any kind of process. So it sounds kind of like a made up term that sounds plausible. Customer production system.

So I don't think a C is clearly something we've probably heard of just in time production and it may be the case that just in time production is being used. That does allow us for some more customization. But this really has to do with how fast we put things together, how we put together our system and our process and not so much to deal with with the type of system we're having. So we could use it just in the time system, not necessarily because of that customization. However, using a job order production. So final answer production cost cost production of customized products or services for each customer uses the job order production.

Discussion Question - Job Cost System

In this discussion, we will discuss the discussion question of describing key documents used in a job cost system. If we see a discussion question like this or an essay question like this, we can see from it that we're starting off with a job cost system. So we might be able to pick up some points by just considering what a job cost system is, even if we're not really clear on all the documentation for it. So that's where we would start. A job cost system is typically going to be one of the two types of cost tracking systems we will have when we're in a production company. So when we're producing things, we could use a job cost system.

It is typically used when we're producing things that are somewhat customized, somewhat different in nature, we're not making all the same units of items. It could also be used in a service company. When we have types of jobs that we work on that will be different. We're not making inventory, but a service company, we'll typically be focusing on the production process here. So we'll be thinking about us making things, making things that are somewhat customized, somewhat different in nature, and using a job cost system to allocate the cost to the things we are making. So it's useful if we're thinking about forms, then as to think about the process of how the process is going to work, how the raw materials are going to be converted to the finished goods, and then think about the forms that will be taking place along that process.

So there's in essence, there's going to be three types of costs that we need to think about, and those are going to be including materials, direct materials, direct labor and overhead. So we can consider as those costs are applied to the inventory, you know, what type of documentation is going to be there for those costs. So first we're basically going to start off with the materials. When we get the materials, we can imagine them coming into the warehouse and we're going to then fill out a receiving report saying that we have received the materials, we're going to count the materials and make sure that everything is proper. Once we get the materials, we're going to record them.

We could call that into a material ledger card, which is basically us tracking the inventory, similar to how we would track inventory if we were just a merchandiser, just getting the inventory, counting it, tracking it. We're going to have to track it in a similar way as we would inventory for a merchandising company, meaning we might use a cost flow assumption first in, first out, last in, first out average. We're going to have the same kind of issues that we'll have to do when we count the inventory and then assign a cost to it. Now, the only difference is, Of course, the inventory is not going to be then sold directly to a customer.

It's just a component. It's just raw materials. So it will be transferred out of the warehouse, but it won't be transferred to the customer. It will be transferred from the warehouse to the factory where we start to work on it. So if we make guitars, we're going to transfer it then from the warehouse to the factory. So when a new job happens, that's when that happens. And what's the documentation that will drive that? In a large company we can have a requisition form. So the requisition form is saying, Hey, we have this new job warehouse people. We need you to give us some of the wood.

If we're talking about guitars, we're going to say we need some of that wood that was purchased. Here's a requisition form for how many pieces of wood we need to transfer to the place where we produce the assembly plant. And so we're going to then transfer that wood with the requisition form to do that. Then the requisition form is going to be used to record the materials leaving on the material ledger card on the inventory side for raw materials. And it's going to be going to that same form. The requisition form is going to be used to put it to a job. So we know the journal entry is going to go from materials to work in process and it's going to be supported by a job cost sheet. So the job cost sheet is supporting the work in process account.

We can't put anything to work in process unless we know which job it's going to be on. And so the job sheets are going to be used in order for us to apply that material to specific jobs that we are working on. All those job cost sheets, then supporting the work in process account. Once in work, in process, then we can imagine the other items that are going to be added here and that's going to be the direct labor and the overhead. So direct labor is going to be something that we could do. People are going to work, Of course, and when we record their labor, we're going to record it not as an expense but to the inventory in order to track the time, we're going to have to use some type of time sheet. So we're going to have some type of time sheet that's going to be possibly a clock in clock.

Type of timesheet, which is going to have the job that people worked on, the number of hours and the amount that's going to be applied to each job. And that's going to be the documentation we'll use in order to record again to work in process, increasing the main account by direct labor. And if there's any indirect labor, we'll also increase the overhead for the indirect labor using that same documentation. We'll also use it to fill out any job accounts to support the work and process account. So the work in process account is going to have the total number. We'll support it by naming which job will be used by having the time tickets that will allow us to have that detailed information.

Then we're going to have the overhead, and the overhead is going to include things like the materials, the indirect materials, not the direct materials, but indirect materials, which we could use the same type of requisition form, but this time not being able to apply it to the job and then being having to apply to overhead instead because we can't apply it to the job. Same with the time of indirect labor. We cannot apply it to the job. We'll use the time tickets to apply it to overhead. Then anything else that's in the factory on production that we cannot apply to a specific job. Things like paying the utilities, things like playing any other kind of. Well, we already said the wages, but anything else?

Depreciation, those types of things we're going to record to overhead.

They'll be driven by the same types of things that would be normal when we pay bills. So if we had a utility bill that would drive us, we wouldn't record utility expenses, but instead put it into the overhead, which will eventually go to the work and process account. And then we'll use an allocation method to allocate from the overhead to the specific jobs. We'll use a predetermined overhead rate. In order to do that, we can do that specific job. In order to do that calculation and record the overhead per job based on some kind of cost driver in order to do that.

So that will happen on the job cost sheet. Then once the jobs are completed, we will show on the jobs that they have been closed or they're now completed and that will move them from the work in process account to the finished goods account. And then finally, Of course, we will sell the inventory and that will be driven by, say, an invoice which will record the journal entry for the sale typically, and that will be the same for like a merchandising company it recording the sales, half debiting accounts receivable, credit and sales and the inventory half crediting inventory, reducing inventory and debiting the cost of goods sold.

Writing off the expense at the end of the process. Finally recording the expense for all these costs we've been accumulating, we've been capitalizing, we've been putting on the balance sheet instead of the income statement in the form of inventory until this point in time when we actually sold it to help us generate revenue in accordance with the matching principle.

Job Cost vs Process Cost System

Within the job cost versus process cost system chapter of the Book we will compare and contrast. A job costs system and a process cost system. The two major systems that we can use in a manufacturing company for a company that makes inventory the scores will be focusing on a job cost system. But in order to understand the job cost system fully we need to compare and contrast that to the alternative of the other type of system that could be used and that would be the process cost system.

Job Cost Vs Process Cost

In this chapter we will compare a job cost and process cost system. When we produce inventory when we are a manufacturing company we typically will be using either a job cost system or a process cost system and the difference between these two which one we will use will typically depend on the type of inventory that we produce. So let's go through the characteristics that will generally be apparent or be present when we use a job cost system and when we look at these we want to compare and contrast that to when we would use the job cost system. When would we use a process cost system as we start to work through our problems of a job cost system and process costs and we'll start to see why these characteristics of inventory are going to be those that will distinguish whether we choose to be a job cost system or a process cost system.

For now I'll just note that a job costs system means that we're going to apply the cost of the inventory to particular jobs. So we're going to have a particular job. We're going to assign the costs to that job as opposed to a process cost system where we were going to assign costs to a process as we go. So as we think of this we're going to think of the example of custom guitars pretty much anything custom that you can think of. You can say that's one type of thing that would basically usually be in a job cost system. So if we get an order for a guitar it's going to be a specific type of guitar and we're going to custom make this guitar in accordance with the order we would typically use more of a job cost system.

It's also something that if you think of custom for like construction and stuff like that construction jobs are typically going to be different in nature and therefore we typically use the job costs system. So that's the first characteristic we'll have if they're custom order then we're typically going to use a job cost system. Now I would use that characteristic in order to then think about the other characteristics as following from its meaning if we do some type of manufacturing business that's custom in some way then the other things are going to follow from if we make custom guitars if we make if we do any kind of construction it's going to be custom to whatever needs to be done.

Then we're typically going to be doing a job cost system. Our next characteristic is our heterogeneous product products or services and that just means that they're different. And the reason I use this word is because sometimes you'll see it in textbooks so heterogeneous and homogeneous heterogeneous in the opposite meaning different and homogeneous meaning the same. So this Of course follows that we can just say Of course that the types of things we're producing are not all exactly the same. And that follows from the idea that they are their custom; they're different in some way. We've got some differences in the production that we have.

And because of those differences we cannot do things like just allocate the costs evenly to whatever we're making. If one guitar we make is a lot more detailed than another guitar we make then we cannot evenly allocate that cost. And that's going to be one of the reasons we use a job costs system. If we do a construction job and one happens to be a lot larger than another then we can't allocate the same cost to those two jobs. Or we shouldn't we should find some other way and that's why we're going to use a job cost system as opposed to a process cost system low production volume now low production volume means that we're not producing as many of the items possibly as in a job cost type of inventory system meaning if we're making custom guitars then we're going to produce far less of them.

That's OK because we're going to charge a higher price for the ones that we produce as opposed to if we were just stamping out their guitars and they were all the same. Then the idea there is that we're going to have a high volume with less customization. So a job cost system follows from the idea that we're going to have some differentiation, some custom, and that means that the products are going to be different in nature, differences in nature of whatever we make typically would mean that the production volume will be lower. And then we're going to have high product flexibility. Again that's going to follow from the idea that they're custom.

So if something is going to be different in nature of anything that we're making that's going to be different and we might just specialize and even if we're just specializing in guitars and even if it's fairly limited if we have more customization we have within that guitar the more we're going to need to see you have a job cost system as opposed to a process cost. If we're in construction Of course everything we do might be the same type of construction all the time but the jobs that we go to and deal with are typically going to be different just by the nature of the job.

And so we're going to have to have differences there they'll be flexibility that we will have basically based on the fact that they're going to be custom in some manner. Also the job costs will typically have higher value for the products as opposed to a process cost and because that leads through the customization if we're going to customize it that it's going to take more time and it's going to cost more as opposed to if it was all just being the same thing.

Our goal there is to lower costs and have it be typically cheaper. So if we can contrast this to a process cost system the idea of a process cost system is we're going to apply the costs to the process. And the reason we can do that is because all the things that we make are going to be in essence the same. So that's going to be our route again that we want to think about as opposed to something we customized everything it is what it is you get what you get. It's all going to be the same.

So we don't need to apply the costs in the same way we need to apply the costs or even lead to the units. So what we need to do then we can do that by using a process cost system assigning costs as they go through the process rather than two particular units of inventory. Particular jobs. So in this I would think of something like taffy if we're making Taffy or at Carmel Candie's or something like that. They're all the same. We're not going to vary, they are more Candie's they're all the same. So we're producing our inventory.

Other things like oil are going to be like that for processing oil. So all the same at the end of the process so our goal here is to make everything the same and lower costs. So we're going to have repetitive procedures. Everything is going to be the same and our goal here again is just to make everything the same even mechanized If possible have the whole machine make the taffy and go through just the process of making the taffy. And once we automate the system because they're all the same then that should be lowering the cost. We're going to have homogeneous product products or services as opposed to heterogeneous So they're all the same.

And again this is probably the one that you want to focus on. Or the fact that they're not custom. So we don't have custom products; they're all going to be the same in nature and therefore everything else pretty much derives from that. We're gonna have high production value. That's the point of us making everything the same, we're going to say you have no variance. You want Carmel's with different kinds of things in them or what we don't do is that we just make the Carmel's they're all the same and we have a pretty low cost because of that. The more we try to customize the Carmel's then the more it's going to be, you know, difficult for us to automate the process.

And we're going to have more customization. So if we keep them all the same we can have high production volume and lower cost low production flexibility. Again that follows from them all being pretty much the same and not being customized. So we're not going to vary what we produce, we're going to say that these are all we're all going to produce the same thing for every every unit is going to be the same. So if we look at these together then the job costs and the process cost system. Remember that the job cost system has the customer order as opposed to you know and custom motors are just repetitive procedures on the process cost system.

So the side's going to be custom This side is not custom and that means that we're going to have everything be repeated it's just it is going to be what it is and then we're going to have heterogeneous production from for the job costs versus the process cost homogeneous and again this this kind of falls out from the fact that these are custom and these are non-customer So these are going to be all different products and services through that customization. These will all be the same. The job cost system low production volume again because they're all different in nature and a high production volume for the process cost system because they're all the same.

We can then scale up and be able to produce a lot more than the job cost system has high product flexibility. We can vary that the point at the point of having them be custom on the process costs them we have no product less flexibility. And again that's that's a point because that's what leads us to be able to produce more at that time.

Multiple Choice Questions – Job Cost System

In this chapter, we will take a look at multiple choice questions related to the job cost system. First question job cost sheets include each accept the direct labor costs. B customer name C advertising costs for a job D the overhead costs e the direct materials costs. Let's go through this again using the process of elimination. Job cost sheets include each accept. Now what is a job cost sheet? That's going to be the sheets that support the work in process or the finished goods account. In terms of the jobs we're working on, kind of like the inventory items that we're working on. If we're if we're manufacturing inventory or the job we're working on, if it's a service company.

And they typically, if we're making inventory, include the details of the cost of the job. And any inventory we make, remember has three details: direct materials, labor, direct labor and overhead. So those are probably going to be on the job sheet. So if we go through these, we're going to say the direct labor costs that's probably on the job sheet. So, so direct labor. That's not it because it's on the job sheet. B says the customer 's name probably. But you know, we'll keep that for now. C says advertising costs for a job. You know, it's kind of a cost notice. It's saying for a job here we like, we advertise a particular job. So I'll keep that for now. And then D says the overhead costs and that's going to be on the job cost sheet, we would think.

And then E says the direct materials costs, that looks reasonable. So I think that's on there. That's not it. So because those are our main three direct materials, labor, direct labor and overhead. So we're left with B and C, So if we go through this again, job cost sheets include each except B customer name or C advertising costs for a job. Now, of the two, I would think that B would be included. We need to know who the customer is related to the job because we're going to eventually have to assign that, track that and bill them.

So I think B is going to be on the job cost sheet. We're going to know that somehow at least. And then C advertising costs for the job is kind of tricky because they're applying it to the job and not just saying it's general advertisement, but the advertising, whether it be applied to a particular job or not, is not part of production, meaning the job cost sheets are tracking inventory. The cost of inventory and advertising is a general and administrative cost. It's not part of inventory. So we're not going to include advertising typically in the cost of the inventory because it's not something that converts the raw material to finished goods. It helps us to convert a sale once the inventory has been produced.

So the final answer is C, let's go through the final answer. Job cost sheets include each except C advertising costs for a job. Next question: Which industry would use a job costing system? A general contractor? The fruit punch production C yogurt. D seeds for planting small gardening tools. So let's go through this again. Using the process of elimination, which industry would use a job costing system? Now, when we think about this, we're always thinking about this in terms of what the other costing system is, which is a process costing system. And the major differentiation between the two typically will be that the job cost system will have differentiation in inventory, whereas the process cost system will typically be all the same.

Therefore, job costs are tracked by job process costs. We track costs by process because of that differentiation in inventory versus sameness in inventory. So if we go through these, then a general contractor, a general contractor possibly has different jobs that they work on. So I would think that might be a job cost system, fruit punch if we're mass producing fruit punch, unless it's like some customized production of fruit punch, I would think it would be a process cost because the end result would probably be all the same we'd be using to maximize production.

So probably not that C yogurt again, I would think the same thing. I would think that we're trying to make all the yogurt the same and once we get the process down, the system down, we can mass produce it and make it all the same and use a process cost D seeds for planting. And there's a little bit, you know, we might have to do something on it. But, I would think that all the seeds are pretty much the same. We're going to try to make a system to make all the seeds the same and gather the seeds and have the same amount of seeds in. Certain, you know, basket or whatever.

And so I would think that would still be a process cost and not a not a job cost. And then he says small gardening tools.

And as long as they're small and they're all the same and we're making them or producing them again, I would think that we would make them all in the process. So this is one. So I don't think it's that this is one that didn't use customization. If we saw the word customized something, we make customized something, then that's usually for sure going to be a job cost. This one is a general contractor, which by the nature of being a contractor, you know, is typically going to be different. So contracting is a little bit different.

The way the jobs are tracked. But it's a job cost system and all the jobs are typically different. So I think this would be the final answer. Let's go through it one last time. Which industry would use a job costing system? A general contractor. Next question. Cost accounting systems are job order costing and perpetual costing. B Job order costing and job hunting system C job order costing and specific identification. D Job order costing and process costing. E job order costing and first in, first out. So let's go through this again. Using the process of elimination cost accounting systems now all of them have job order costing.

So I mean, this first half is pretty much a given. So we don't really even need to read that anymore. And we're really just saying, okay, what's the second? What's the second half here? And A says perpetual accounting. We may have heard perpetual accounting. I mean, that's a thing kind of we've probably heard of the perpetual system before, so I'll keep that for now. B says job hunting system. And that sounds just kind of silly and a job hunting system. It sounds like it's something that was made up because they ran out of options or something. So I think that one probably is not it and C says specific identification.

Um, we may have heard specific identification, but that actually has to do with tracking inventory in a merchandising company typically where we specifically identify the inventory as it goes. So it's actually not going to typically be a cost. Typical cost accounting, it's more of a merchandising usually. D says process costing. And again, we may have that. That sounds familiar. So I'll keep that one for now. And E says first in, first out. And again, we probably heard a first in, first out. But it's not it's not usually a cost accounting system. First in, first out is how we track, again, like specific identification in a merchandising company.

Typically it's some kind of cost flow assumption. So I don't think it's going to be first in, first out. So let's go through this again. Cost accounting systems are job costs. And what's the other one? Perpetual costing. Now that's kind of alluding to perpetual versus periodic, which has to do oftentimes, again, with the merchandise, with a merchandising company that has that option. So it's not going to be that specific identification has to do with typically a, you know, how we're tracking the inventory and a merchandising company. And then Of course, it's going to be the process costing.

So the job cost system and a process cost system, those are the two that we're always contrasting when we think of a job cost system or when we think of a job process cost, whichever one we're working on, we're often going to be asked questions or thinking about its opposite, or it's the other one comparing and contrasting to the other one. So we're always thinking between job cost, process cost, the difference Of course being the differentiation typically in inventory and other differences that result from it.

Discussion Question - Job Cost System

In this discussion, we will discuss the discussion of the two primary cost systems for manufacturing companies. If we see a discussion question like this or essay question like this, we can look through and think through what a manufacturing company is and then think through what the cost flow systems would be. And hopefully that will lead us to the two primary cost flows that we have, the two primary forms that the cost flow systems will take. So when we think about a manufacturing company, we're thinking about a company that manufactures inventory that's going to be different from other types of companies. We can contrast that to a merchandising company, for example, which also has inventory but does not make the inventory.

So now we have the added step, Of course, of making the inventory. And so that's going to lead us to then how are we going to do that? How are we going to track the costs of inventory? We're not just going to be buying the inventory and then selling it. We're going to have to then track the cost of the inventory in some way. Now, there's two primary ways we can think about that. If you look at how we would do that, we can break the types of products up into two categories, in essence. And we will typically be using two types of systems in order to track the inventory based on the characteristics of the inventory we are making. For example, if we make very customized types of items, if we make custom jewelry, if we make custom guitars, if we were working in construction where all the jobs are different, we have different size jobs and that kind of thing, then we're going to have to apply the costs to the job, to the specific jobs.

When we start a new job, we're going to need to somehow apply the costs to whatever thing we're starting to work on. So you can think of it like as the specific inventory we're working on, we need to apply the cost to that. And in essence, we can think about that as basically a type of job we're putting together. They're not the same as other types of jobs. They're probably similar, but they have unique characteristics and therefore the costs will not be the same from inventory piece to inventory, from job to job.

If we make two custom necklaces, one could cost much different than the other and therefore we have to track the costs separately. And that's going to be a job cost system. The other system is that if we're making something that's really the same we're making for processing oil or something like that, if we're making any kind of processed food, you can think if we're making taffies or if we're making any any type of candy or anything like that or processed candy will typically be all the same. Our goal is to have the finished product where it's all the same, and therefore our goal is to really systemize that process down, to be able to do it as easily as possible, to scale the process so that everything is conforming to uniformity, not differentiation. And if that's the case, then we don't need to track the cost to each unit or each job. That wouldn't make sense because they're all the same. So our goal there then is to track the costs, but not necessarily by each unit because all the units are the same and we can just basically apply the same cost to whatever unit. So therefore, we're not going to tie the costs in production to when the production processes take place to the process. So that's going to be a process cost system. So those are the two primary systems. Now, it could be the case that we have types of things that have a more of a processing component and a more of a standardized component. We might have types of inventory that we make that have two, two layers to it. We make some component that's all the same and some component that is customized partially, but just in essence, those are going to be the two major types of manufacturing that will have and will distinguish them typically by how unique the inventory is, how customized something is going to be as the driving factor as to whether we want to use a job cost system or a process cost system.

Cost Flows for a Job Cost System

Within the cost of Flo's for a job cost system chapter of the Book we will take a look at cost flow related to a job cost system focusing mainly on manufacturing companies. Those that produce and make inventory it is possible to apply the same concept to some service companies such as a law firm or a bookkeeping firm that tracks costs by job. But we're going to focus on job cost systems that make something make inventory because that adds a level of complexity to it. And if we're going to apply the same system to a service company we can easily just remove the inventory factor in the same kind of concepts.

We're going to have to track that inventory from the raw materials to the finished products going through the work in process as we go to finished goods to cost of goods sold within a job cost system we're going to have to support that process with the job sheets the job sheets are then going to be used to support the G.L. accounts as we move the raw materials to the costs related to work and process to convert the raw materials to finished goods and finally to the cost of goods sold at the end of the process when we sell the inventory.

Job Cost System Cost Flow

In this chapter we will take a look at a job cost system cost flow. Well look at this cost flow a few different times a few different ways but now we want to get an overview of that cost flow. So we get an idea of where we're going. Well then look at their costs low as we go through a comprehensive problem. When we go through a comprehensive problem however we often start to look at the very specific component that we are on in a fairly long problem. So as we do that we want to get an idea and keep an idea in our heads of what the overall cost flow will be so that we know when we're focusing in on one particular component how it fits into the big picture that will give us more context more motivation to learn the particular step that we are looking at.

So whenever we think of manufacturing costs we want to think of materials overhead costs and labor and just start any inventory that we think of not just in terms of if we are the manufacturer they include these items in it. It's easy to think of inventory as materials. So if we think of TV we think of the materials that are in the TV but notice that a lot of that is going to be due to overhead and labor costs a lot of the value. A lot of what it is we just took the raw materials of a TV that wouldn't amount to much unless they were put together to format a TV. So it's important to know when we do a manufacturing company Of course we are providing some of those products with some of that value.

So we have the raw materials. We're going to have the overhead we're going to have to labor. We're going to have to account for all three of those indirect costs of whatever we make. We make a TV we've got to include all of those and the cost of the TV we have to track all those costs so that we can include them in the cost of our inventory. How will that work then? Well if we start with our materials here clearly we will buy the materials whatever it's going to be used to create our TV, the plastic and whatnot that are going to be used to create the TV. We're going to have those and that's going to be a part of inventory. And then we're going to start to work on those and once we do that we're going to put it into what we call work and process.

So work in progress is starting to converge. Whatever the raw materials are to the finished product the TV. So now our materials over here are going to be taken from the materials and put into a working process. As we start the job as we start to get going with the process of making it, we want to keep in mind that this work in process is going to be an account called work in process. And when we're thinking about a job cost system we're not going to be able to apply anything to this work in process unless we can assign it to a job. So if it's within the working process we need to have it be supported by a job and that's going to be similar to if we had say an accounts receivable account we can't apply anything to our accounts receivable account unless we also have a subsidiary ledger and a customer to apply it to.

We need to know who owes us the money. But when we go to a job cost system for work and process it's similar. If I put these materials from the materials to the working process account I need to know which job that we're working on. And so that's going to be our criteria. Now if it's direct labor, if we're making, say , let's go back to their guitars. If we're making a guitar and we're putting the wood in the guitar, we know exactly which guitar the woods are going to. On the other hand if we're talking about some of these materials that we don't know exactly which guitars go into things like glue things like small components that are going to be included in the guitar. It's not worth us to track exactly which guitar they go to.

We're not going to get a requisition form and say I need this specific amount of glue to put together this guitar. It would not be cost effective to do so. So what we'll do is we'll take some of this material and we'll put it into overhead. We can't put it up here yet we can't put it into the working process account because we don't we can't assign it to a particular job and nothing goes over here until we can assign it to a particular job. This overhead is also going to include any other type of overhead that we have. So when we think of overhead in general these are all types of things that we basically spend on the warehouse where we make things. So if that's going to include things like depreciation on the warehouse if we have a supervisor salary in the warehouse we don't know which job that we're working on.

So it's going to go into overhead. If we have maintenance in the warehouse then all of that is going to go to some inventory but we don't know which job to assign it to. So it's going to be in there if we have utilities in the warehouse it's going to be in overhead and that overhead then Of course is going to be a cost that will be included in overhead. Then we're going to take that overhead and we will assign it to the working process. How will we do that? That's going to be one of the things that we'll have to figure out because we cannot just take this overhead. It's a work in progress. We can generalize it there and put it into that account. But we need to know which job it goes to and that's going to be one of our problems. One of the things that we'll have to figure out from this step here is assigning the overhead to a job we're going to have to figure out which job gets how much overhead.

Because some of the stars are custom guitars. Some of them are more specialized than others. It would be similar if we had a construction company. Some of them are never larger companies, some of them are smaller projects and larger projects. We need to know how much of the supervisor's salary or how much of the small materials we use. How much of that truck and gas possibly would go into each individual job when they're not all the same size. And we don't have any way to assign them particularly to each job. So that's going to be one of our problems that we'll talk through as we work through the job cost system.

Same thing we're going to take the labor and we're going to assign it to the work in process and that's going to be direct labor. So any time we have someone working on a particular guitar it's pretty easy for us to see which job which guitar that person is working on and therefore be able to assign their cost directly to work and process and back it up by job costs sheets. However we may have some people working in the warehouse that we cannot assign to a particular job. And those would be things like possibly the supervisor salary, possibly the maintenance in the in the in there because we don't know which job it goes to. And therefore we're going to say well it's still labor it's going to be labor. We're going to have payroll happening.

But some of that labor is going to be directly to the job direct labor and some of it will be indirect. If we can't assign it directly to the job then we're going to include it as well. And there's overhead. So you can see this overhead is a big bucket of stuff that basically we cannot assign or it would be not cost effective to assign directly to a particular job and therefore we will use some other format. Once we have these items in process at some point in time we are going to finish them within the working process and we can then transfer them to the finished goods. So once weren't finished goods then the finished goods are going to include all of these items, raw materials overhead and labor within the job but we're basically going to have a job that will be completed and that job will be in finished goods. We'll have that concept or the account of finished goods.

Note that these two accounts on the general ledger are just going to be one account on that. On the general ledger we're going to have work in process but within the working process it's made up of a job cost sheet. So these are like sub ledgers that are backing you up in a similar way as accounts receivable would be what they count on the general ledger but it's supported by a subsidiary ledger. Breaking that information up by customer. So in this case all of these accounts remember are going to be broken up or backed up supported by a general ledger account.

Breaking the information out by date but these are also going to be supported by another account, another Ledger, another source document that's going to give us the information in terms of jobs. So the finished goods then is going to be one number we're going to transfer it from work in process to finished goods. But we will still know which jobs are going to be applied to the finished goods and those jobs Of course are made up of materials overhead and labor. And then once we have the finished goods we're kind of at the end product now. Now we can sell them. If we're talking about guitars we can sell them right now. So now the final step which is similar to a merchandising company we sell and that will go to the cost of goods sold.

Now as we go through this process it's easy for us to forget about just the normal sales journal entry because this whole process leads up to us selling the inventory that's the point of the business. But none of this is tracking the sales price. We may use the cost sheets to derive this sales price but the sales price is not directly related to what we're tracking here we're tracking the cost. So at the end of the day the last journal entry is going to be increasing sales credit to sales and debit the accounts receivable or cash. And none of that journal entry is not being represented here because we don't know exactly what the sales price is based on this information.

What will be here is when we make a sale in a perpetual system the second half of that journal entry is debit to the cost of goods sold. The expense related to the sale. That's what's here and I credit the inventory reduction of the asset related to the sale. And Of course that cost of goods sold then is going to be composed of jobs that we're going to be selling . You know a particular job where we made particular guitars, particular construction jobs, those jobs consisting of materials overhead and labor.

39. Transcript In this chapter we will take a look at multiple choice questions related to a job cost system. First question job cost sheets include a direct loan materials direct labor finished goods the direct materials estimated overhead selling costs C direct labor actual overhead administrative costs the direct materials direct labor estimated overhead e direct materials direct labor cost of goods sold. OK so here we go. We're going to use the process of elimination to see if we can cancel some of these out and so the job cost sheets. Include now as we do this we can.

This is one of those questions that have a lot in common and we can try to use the process of elimination here between the choices if we had no idea which one to look at. Now as we see this in a job cost system we should think that we're talking about making inventory and the three things involved are going to be direct materials, direct labor and overhead. So as we go through this we probably have an idea that that's what we should have an idea of that's what I would expect to see. So the first one is the direct material direct labor and finished goods and finished goods. Doesn't doesn't seem right. That's what you know once the job is complete it is finished goods.

That's not what's on the job sheet. So we're kind of missing out and say OK we're missing overhead on that one so I don't think that's going to be it. Second one says direct materials estimated overhead and selling costs. Now this one looks good. I'm not sure on this one with the estimate I know overhead possibly would be there you know selling costs. However I'm pretty confident they are not on the job cost sheet because those are period costs not part of the cost of production which is what the job cost sheet is tracking. So I don't think it's b c says direct labor actual overhead and administrative costs. So now we see these two kinds of overhead: actual and estimated.

But again I can eliminate this one not based on that but based on the fact that it's administrative costs which are period costs not part of production not therefore on the job cost sheet. So it's not see D-cells direct material direct labor and estimated overhead. So maybe I don't have an idea of what this estimate is overhead but that looks pretty good because those are free. But I would expect to see. So then the last one you said direct materials direct labor cost of goods sold. And that one is we wouldn't think it's the cost of goods sold because that's what's going to happen once we finally sell it. So again that's not on the job cost sheet. We use the job cost sheet to determine the cost of goods sold once it is sold.

So it's actually Ian and I was kind of thinking they would have one that would be direct materials direct labor and actual overhead. And if they were to do that just recognize that it would be the estimated overhead here that we were looking for because when we applied to the job Quashy we didn't know what actual overhead was. We used an estimate to do so. So if there was a question between D and another one that was all the same except this was actual overhead. Just note that the job cost sheet will be using an estimate, not the actual overhead. We don't know what the actual cost should be applied to the job. That's why we have to use an estimate. That's why we have to use overhead in general.

OK so final answer job cost sheets include the direct material direct labor and estimated overhead. Next question: a source document to request materials for production a job cost sheet B purchase order C materials requisition the materials and summarizes the new job notification. Let's go through this again using the process of elimination. A source document to request materials for production is either a job cost sheet. Now we might think well that's what we're working on. So maybe it is a job cause you know I'll keep that for now because you know that's the main thing we're working with here in the job costing system, be it a purchase order. And again we might think the materials are the first step that we might need a purchase order for.

I'll keep that for now she says a materials requisition and again materials requisition software we're requesting materials. That sounds kind of reasonable. I'll keep that for now. Dee says a material summands and I'm not sure that sounds funny to me. Some of the summands are like if there's someone that quite sounds kind of serious type of terminology for requesting materials I don't think that doesn't sound right to me. I think that's a made up thing. So and then he says new job notification, new job notification and that might be the reason for us requesting materials but I don't think we request materials with a new job notification.

We got notified we got a new job and therefore our request meets. I don't think it's easy. So if we go through this again then we're going to say a source document to request materials for production is either a job cost sheet, the purchase order or C materials requisition. Now of those three I don't think it's because he's going to include all everything on it's going to include materials labor and overhead that's where we track it. So it's not going to be the requesting document or a form purchase order or materials or requisition of the purchase order is the one that we use to request from the vendor.

So when we are buying the materials from the vendor we may use a purchase order to request the materials that they will then ship but when we're getting the materials from the warehouse to the production to the factory then that's the one we're going to use the materials requisition form. So we're going to request the requisition from materials. So this is going to be the answer. Final answer. A source document to request materials for production is C materials requisition. Next question. Journal Entry to record payroll costs for labor in the factory a payroll expense is debited and a work in process inventory is credited to work working process inventory and factory overhead are debited and payroll payable is credited.

See cost of goods sold is debited and payroll payable is credited the direct labor and indirect labor are debited and payroll payable is credited or even work in process inventory is debited and overhead is credited. Okay let's go through this again and see if we can use the process of elimination journal entry to record payroll costs for labor in the factory. So we've got a payroll journal entry for people that work in the factory. So a payroll expense is debited and the working process is credited. Now we might think that sounds reasonable if we're paying payroll that's normally the payroll Journal actually.

We're not talking about withholdings; they didn't put anything in here with Social Security and Medicare payroll taxes. But if we eliminate all those That's usually what we think of as payroll debit expense. Wages payroll expense credit work in process. So we would credit cash you would think. So the second part of the working process is kind of unusual; the debit payroll seems like the norm. So let's go to the next one. So when we say we'll keep that one for now. This says work in process inventory and factory overhead are debited and payroll payable is credited.

Now you know this might seem reasonable in some ways because we're going to put it in work and process's is where we want to apply the wages somehow because we want to put it into work and process an inventory account and then we're going to credit wages payable which may be instead of credit in cash because we haven't paid it yet. Possibly. So I'm going to keep this for now and then say the cost of goods sold is debited in payroll payable. That doesn't seem reasonable really because the cost of goods sold is where we would expense the inventory at the end. We haven't sold it yet.

So clearly if it's going to be an expense you would think it be payroll not cost of goods sold at this point. So I don't think it's because the DSS direct labor and indirect labor are debited and payroll payable is credited. Now that actually sounds kind of reasonable here because again it says that's what we have here. You would think I mean if we were paying payroll it would be direct labor and indirect labor. So I'll keep that for now. And then each says work and process inventories debited and overhead is credited and in this case work in process it might you might think well something should go to work and process and Sumption something should go to overhead.

But you would think they would both be going the same direction because you know we're increasing them both and they're both inventory accounts. So it doesn't really make sense that one would be debited and credited. So I don't think it's easy. So let's go through this again we've got a D A B and D. JOURNAL ENTRY TO RECORD payroll costs for labor in the factory. So first one says payroll expense is debited and work in process. Inventory is credited. Now this one the payroll makes it sound kind of like it's possible and the fact that we have work in process is part of inventory sounds kind of plausible but if this was the journal entry when are they going to get paid. How are we going to pay them?

There's no cash being credited and there's no payable. So it would never be payable Plus the work in process is going down or has a credit and it's an asset account. So we should be Deben in the work in process and payroll expense is actually wrong because we're not going to be expensing it even though we're processing payroll we're going to be putting it into an asset. We're not consuming it to help us generate revenue. So that's why it's not a. And then we're left to be NDB says work in process inventory and factory overhead are debited and payroll payable is credited which is similar to D which is say in that direct labor and indirect labor are debited and payroll payable is credited.

Now of those to be is actually the correct one because D is really telling us why we do the meaning. In other words the same direct labor and indirect labor are the types of wages we could be paying. Meaning we're either paying people who are working directly on a job or people who are working indirectly and if they're working directly on a job we determine that so that we can do it work and process. If they're not working directly on a job we determine that we will have the Tebbutt factory overhead. So these are the determining factors; these aren't actual accounts. These are just telling us which accounts we should be hitting based on the fact that we can apply these to a job we can't. So the correct answer is actually the final answer. Journal Entry to record payroll costs for labor in the factory B work in process inventory and factory overhead are debited and payroll payable is credited.

Discussion Question - Job Cost System

In this discussion, we will discuss the discussion of what a predetermined overhead rate is and how it is calculated and used. If we see a discussion question like this or an essay question like this, even if we don't know exactly what a predetermined overhead rate is, we could start by thinking, well, it has something to do with overhead. Overhead typically has something to do with production. So we might want to start there. We can say, Well, how does overhead fit into production? How might we use a rate? What is overhead? And by starting there, even if we don't know exactly where we're going, that might give us some points if we're talking about an essay question. So if we're thinking about overhead, we're typically thinking about some type of manufacturing process.

So we can think there, we can at least say, well, overhead is typically going to be used not in a company that doesn't have inventory, but one that creates the inventory. So it's going to be in a manufacturing company and it's not just going to be in a company that purchases and sells inventory. So that's the first thing we can get to. We can typically say, well, overhead is going to be related to us producing inventory in a manufacturing type of company. Now there's going to be three types of things. When we produce inventory, we always whenever we think of inventory, we want to think of three things. There's going to be direct labor, direct materials and overhead.

That's what inventory consists of, the things the Labor put into it and everything else that we had to put into to basically convert it from raw materials to whatever the end product is when we make it. Now, Of course, here we're focusing on the overhead. So the overhead is everything else. So we can say, well, overhead itself is going to be everything else. Our goal is to try to track everything else that's within the production process that we cannot apply, like to a specific job or we cannot apply to a specific process. And therefore, we need to put it into this bucket of overhead. And that's the problem with overhead. We don't know. We don't know where it should go.

We can't apply it to the job directly. It's not direct labor. It's not a direct cost. It's some, it's some. We don't know which. If we think of a job cost system, we don't know which job to apply it to. That's the problem. That's why we can't put it directly into work. And then Of course, we're going to have to apply it to work in process, but not using the direct process because we don't know exactly what it is, but some type of estimate. And Of course, that's what this calculation is going to help us do. The predetermined overhead rate is going to help us to estimate how much of this overhead should go into each job.

Now, when you consider that problem, if we have if we have a set amount of overhead, if you imagine, well, we got this much overhead and we need to apply it to this many jobs, if we have five jobs and we've got 1000 in overhead, then if you if you consider that problem, you might say, well, that's an easy problem to solve. I'll just take the overhead and divide it by five jobs and then apply it out to the five jobs evenly and that'll be it. But Of course, we cannot do that for a few different reasons. One, the jobs aren't the same. If we're using a job cost system, the jobs may differ, so we don't know. Some jobs will be larger, some will be smaller. Doesn't seem proper to apply the same amount of overhead to them.

And two, we're going to be finishing jobs as we go and we want to apply the overhead to it, even though we may not know what the actual overhead is until the end of the time period, meaning things like paying the utility bill, things like recording depreciation, those types of things we don't usually do until the end of the month, but we want to apply overhead as we go. So even though we're using the utilities in the factory, we don't really know exactly what the utilities bill is until the end of the month. That's going to go into overhead and then we're going to apply it out.

So we don't even know what the end month overhead is to apply out to the jobs that we're making in this month. So for those two reasons, we're going to have to come up with some type of estimate that will be allocated more to the bigger jobs, less to the smaller jobs. And two, it'll allow us to allocate during the month, even though we don't know what total overhead is that we're actually using on the current jobs that we're working on. So the way to do that is we're going to have to use this estimate. We'll use this predetermined overhead rate and the predetermined overhead rate is going to be us using the estimated overhead and dividing it by some type of estimate of a cost driver.

So we're going to take the estimated total overhead for the month and divide it by some type of allocation factor, some type of cost driver. So an estimated cost. So let's think about how that would work. Again, we don't we don't know exactly what the total overhead cost will be. We can estimate that. How would we estimate it? Probably look at last month, we'd probably look at last month and then make projections into the future. So we would say this is what we think overhead costs will be. All the stuff will add together. And then we're going to divide it by some kind of cost driver, some kind of allocation basis. And this is where we're going to try to figure out which jobs are going to be larger or smaller based on this allocation.

So common usages would be direct labor, either cost or direct labor hours or direct materials. And the idea being that if we take the total cost that we think is going to happen throughout the time period divided by this allocation driver such as direct labor, then we can use that ratio to allocate out the cost. So we're basically just using direct labor as an allocation ratio so that we can see larger jobs than we would expect to have more labor, smaller jobs, and less labor. And then we would divide this out and that would give us our predetermined overhead rate. Once we have the predetermined overhead rate, then we can just have our jobs.

And as we create our jobs, we'll have direct material for each job. We'll have direct labor for each job, and then we'll multiply our predetermined overhead rate times the cost driver, the activity based driver that we're using. If we use direct labor, we can multiply that rate times the direct labor in order to get the amount of overhead we're going to allocate to the job. So remember that the the overhead doesn't have anything to do with direct labor specifically, but direct labor is used on a ratio basis to see how big one job is in proportion to another job and therefore apply more of the estimated overhead that will happen throughout the time period to the larger jobs and less to the smaller jobs.

Job Cost Documents and Forms

Within the job cost documents and forms chapter of the Book. We will discuss documents and forms that will be used within the job court system. We'll also take a look at the journal entries related to these documents and forms meaning the documents and forms will often be the driving factor to tell us when something is happening when we're going to be moving costs from one area to another and therefore when we need to record the journal entry and possibly record that information to the related job for example we may have a form that we will need in order to take the materials out of the warehouse move them into work and process out of materials inventory go to work and process inventory a form to help us to record the direct labor. So we'll take a look at those forms that will drive the recording.

We'll talk about the recording of that information and we'll talk about the related job cost sheets which will support the documentation and the recording that we will have on the trial balance and the financial statements. We will also have examples of the documents and we'll have problems in forms of Excel worksheets that we can work along with as examples for these problems as well. So we will have a chapter and if there is going to be a related transaction that we can practice we will then have a practice Ixo worksheet which will have instructional chapters for it and then Excel worksheets which typically have at least two tabs one tab with the answer to it so you can see exactly how it's put together. And then another tab that will be pre-formatted that you can fill out a Along with instructional chapters in A Step-By-Step format.

Job Cost Sheet

In this chapter we will take a look at a job cost sheet. A job call sheet is going to be used to help us to track the costs of inventory or jobs to a particular job or a job cost sheet or job costs system could be used for a manufacturing company that produces inventory. It can also be used for a service company that's tracking say time that goes to a particular job say a legal firm or an accounting firm that needs to track the time that they put in to a particular job. Would you use a similar system in order to track those costs by job in a construction company. Oftentimes we're going to use a similar job cost system because again those jobs are all going to be different in nature.

We'll have to track the costs to jobs if we make something like custom anything that's going to be customized guitars or something like that. If we produce inventory in other words we're going to have the same kind of issue that we're going to need to be able to track the costs to the particular job. The inventory is usually the one that we work with in a manufacturing company that makes inventory because it needs to track the costs to the job and has the added complication of dealing with inventory meeting materials that will have to be dealt with. Now the job cost sheets are going to be a type of subsidiary ledger if we think about all the job cost sheets put together.

They are going to support amounts that are going to be on the balance sheet. In other words when we have work in process when we start to get the working process the inventory count that's going to be tracking what we're doing in terms of the inventory for putting together guitars and we're tracking the cost to direct materials to direct labor and the overhead of those guitars on the trial balance on the financial statements as an assets in inventory then that number needs to be supported by something like a job cost sheet cost sheets multiple sheets that will be reporting and supporting that in a similar way. As one every account has a G.L.

Every account has a G-0 account and that gives support to those accounts by date of transaction. Some accounts need more than that. However for example accounts receivable is not enough to have a G.L. account. We also need to know the supporting subsidiary ledger by which customers owe us money so we can track that and hopefully collect when we talk about the inventory account. We're going to break that out to work in process and finished goods whenever something goes in the working process. It's not enough for us to just know the date of the transaction as will be on the go to General Ledger. We also need to know which job to track these costs to.

So this is similar to tracking the accounts receivable by customers. Here we're tracking the work in process by job that we have the job that we're applying this to. Now the job Quashy could have a customer here. It may be the fact that what we're making was a sign in job for making jobs and maybe we don't have a customer we might be in a system where the customer custom orders the job and therefore we have the customer that we're going to start to create the job for. And that's typically the case because if we're in a construction company if we make customers anything we're typically going to get the order we're going to know the customer and then can create the job typically with the job number from it.

But it's possible for us to make a job for something that we're going to have that on display or something like that. And and and not have the customer at this point in time. But we would have Of course the job number we need for the job that we're going to be working on. So it would be depending on the industry in terms of how these job cost sheets might be formatted we could have the addressed the job description depending on what we're making if we're making custom guitars we might say that type of guitar that we're making in general we might have the date of the proposed date the date started and the date completed on the job and Of course when it's completed that's when this job then would go from working process to finished goods.

It would then be done and we can make the general ledger transfer from what's in process to the finished goods. Now the job. Any job cost sheet no matter what we're dealing with is going to have the three components unless it's a service company. Right if it's a service company or if we're a law firm or for a bookkeeping firm all we really need to track is the labor is the hours to labor that we had. So if we work on bookkeeping we need to know how much time we spent and who spent the time and what their billable rate is for any particular job.

So we would have this. And then we're going to have the overhead of like the office face and whatnot that we could we may include in a job cost sheet. So those would be for a service company Of course. It's a little bit more complex for a manufacturing company because they're going to be dealing with materials. So if we deal with a manufacturing company making something like custom guitars than anything, any time you think of inventory, anything that deals with tracking inventory. What's the value of inventory? Its value is the direct materials, the direct labor and the overhead. All the other stuff.

So those are going to be the three components of our job cost sheet: direct materials, direct labor and overhead. And then we're going to have to track that information in some way. So the direct materials we may track by the date that we brought the materials in. We have a long job that we're working on. We may have multiple dates that we're going to have here something like a construction company might have Of course multiple dates of materials requisitions meaning we might have you know that's going to be the document that we're going to use in order to requisition materials for an a large company then we're going to have to get the materials from you know purchasing or that materials Department we're going to have to ask for those to happen we're going to have to requisition those.

We might list out the requisition number if that's the case. But at the minimum we probably want the date and the cost of the materials per job and then we're going to have the direct labor that we're going to have. And again if it's a construction company we might have multiple dates and multiple people at multiple different rates that are working on a particular job. We're going to want to date and then we're going to want the time ticket or some kind of tracking to a source document to be able to know how much time and what the billable rate that we're using is for these so we're going to source these out again and these time tickets are going to help us to know exactly how much to apply to these particular jobs.

And again this could get kind of complicated because we might have multiple people at multiple different billable rates and Of course a computer system can help us out with this. But at the minimum we need to date and we need the cost that we're going to have for the hours that will be worked and the hours worked we might be charging just per hour on our own direct labor. It's basically the payroll that we have here. We're processing the payroll and allocating the payroll not to an expense as we process it but to whatever job we're applying to and then we've got the overhead which is always the most confusing part both to us creating it and then when we try to explain something like this to a customer how much it cost us and the overhead we're going to say is we're going to have a predetermined overhead rate.

And here we're going to say that 160 percent of direct labor should favor costs. And notice that it has nothing to do with labor in particular but labor can be used as a way for us to know how big one job is compared to another. So for example if total labor was 1000 for this choppiness 2000 for the second job that might be a good way for us to say well that means that we should be applying twice as much of of of overhead to the second job not because there was more labor but because the more labor indicates that it's a bigger job. So we're using direct labor as an indicator to allocate the overhead. We'll talk more about that allocation and how that works how we get to this number here.

But just note the overheads going to have to deal with everything else that's involved. So if we make the guitar everything in the factory. So the depreciation on the factory. You know the small materials that we use in the factory, those indirect labor in the factory, the indirect material in the factory in anything. Utilities in the factory, anything in the factory. And then if we sum these up then we've got the materials we've got the labor and we've got the overhead that's going to be our total cost. Now if you look at this you might say this looks a lot like an invoice or like a bid that we might make on say like a construction company or something like that and it is very similar. But note that this is basically tracking the actual costs here.

So this isn't a bid which would look the same but it would be before you know before we do any work this is basically the actual cost is close. We can't Of course this is an estimate over here on the overhead but this is the actual cost. And note that a bid or an invoice won't stop here because this is only the cost. We might include this in our invoice. We might tell our customers hey here's our invoice. The materials cost , the labor cost is the overhead cost. This is our best calculation of what our cost is and our markup is whatever it is. Right if we have a 30 percent markup we might say that then how much should we charge you three to six six times a 30 percent market 1.3 and then get to the amount that we're going to bill.

So this might be the start of the bill. In other words. But then we're going to say that based on that we're going to give our markup. And this is the actual amount that we might have said if we were using this to create a bill. So note that Of course if we had a process in a construction company if it was a big job we would probably set a price at the beginning based on an estimate that would be similar to this but it would all be estimates. And then we might tell our customer that we're either going to, you know, abide by the estimate or we are going to make adjustments if the costs run over the estimate. And then once we have the end product here, the end product here is at cost. We might use this then for the invoice basically and mark it up.

So this looks similar to the invoice but this might be used for invoicing a similar type of process. But this is going to be actually used for the allocation of the job. What we will definitely use this for is when we sell this if this was a guitar or something. If this was a job once the job is done once we sell the inventory at the end then we will debit accounts receivable or cash more credit sales not for this number possibly for that other number that we just looked at. But then this number will be used to debit the cost of goods sold. The expense on the income statement is the cost of the inventory we used and then we'll credit the inventory lower in the finished goods inventory by this now also note that this is only one job here.

So when we think of the work and process account of what's reported on the balance sheet in the work process it's going to be the sum of all these jobs. So this would be like one customer this amount would be similar to one customer on the accounts receivable subsidiary ledger and we'd have to add up all of the customers to get to the number on the balance sheet. This is like one job on our job sheets and we would have to add up all the jobs that are open that haven't been finished yet in order to add up to what is being included on the balance sheet in the work process.

Materials Ledger Card & Materials Requisition

In this chapter, we will take a look at a materials ledger card and materials requisition form. This is going to be an example of a materials ledger card. And you can note that it's going to look very similar to us tracking inventory. We're basically tracking the inventory of materials. So if you work with a merchandising company, a company that purchases and sells inventory, we'll have a similar kind of tracking system that we might use for the tracking of inventory. In this case, Of course, we're using it for one component of inventory, one component of in this case, the type of services or the type of inventory that we make. So if we make guitars, for example, the major component might be wood. And so we would have to track that major component in a similar way that we would have to track the entire units of inventory for a merchandising company.

So we might have things like on the inventory items. In this case, we're going to say it's the wood planks. We might have a stock number, we might have a location in a store room. If we have a large store room, maximum quantity, a minimum quantity and quantity to reorder a reorder point when we want to reorder. And then we're going to break this out then to the received issue and balance. So this means received like we purchased it and we have received it. So this is when we're getting the inventory issued would be similar to our sales type of item or their cost of goods sold if we were a merchandising company.

In this case, we're not selling it. It's not leaving the company. It's going to another department. It's going from our warehouse basically to the production department to the factory to the work in process. And then we're going to have the balance here, which is going to be what is kind of on the balance sheet as of the ending product. So if we think of the balance sheet, this is going to be what is still included in our inventory items of just raw material. And then we might be tracking this information for example, on March 4th we said we had received.

So we have a receiving report and this is going to be the documentation we might use in a large company to tie this out to the receiving report. So in other words, this came from a receiving report. The warehouse would have received this information, counted it. We have then received the report to units and then we're going to have the unit price 225. And then the total price is two units times 225 or 450. Now, if we bring this over to the balance, we started with one unit at 225 or 225, and now we're bringing over these two units. So now we've got the two units and the one unit or Of course three units.

They still all cost 225 and therefore three times the 225 means we have a total of 675. So as of March 4th, we have $675 worth of inventory for wood planks. And then we're saying this time we have an issuance. On March 7th, we had an issuance. Why would we issue? Well, there was a request from the work in process for, say there's a new guitar we need to make, and they ordered some planks of wood, one plank of wood, apparently. And we then have a requisition form that's going to be the form from the work in process, the factory saying, Hey, we got a we've got a project that we need to work on.

Here's the form. We're going to say this for one unit, one plank cost 225. Notice this isn't the sales price. We're not dealing with any sales. This is all internal purchasing, going from one department, department to another now to work in process to the factory. Here's the total. If we go to the balance, then we have three units. We just issued one from the warehouse. So how many are left in the warehouse? Only two times the 225. And that gives us the 450. Now, a couple things to note here. Note that obviously you might think, well, wait, we still have three units because it only went from one department to the other.

And that's true. But we're not going to be tracking it here at work, in process now. It's not going to be included in the balance sheet account of materials. It's going to be included in the balance sheet account of work in process. We're going to apply it to this one unit. Now, it's going to be applied from these materials to the work in process account and be supported by a job cost sheet as opposed to being tracked in our just materials ledger. Also note that this system works well if these units' planks of wood don't change in value, meaning if the planks of wood become more expensive over time just because of inflation, then we're going to have similar issues that we have with inventory tracking.

We're going to have to use some type of method, actual cost of the inventory and track it specific identification or probably some kind of cost flow like first in, first out, the assumption that we have. First and first out, assumption last in, first out or average. So we'll have those same kinds of inventory tracking problems that we have for the materials ledger as we would for just inventory in general. And then we got this would be the requisition form. So when we had this item here, this isn't going to be the same form, but when we had this requisition, this is the type of form that we would use for the requisition. And remember, in a big company, then we would have to have this process of one department requisition.

So if I'm in the warehouse and I'm asking for a plank of wood, I have to go, I'd have to go. I mean, if I'm in the work process, the factory and I need a plank of wood to make our project, then we might have to use a requisition form to get that from the warehouse. Now, Of course, the smaller a company is then, and if we're a construction company working on a job, then the requisition forms might be similar to just the receipts, you know, that we're using in order to purchase materials that will then be supportive of of what we're going to be using in the in the work in process. So the requisition form here is being used for us to take it from the warehouse that it's already been purchased from.

But it's also going to be the form that we're going to use in order to apply it to a job when we create the job cost sheet. So the requisition and so when we create if it was if we were a smaller company, we might use receipts to create,

Of course, the job cost sheet for the materials that we would be purchasing. So we're going to have the job number that we're going to have on here, the materials, the quantity that we need, one plank of wood quantity provided. Hopefully they're the same, unless, you know, the department didn't give us. Maybe they didn't have the warehouse, didn't have all we needed, and then we usually have it filled out because we want to be able to track an audit trail that we have here.

And then we've got the date, the materials description, the plank of wood. This is the requester and this is filled by. So obviously we want to have the two individuals. We want to have someone requesting one, one filling it out. That gives us a system of controls, meaning it would be difficult to steal the plank of wood if we have to have two people involved in the requisition process without having some type of collusion in order for that to happen, date provided and material received, date and any remarks that we might have. So this would just be the form, just just a form for us to get that wood from the warehouse to the work in process so we can start working on it.

And remember that all ties out to this form as well. So this requisition form is going to be used here on the material side to get the materials out of there. And it's also going to be used on the supporting document, not that this isn't the actual form we'll see here, but it'll also be used in this document, which is the job cost. So we're moving the materials over here to the job cost system. So we still have our job 15 and we're going to allocate this requisition form to it. And that will mean that we're still tracking the wood, It's still there.

It hasn't left the company because we haven't sold it yet, but now we're tracking it in the account of work in process, and that account is not supported by us, we are tracking the inventory and just planks of wood. It's supported by our job cost sheets. So our job cost sheets are now supporting that piece of inventory and we're going to have it in this job cost sheet up until it's finished and then we'll have the job move to finished goods and it'll still be supported by this job cost sheet. And then we'll finally sell it. And once we sell it, we'll then move this. All these costs, all the inventory that we bought and all the material we bought, all the labor we did, all the overhead will then be finally expensed in the form of the cost of goods sold at the point of sale.

Now we'll take a look at a journal entry related to the materials requisition. So every time we have a materials requisition, we're going to have a journal entry for it. For the general ledger accounts here, we're going to say for all these different jobs. So we're looking at all these jobs and we had all these requisitions for these jobs. We're going to sum up those requisitions. So we're just taking these documents and summing up the materials that were requested. And that's going to come up to a total of 2230. So the journal entry then we will have is going to be the raw materials going down. The raw materials here are going down and then it's going to be moved to the work in process account.

So raw materials are an asset account. It has a debit balance. We're moving it from the raw materials from the warehouse. So that's going to decrease and we're going to move it not too far to another inventory account to work in process. So work in process is an inventory account, it's an asset account. It represents the inventory we're working on. It's going to increase. Now that's going to be for the direct materials, those that we can apply directly out to the guitars if we're making guitars. Now, there also might be some materials that are indirect, meaning something like glue or something like that. If we're making guitars and if we say that there were requests for glue or something like that, that was indirect that we couldn't assign to a job we didn't know Job applied to.

We just are basically taking stuff from the warehouse and assigning it just in general to be in the where we just gave them glue. That can be assigned to anybody who wants to use it in the middle on any guitar that they start to work on. Then we don't know which job to apply for here. And so those may still come out of just the materials. We might still have just materials that will be there or we might try to track those types of materials separately. So in other words, we might have a materials account that includes all materials, direct and indirect, or we might try to have another account that just has the indirect stuff and track those separately.

In this case, we're going to say they're all in raw materials and then the indirect materials, we're going to say, okay, that raw materials is going down by 550 and the debits are not going to work in process. Why? Because we don't know which job to assign it to. It just went into the warehouse. And anybody who's making a guitar, any of these jobs that are working on a guitar can use the material. So that means that we can't assign it yet. We can't put it to work because we cannot support it. We can't back it up by particular jobs. So therefore, we're going to put it into the bucket factory overhead. It's still kind of an asset because ultimately it's going to go into the work in process. It's just that we're going to have to assign it to a job first.

We're just going to put all the stuff into a bucket and then find some way to assign it to a job. So if we look at those journal entries, then we're going to post out the work in the process that started at zero. It's going to go up by 2200 to 2200. And you can see that work in process then is here on the trial balance and then the raw materials. Here's the general ledger for raw materials. It was at 1500, 150,000. It's going down with a credit, 2002 32 147, 770. So we just moved it from raw materials to work in process. And then this side factory overhead went from zero up by 550.

So here's the factory overhead at 550, and then the raw materials are going to go down again. So raw materials 147, 770 going down by 552 147 220 And that then is going to be the 147 220 So it was one 4777 two before now it's down to the 147 220 that's represented here on the trial balance after both of these have been completed. Note that none of this whole process is not doing anything to the income statement. We bought the materials we were starting to use, the materials never going to hit the income statement, never affecting net income until when it's going to affect net income.

When we're finally done, we move these from work in process to finished goods and then we move them from finished goods to actually selling them, moving them to cost of goods sold. Now we will sell it. Sales will increase at the same time at that point. But what we're working on is the cost of goods sold that will ultimately be the cost. So all the stuff we're doing here is just kind of shuffling around on balance sheet accounts, just shuffling around basically an inventory asset type of accounts to track this process as it goes through and being able to support the process with job cost sheets.

Materials Ledger Card Requisition

In this chapter we will record a journal entry related to the requisition of materials in a Job Corps system where you have the information on the left. We're going to enter the journal entry into our general journal here then go into the general ledger and the general ledger will be used to create the trial balance. We can see the trial balance is going to be in order in terms of assets, liabilities , equity income and then expense accounts in the trial balance. We're going to have the debits represented with non-branded or positive numbers credits with bracketed numbers or negative numbers for Excel and therefore the total debits and credits are equal to zero at this time no net income at this time.

Nothing in sales costs of goods sold or any income statement accounts. Our focus here Of course is going to be on the tracking of inventory through the job cost systems so we're going to be working up here and the work in process and the raw materials finished goods overhead as we work through this problem. Our goal here is going to be taking raw materials and the raw materials that are going to be in our warehouse represented by the raw materials accounts. And we're going to be transferring them to the jobs and to where we can transfer them to the job.

And anything that we cannot transfer to the job we're going to put into overhead. So when we transfer things to the job that means that it's going from the warehouse. We want to take this stuff from the warehouse and we want to put it into the factory where we produce things so we're making guitars. We would take the wood or whatever from the warehouse and put it into the factory where we're going to start to make the inventory. So that's going to be our idea here. Now if we can apply to a particular job within a job call system then we're going to apply it out to overhead. So first let's just take a quick look at the example of a form that might be used to do this. Remember if it's a large company we're going to have to do this with documentation to have a requisition form in order to transfer the inventory so the inventory we imagine is in the warehouse.

We might have something like a requisition form. Something like this is just an example of a requisition form which would have the job number and the materials the date of the requisition. And what we want if its clanks would be requested by and it's going to be filled out by that we have to check and balance here. So in a larger company we would have this requisition and this would be what the documentation would be to allow us to take the raw materials from the warehouse and put them into a job. And notice we're referencing a particular job here and that's going to be allowing us to assign it both in terms of the materials Ledger card which is kind of like the material tracking the material within an inventory type system in the warehouse.

It's also going to be used as a requisition form for us to apply for the job and we'll see that process here. So we need to know which job it is so that we know what job it's going from out of the warehouse and how it's going to end at work and process. And then we might have a materials Ledger card that is just showing the inventory just again, just an example form that would say that we're tracking basically the inventory in a similar way in raw materials as we were just in a merchandising company. So for example we have anything that's going to be received here. We have a receiving report number of units received. And then we're going to add that to the total here.

So that this is what's on our balance sheet at any given time at any given date. So on the balance we started with one unit at 225 or 225 and we got three more units. I'm sorry we got two more units to add up to that three at two twenty five or six hundred seventy five dollars worth of inventory. And then when the inventory is taken out we do that with a requisition form similar to this. And these are just examples. And the requisition form says we're going to want one unit at 225 and that leaves us with three minutes to one or two units that are still left at 225 for 450.

So these are just an example of us having to track the inventory within the warehouse. And it's similar to us tracking inventory if we were a merchandising company and tracking inventory if the prices change we have the same flow assumptions that problems that we'll have to deal with first in first out last in first out average cost. Our focus here though is going to be on the job costs. These are just going to be some examples of the types of formants we would need and now we're just going to basically say I'm going to scroll all the way to the left that the requisition forms that we got are these these requisitions Fordham's for these jobs job B 15 16 17 18 and B 19.

We're going to start these jobs. And we asked for materials for them with requisition forms. And so then we also have some materials that are our small materials that we're not going to apply for a particular job of 550. And so that could be stuff like we're making guitars or something. It's like glue or something like that. The things that go into the guitar. We're talking about construction. These might be small small materials and whatnot. It's not worth tracking two particular jobs. OK. So that means that what we're going to do is take it from a journal entry standpoint the journal entry is the easiest part of it is we're just going to take the information out of the raw materials and transfer it to work and process both of these big inventory accounts raw materials is an inventory account with a debit balance.

We're going to make you go down doing the opposite thing to it which will be a credit to right click on raw materials right click and copy. When I put that on the bottom so it's on the 5 right click. I'm going to paste one two three just the values and we're going to credit this amount to two thousand two hundred thirty not including the five hundred and fifty. So it can be a credit of 2 to 3 0 and then we're going to debit something for that same amount. I'm going to do that by saying negative of this number. Or we could just type in there 2 2 3 0 and it's going to go into the working process account.

So is the working process account that's where it's going. It's a debit, it's another asset account. It's going to increase. So we're going to do the same thing to it as it's normal balance or debit. So all right click on that and copy it. Put that in before right click and paste one to three. So there's going to be our first journal entry. Let's go ahead and record that to the general ledger. So we're going to go to the general ledger for the working process. It's going to be one two three four accounts over so it can be for accounts to the right as well. So if I go to the right here's work in process I'm going to go back and forth from the screens a little bit. We could freeze the panes or you could make the screen smaller like this.

So you can see more but I'm just going to try to scroll back and forth here. So we're recording this right there and s 9 going to say equals and point to that 2230 and going to scroll to the right a little bit more that's going to go from 0 up by 2000 to 30 to 2000 230. This amount then is what's being used to create the trial balance. And we're Of course out of balance by that amount. Now will record the other side and these you may not be able to use if it's locked but they're in there in the formulas chapter here. I've put them in the quick toolbar. OK. In raw materials raw materials are here. Here's raw materials. Third account. It's the same order on the general ledger. So raw materials are going to be down here. So we want to be on the credit side. So I mean sell P 24 P 24 and I'm going to have to scroll up just a little bit to do this.

I'm going to be in 24 here and say Beagle's and I would highly recommend you put just a dollar amount here but I would use formulas as much as possible. Scroll up and we want that two thousand to 30 on the credits and enter. And that brings it to 550 down by 2000 232 147 770. That van can be found on the trial balance and it's going to put it back in balance here Deb it's equal in the credits. No effect on net income no effect on net income. Now I'm also going to represent this on the jobs as well. We're just going to be a quick little job sheet so that we can track these jobs. So 15 16 17 18 19 700 450. So it's 671 18 to 30 and hey coffee please I'm going to go all the way to the right and here is going to be our jobs. So I'll put this down here again just so we could see it.

Sales jobs are going to be our job sheets now; these are just fairly simplified sheets. But notice what we're going to have is the job number that is going to represent whether it be opened, closed or shipped and we sold it and then we've got the direct materials, direct labor and the factory overhead. Every job is going to include those three things. When we start the job we generally start with the materials that's the first thing we do. So now it's in progress and we're transferring these materials and we know which job they should go to because they're right here. So we're going to say okay materials for jobs are 15. It's going to be that 700 so 700 we're going to safely be 16 is 450 450. The 16th is going to be here.

And that was 617 we're going to say that this is 18 and that's going to be one 80 and then 19 is going to be that 230 so he'd be 19. Two hundred and thirty. Now if we did this correctly if we add up these jobs which is this all adding them up there's the total for all the jobs which only includes you know the direct materials at this point that should be equivalent. See what's on the G.L. at this time. So here's the geo or here's the balance which is equivalent to the goal. And that's going to be the same as what's on the job sheet.

So notice that this number is being derived from this number and this number is going to be supported if we look at if we look at this number of on the trial balance we need to support it with with a subsidiary Ledger in a similar way that we need to rip to support the accounts receivable with a subsidiary ledger. In other words the accounts receivable we need to support it not only with the G.L. given it's detailed by date but by who owes this money. When you insist on your ledger telling us by customer the same thing is true here we need the DL to tell us by date what happened but we also need it by job because we need to track this information by job.

That's what these job cost sheets are doing. So we're going to track each thing here by job. The job cost sheet has to match all the job cost sheets if we add them together to match what is in the work in process. OK, I want to scroll back to the left now and I'm going to the last piece of this, which is this indirect material that's also going to come out of the materials warehouse but we couldn't assign it to a job. We can think of it like binding the glue for all of the guitars we're making. They just needed more of it in the warehouse. We don't know which job it's going to go to, we're just going to put it in there and whoever needs it can use it.

So we've got the work in process. I'm sorry the raw materials are going to go down. So when I right click and copy my skip a line and skip another line to have a new journal entry

I mean the eight right click and paste one two three. So the raw materials are going down again by this 550 but then there's going to be a debit. So I'm going to do that with a negative of this number or we could just type in five 50 and now we just need to know what that account is going to be. It's not going to be a working process because we can't apply it to a job. So we have to put it in the overhead bucket. We will apply to a job at a later time but we'll have to do some type of estimate in order to do so.

So when I right click and copy the factory overhead, put that in B-7 right click and paste one to three and now will record this out. So here's the factory overhead. Here's the factory overhead. It's like one two three four five six over. So it's going to be the same order on that on the G.L. and the factory overhead is going to be down here actually it's in s 25 factory overhead debit side. So I'm going to put my cursor as 25 and say equals and then go left and I'm just going to scroll up till I find this. And so there it is. I mean see 7 and enter. So it went from zero up by five to five hundred fifty to 550 and it gave you double click on it see seven this number then is being used to create the trial balance here and we're out of balance Of course by the 550 till we record the other side.

So then we're going to go to raw materials. Here's the third account of raw materials. It's going to be the same in the G.L. tuner's raw materials down here. It's a credit again so we're in the 25 P 25 we'll say equals going to scroll up just a bit and pick up that 550 and it's going to bring this 147 770 down by 552 147. Two hundred and twenty. That number then Of course used to create the trial balance here. And that puts it back in balance debits equal in the credits. And we have net income nothing right now. And notice that's going to be the case for pretty much this whole like Job cost system until we sell the finished goods and then it'll be affected by the cost of goods sold. So all this activity we're doing here is really just going to be moving throughout the assets more specifically moving throughout inventory asset type accounts.

Time Ticket & Labor Journal Entry

In this chapter, we will take a look at an example of a time ticket and the recording of a journal entry related to labor for a manufacturing company, for a company using a job cost system. So when considering a time ticket, we want to keep in mind, Of course, that when we track the time of workers that are going to be working on a job, we need to be able to apply it to a particular job. The time ticket here is going to be used for us to track the cost so that we know the cost of the job. Now, Of course, we also in a job cost system would be tracking this out, probably to help us to build the job as well. They're going to be related in some way. But notice here, what we're trying to do is get to the cost of the job with the time ticket. Everything we're tracking here is the actual cost of the job.

So when we consider the time ticket, then we're going to have, you know, any employee that works on the job and we're ultimately going to take their wages that we we pay them, which we usually record as wages expense or something, or, you know, hourly wages expense to not an expense but to the job to work in process. So that's in essence what we're doing here. We're tracking the time. We're going to apply that time not to an expense at the period in which we paid the employee or even in which they worked, but to an asset inventory, not expensing it until we sell the inventory in the form of cost of goods sold. So this is going to be a time ticket.

We're going to have the employee here, we'll have the employee number if we have one, then Of course, the job that's going to be the important component, the job that we're going to assign it to. You know, we have the similar punching in the time in, time out, the time that elapsed, the rate, and that will give us the amount that we're going to apply to each job. Now, Of course, this could be used in a computerized system. We could have a, you know, an old time ticking tracker that we're going to have. So whatever way that we're going to use to format this, we have to make sure that whatever time we have, we're applying it out to the correct job so that we can then post this to work in process and have it be supported then by the job sheets. So here's an example of the job sheet. I'm not tying this ticket in directly to it, but it's just an example of a job sheet.

Then this is a particular job that's going to support all the work in process accounts, everything that's on the work in process in a similar way as a subsidiary account by customer supports, what's in accounts receivable, the job sheets are going to report what's on the balance sheet, what's on the trial balance for work in process. So in this case, we're talking about labor. So we're tracking labor here. So these time tickets are going to help us to track the labor we might have if we're working a big construction job or something like that, we might have multiple time tickets that we're going to have to track and we're going to have to apply them to these job sheets.

And note what's happening here. Again, when we record the journal entry as we'll see, we're not going to record it to wages expense, meaning when we process payroll, we're in essence debiting not an expense, but inventory in the form of work in process, supporting it by the job. We won't expense it until we sell the inventory at the end of this process. So that's going to be what the time ticket function will be and we need some format to do that. If we're just doing a construction job, then we've got to apply that, apply it out some way. If we have a service, a bookkeeping company or a law firm, then again, we have to apply some way the wages out.

Now again, the billing is going to be similar to if we had a construction company or a law firm or something like that. When we create the invoice, we might have a billable rate which may or may not be the same as the rate that we're using to apply the cost to the job. But here again, we're looking at the cost. So we're looking at the actual cost meaning in other words, this looks a lot like an invoice. We may use this to create the invoice, we may take the bottom line number of actual costs as close as we can except for the overhead and mark it up. So we might say we're going to mark it up 30 or 40% and that's going to be our sales price. Or if we're a bookkeeping firm or a bookkeeping firm or something like that or a law firm, we might be tracking the time of our multiple employees.

And on the invoice, we might be having a similar tracking, but we might use billable rates that are different from the pay rate in order to create the invoice. That might be a way that we basically create invoices. But here we're tracking the actual cost of the employees here because we're tracking the cost of the job. Okay. So if we then took this, the direct labor and we took all of the labor that we're applying to these jobs, we took all the time tickets and we applied them out to the jobs. So we have a list of jobs. That we're saying all these jobs now are listed out and we know the direct labor applied to them. In other words, we can think of it this way.

If we're saying that the payroll for this time period added up to 5000, that's what we have in payroll for these individuals. Then we're breaking it out between these jobs. That we paid for, and this much is indirect that we couldn't apply to a particular job. So we're processing this now with a journal entry, just like we would with payroll, meaning we're going to credit, we're going to say wages payable in a simplified journal entry. It might be a credit to cash, right? Or but wages payable will show us that it's for wages because we're processing payroll. And then the debit usually we would think, well, it's payroll, it's going to go to, it's going to go to wages expense.

And again, we're not getting, we're not getting into the withholdings and everything right now. This is a simplified payroll journal entry. And we're just going to say, well, the debit would normally go to payroll expense, but now we're going to say no, it's going to go to work in process. Why is it going to go to work in process and not payroll expense when we're basically recording the payment of employees because the expense isn't there just because it's payroll at the time we pay them. It's an expense because we use that work, that work in order usually to help us generate revenue in the same time period.

The matching principle here, we use this labor not in order to help us generate revenue, yet it helps us to make inventory, which is work in process. It's part of the inventory. So the labor, the wages that we're paying is part of inventory. We will expense it when we're going to expense it when we sell the inventory in the form of the cost of goods sold. Then the other side, this is going to be the labor that wasn't applied to a job, meaning like supervisor salaries or possibly maintenance in the warehouse. We couldn't apply it to a job. So it just is going to go indirect. So it's going to go we're still going to go to wages payable because we're going to pay these people. And so it's going to eventually go to cash that you can think of as cash.

We're going to pay them as well. It's going to go out of payable and then into cash eventually. And then the debit is going to go to the factory overhead. So it's going to go to the factory overhead. Again, it's not going to go to wages expense because we haven't used it. It's going to go to inventory eventually and we're going to have to apply it out from factory overhead to inventory in some way. So if we look at posting the journal entry to the general ledger, we've got the work in process here. So we've got the work in process at 2230. It's going to go up by 4200 to 6430. That then is what we have here 6430 wages payable. So here wages were at zero.

It's going to go up by 4200. And again, you can think about it as if we were paying cash, right? So wages payable is just going to be an intermediary. If this was a very simplified transaction, it would just be a debit to the work in process credit to cash, and that would be similar to us, again, just processing the payroll. We're not dealing with anything else like withholdings or anything. We're just looking at a very basic kind of payroll journal entry. The main thing to note, however, Of course, is that the expense here is not going to be an expense. It's going to that inventory account. We also note that book problems will often use a payable account when working these types of systems because what they're trying to do is show us just what the journal entry without having to have a note in the journal entry that what this is related to.

And if we just debit work in process and credit cash, then just by looking at the journal entry, we wouldn't really know what's happening. So we use the payable. Now payable is fairly often used, but we might see it in some other areas where it's less, you know, something like utilities. We might see utilities payable or something like that because that helps us to know that the part that's going into work in process is related to utilities in that case. And usually we wouldn't have utilities payable because we would just pay the utilities. It would be a credit to cash. We might do it with a note. So just be aware of that. So we're just processing the payroll here, wages payable. Then we have the factory overhead.

1000 to 200 was at 550. We're going to debit it, 1200 to 1750. That's the amount of factory overhead. And then we've got the wages payable again, which was 4200. We're going to credit 1200 to 5400. So now we have wages payable, which we will pay soon. When we do so, we will debit this, making it go down to zero and credit cash.

Time Ticket and Labor Entry

In this chapter we will record journal entries related to wages both direct and indirect within a job because this term information will be on the left. We're going to enter that into our general journal and post it to the general ledger General Ledger being used to create the trial balance. Here is our trial balance: it's older assets and then liabilities and in equity income and expenses we Of course are focusing on the asset accounts more specifically the inventory accounts as we take a look at the flow of a job cost system. What we're doing here is looking at the wages that are paid to people that work in basically the we're in the construction of whatever we make or we're making guitars in the construction of where construction jobs within the construction process the people that work directly on that as well as the people that work indirectly.

Going to have to sort those two out and record this information to understand this we first need to think about that we're really kind of just processing payroll here we're processing payroll to people that work on the jobs that they work in the factory and they're making guitars. They work in the factory where we're processing the payroll. Now when that happens typically we think that the journal entry if we take out all the withholdings we're not going to get into payroll withholdings or whatnot but if we think about the simplified transaction of the payroll transaction it would be we're paying someone credit in cash. We instead are going to make wages payable and then debit.

Traditionally we would think it would go to wages expense or some other type of expense in this case. That's Of course what the difference is going to be. And it takes a little while to really understand that this is going to happen a lot in a job cost system because we start to memorize if we've worked in other types of industries, such as a service company merchandising company, that every time we have payroll it's just going to be a wage expense. But in this case when that's because of the matching principle before it used to be that we used those wages in order to help us generate revenue in the same time period. And this time they're not generating revenue yet. They're making an asset, they're making inventory. So that's the first thing we need to realize.

We're kind of processing payroll but it's going to look different and we're going to have to just basically unlearnt if we're just memorized kind of the payroll journal entry which is the credit cash or credit which paypal and debit the expense we're not going to debit the expense because it's not an expense type. What we're going to have over here is the jobs that they worked on and that's what we will have to track. So let's take a look at that. Real quick on how that might happen from a foreign base is just an example. So we're going to go to the right over here all the way to the right and we're going to have something like a time ticket Of course and the time ticket is going to give us an idea of the jobs the people that worked the jobs that they worked on so that we can track what job is being worked on.

So just know that we're going to need some type of system within a job costs system to track which jobs are being worked on so that when we process the payroll we can process it and and select the correct account to hit which is going to be the correct job account when processing their payroll process. So this individual worked on Job B 15. And that's where we need to apply the expense of the wages we're going to pay for this individual. Note that this could happen for a company that makes stuff or for a service company like a service company like a bookkeeping company may have a job cost system in a similar fashion. Also note that if you were applying out the actual cost. If we work in a bookkeeping company or something like that or a law firm we may have a billable rate for people that might be different meaning we might make our invoices using some type of billable rate.

That's different from the actual pay rate or we might make our invoice with what we actually pay an individual and then market up to you some kind of markup in order to record it here though we're tracking the cost to the inventory and the cost to the job. So we're really using the actual number that we pay our employees here. So I'm going to go all the way to the left again. So I scrolled all the way back to the left. Now we're just seeing the documentation that might be used to create this. We're going to just look at the jobs here. This is the jobs and the direct labor that we are applying to them which we're putting together by basically tracking as we as the employees work.

Typically in a database program of some kind what job they worked on. So Job B 15. We've got one thousand two hundred that's going to be applied for direct labor jobs 16

900 B-17 5 60 the 18 850 and B 19 694 a total of four thousand two hundred. So the journal entry then is pretty straightforward. We don't need to break it out for the journal entry but we do need to break it out for the supporting documentation in each job. So the journal entry we're just going to use this total here. It's going to go into work and process and that's usually that's going to be kind of the confusing thing here because again typically we would think of it as an expense here where you are using these wages in order to help us generate an asset which is going to be inventory which is represented here by unfinished work in process.

So it's a debit balance. We're going to make it go up by doing the same thing to another debit. So we get a right click and copy. We're going to put this in the 10 right clicks and paste one into the story. The amount in cetane is going to be that 4200 then we're going to credit something for 4200. I'm going to use the kind of plug formula of negative of that number and enter. And then we just need to see the amount. Now we could say that we paid cash but typically had a lot Of course problems and in practice we may go into wages payable first and then pay it at a later time. So I'm going to put wages payable. So Jay 14.

Right click and copy. We're going to put that in the 11 or right click and paste one to three values only. So again if this was a normal payroll journal entry for a non manufacturing company we would credit which is payable or cash and debit wages expense or something like that. And then we would have withholdings to simplify the kind of payroll entry here but we would debit wages expense here we're not debiting the expense. And that's kind of the tricky thing that we're going to have to see a few times over as we go through a manufacturing company and that's because of the matching principle we haven't used those wages to help generate revenue yet.

They're going to help us generate revenue in the future. When we finally sell the inventory we will expense it in the form of the cost of goods sold. So the value of that work is going into the inventory which is currently in process and therefore going into work in process. So let's record that out. Here's the work in process account. It's going to be one two three four accounts down here. It's going to be 4 accounts over on the G.L. then we're going to try to just scroll back and forth if you want to make the screen smaller that can help to record. I'm going to try to keep it full size and use scrolling to do this. We could also freeze the panes but we'll do it this way.

So we're going to go to work. Here it is. We want to be in the debit we are selling as 10. I'm going to say equals and point to that four thousand two hundred and that's going to bring the balance from 2002 30 up by 4200 to 6000 430 that the end is being used to create this trial balance number and we're out of balance by 4200. Then we'll record the other side of this which is wages payable. That's going to be our only liability account is a pretty simplified trial balance. But there's higher wages payable. We're going to scroll over to wages payable. It's going to be a credit. So here's wages payable we're going to be on the credit side of x 19. So within x 19 equals I'm going to go all the way to the left until I find wages payable the last journal entry 4200 and enter.

So there it is wages payable 4200. This number is then used to create wages payable here. And we're back in balance. So our journal entry is back in balance and has been recorded here OK so there's our process now. Once again we did something to work in process and whenever we do that we need to support this not only with the guild as we have here but this only gives us the details by date. We need to break it out by job. And remember it's similar to the accounts receivable being broken out not only by date but by the customer who owes us the money. The working process needs to be broken out not only by date on the goal but by the job which job we are applying these costs to. So if we do that, that's where we're going to need to separate out here in the sub account. So I'm going to go ahead and copy this and we'll bring it over. I'm going to go all the way to the right to where our jobs are.

So here's our jobs over here. And I'll paste this down here. OK. So. So now we're just going to apply this out that 4200 have broken out of job B 15 were in the 15 direct labor and we're going to say this was 1200. And then 16 900 years 16 direct labor 900. And then we're going to say the 17 560 B-17 560 and then the 18 850 the 18 850 and finally 19 690. So we're going to go over here to be 19 and say 690. Now if we add up our total jobs they add up to direct materials direct labor. These two add up to 1000 230 being summed up across being summed up vertically. Here's our total 1000 230. That's the case for all jobs. If we add up all of them they're all open to all these jobs you do it this way. All these jobs add up to this amount that should be equivalent to what's on the trial balance and NGL so we can see over here we noted that this work in process was used to create this number and this number should be supported by this number.

And by the work in process the jobs. And it still looks good there. The last piece of this then is we're going to record this amount. This is indirect labor and that can be anything in the factory that we couldn't apply to a job. So if we have supervisors salaries or something like that we don't know which job they actually worked on if any other they're working on multiple jobs. So we have to basically apply their salary to those jobs. If it's maintenance or something in there we might need it, if it's anything that's in the factory where we make things, if we're making guitars or whatnot we need to be able to apply those salaries out to the jobs. So that's going to be the indirect labor here.

So it's still going to be wages payable because we're processing payroll but the debit now is not going to work because we don't know which job it's going to. It's going to go to the bucket which is factory overhead. So all right click and copy factory overhead. We'll put that in the 13. Right click and paste one two three and then the amount is going to be 1200 will credit something run 1000 200 as well and do that with a little like negative of that number. That's like the negative Flugge formula. You could put just a negative 1200 that's fine too but then that's going to go to wages payable. Again it's kind of like processing payroll like work. We could get paid cash. We're not dealing with any other withholdings here, we're just having a simplified payroll journal entry rather than debiting expenses. However it's going to an asset account and an inventory account.

In this case overhead until we figure out a way to apply that overhead to a job. So when I right click on wages payable We'll put that in before right click and paste one two three. And there we have it now let's record this one. We're going to post it to the general ledger. Here's the factory overhead. It's like the third to last asset account. Same order on the G.L.. So factory overhead is down here. So it's right there in s 26. So within s 26 minutes equals go left to find that last account there it is factory overhead and pick up that see 13 enter. So within as 26 it equals C 13 bringing the 550 previously and they're up by 1200 to 1000 750 that 1000 750 then is being used to create the trial balance out of balance by 1200 until we record the other side. So here's the other side and wages payable. It's our only liability account which is nice and this nice small trial balance.

So we're going to kill field wages. There it is going to be on the credit side again I mean X 20 x 20 minutes it equals and then we'll scroll left and find back that accounts schoolmen left wages payable. We'll pick that up on the 14th and enter here. So here's wages payable equals D 14. It was at a credit of 4200 going up in the credit direction 1200 to five thousand four hundred. That then is used to create the trial balance and the balance is back in balance debits equal in the credits debits minus the credits equals zero. Still no effect on net income here. And again even though we kind of paid wages and you might in our thinking if we've thought about companies other than manufacturing companies is probably that there should be an expense related to wages expense. But no, there's not an expense because that was part of the inventory. Anything that we had to pay for in order to conform or convert the raw materials to inventory is not an expense until we sell the inventory. It's part of the cost of inventory.

Multiple Choice Questions – Job Cost System

In this chapter, we will take a look at multiple choice questions related to a job cost system. First question: labor costs in production are either high or low. B indirect or hourly. C salary or hourly D indirect or expense, and E, direct or indirect. Okay, let's go through this again using the process of elimination. Labor costs in production are either high or low. That's possible. They could be in between two, Right? So labor costs within there could be high or low. This seems kind of arbitrary.

You know, it might seem correct. It could be either high or low. They've got to be one or the other or in between. But it'll seem like they're kind of made up terms. So high or low doesn't seem to be the types of terms we're looking at here. So let's see, B says indirect or hourly. And those seem like two payroll terms. There are two payroll terms, but they're not really contradictory or they don't seem to match indirect or hourly. Hourly is a type of wage. Indirect would be whether it's applied to a specific job or not. So I don't think it's that they don't seem to go together.

C says salary or hourly. And those are two payroll items that seem to go together. So I would think that, you know, maybe that maybe that would be it because how else do we pay people either hourly or salary? So and then D says indirect or expense. And again, these two don't seem to exactly go together. Indirect is a payroll we apply to payroll and expense. Those two things don't seem to be two terms that are exactly related. So I don't think it's D and then E says direct or indirect. And again, those two terms kind of ring together. That sounds direct or indirect. Those are two terms that sound like they go together. So I'll keep that.

We're at C and E, So let's go through this again. We're going to say direct costs in production are either C salary or hourly or E, direct or indirect. Now the key here is that it's in production costs. So if we're talking about the production costs, I think the more proper one, the one we're looking for is either direct or indirect, which is a little deceiving because probably this one sounds pretty reasonable too, because how else do we pay people either salary or hourly? That would make sense, but that's not really applying that.

That's true for all payroll, really. I mean, we're paying people either on a salary basis or an hourly basis. It's not something that applies to costs of production, which we're talking about here, cost of production. We're typically trying to think of how we're going to apply this stuff out to jobs. And either we're talking about labor that is directly related to a job or labor that is indirect. So given those terms, I think He's the one that we're looking for. So we have labor costs in production that are either direct labor or indirect labor.

And by the way, this is just one of those where you might see this and say, well, this you know, this isn't technically wrong, possibly because there's and we could pay people some kind of hybrid between the two. You know, we can have different kinds of payroll topics. But you might say, well, this seems right from a completely standpoint of it being true or not. But this is one of those questions as many multiple choice questions are, which will be we're looking for the most correct answer, the one that fits the picture the most. And so you're usually going to lose that argument and you might as well try to go for the one that's going to be related to the topic we're working on. Next question.

A perpetual record of raw materials is A materials ledger card, B materials, requisition, C purchase order D materials list G, General Ledger. Let's go through this again. Using the process of elimination, a perpetual record of raw materials is either a materials ledger card. Now, if we hear that, we might think, well, that sounds like a thing. That sounds like a term material ledger card, so I'll keep that for now. B says materials requisition. And that should sound familiar too but it doesn't really sound like a perpetual record. It sounds like a requisition is requesting. So it sounds like a request. Doesn't really sound like the perpetual record of inventory.

It kind of goes as we go. So I don't think it's going to be b, C says purchase order. And that has to do with materials too, possibly. But that's really the request for us to purchase the materials from the vendor. So it's not really a perpetual record of our materials. That's the form that's going to tell the vendor, Hey, we would like some materials please. So I don't think it's going to be that one D says materials list. That sounds kind of, kind of reasonable. It's going to be a list of materials, could be a perpetual perpetual list of materials. And then E says the general ledger, the general ledger will be kind of a perpetual ledger in some cases, but it's not really a subsidiary ledger, which we would think of, that we would need for inventory.

We would need the general ledger. Every account has a general ledger that gives the details by date. But we really need the detail by the cost of inventory tracking inventory items, we need some kind of subsidiary ledger. So I don't think it's E. So let's go through this again. A perpetual record of raw materials is a materials ledger card or D materials list. Now of those two, I think A is actually going to be the one A materials list sounds like it's just going to kind of list out the materials we have. But what we really need is the cost of those materials as they go through the system.

So what we what we purchased, what what's still on hand versus what we have sold and the cost of those and this is the materials ledger card is going to be very similar to what we do in a merchandising company and we might have to use a similar cost flow assumption like first in, first out, last in, first out average cost method. The only difference being that we're still using the purchase order. The inventory is still coming in to us in the same kind of similar process as with a merchandising company. But of course, we're not selling the inventory. With the inventory still leaving the warehouse in a similar fashion as with a merchandising company.

It's just that it's going to the factory, to the production process instead of to a customer at that time. So we have the same kind of issues with inventory that we would have with a merchandising company, tracking the inventory and finding methods to do that. Next question. The balance in the work in process inventory is equal to once again, the balance in the work in process inventory is equal to the sum of the costs for all jobs finished, but not yet sold. B raw materials used in production. C the sum of costs for all jobs in process but not yet completed. D The costs of all jobs finished during the current period. E says the sum of all materials, labor and overhead costs paid during the period. Okay, let's go through this again using the process of elimination.

The balance in the work in process inventory is equal to either the sum of the costs for all jobs finished, but not yet sold. It sounds kind of like it's possible, so I'll keep that for now. B says raw materials in production. Now, you might think, well, that's if they're in production, they're in process. So the raw materials are included in work in process, but the raw materials aren't going to be the balance of the work in process account because the work in process account includes everything that's going into the process, including raw materials, but also the factory overhead as we go and the labor. So this would just be one factor. It can't be that it can't be equal to the total. So he says the sum of costs for all jobs in process, but not yet completed. So that sounds kind of reasonable. I'll keep that for now. D says the costs of all jobs started.

I think it should be finished during the current period. So the sum of the jobs that were both started and finished. Now this might be something that if you looked at a process cost system, you might be that might start to ring like something that sounds familiar. If you're using a first in, first out process cost system or something, but it's not really something we do at a job cost. I mean, whether it was started and finished during the same time period doesn't necessarily tie out to the work in process. It's a permanent account, work in process, a balance sheet account. So it's not it's not D And then E says the sum of all materials, labor and overhead costs paid during the period. And again, that might sound reasonable. I'll keep that for now.

So let's go through this again. The balance in the work in process inventory is equal to either A, the sum of costs for all jobs finished, but not yet sold. And note that that one's very similar to C, which says the sum of costs for all jobs in process but not yet completed. The fact that these two are very similar in the form could make us suspicious that one of those are going to be the answer as opposed to e that says the sum of all materials, labor and overhead costs paid during the period. So of those three, I'm thinking that A or C are probably it, given the fact that they're similar, it doesn't have to mean that they're it. But that's often the case. If the two answers are very similar with one kind of twist, then one of those is probably possible a lot of the time.

E says The reason this sounds good is because it has materials, labor and overhead, which are the three things that we kind of look for in the work and process account. The reason it's not correct is because it's costs during the period and it's not necessarily the work in process could go over the like it could be work in process. Some of the costs were there from last month. It's a permanent account, so it's not like work is going to clear out at the end of the month like an inventory or temporary or income statement account. So it doesn't necessarily need to be the case that these costs all happen during this period.

And again, the reason this one might sound more familiar is if you have looked at a process cost system where we have instances in which we need to look at costs that happen during a period, so it's not going to be E so we're left with A and C and between these two, we're looking for the for the ones that are still in process. And that's going to be the sum of costs for all jobs in process but not yet completed. So if we add up all the jobs that were still working on, they're still in process, they're not completed, then that should add up to the work in process amount. On the trial balance. In other words, the trial balance represents all the open jobs which are supported by the job cost sheets, all those job cost sheets. Then that we add up, which have not been done yet, are these as opposed to a which is the sum of all costs for all jobs finished but not sold. That would be the finished goods.

So if we summed up all those jobs that were done, that would be equivalent to finished goods, not work in process. So the final answer. The balance in the work inventory is equal to C, the sum of the costs of all jobs in process, but not yet so. But not yet completed.

The End

Within this discussion, we will discuss the discussion of what it means for overhead to be overapplied or underapplied and how to deal with it. If we see a discussion question or essay question like this and we don't know exactly what it means for overhead to be overapplied or underapplied. We can start off with the definition or thinking about what overhead is, what type of company overhead would fit into it, and then hopefully that can help us pick up some points and possibly jog our memory as to what underapplied or overapplied might mean. So if we think about overhead, we're thinking about a production company.

Typically we're thinking about a company that's using production or a job cost or a process cost system. It's possible to have overhead in a service company as well. But we'll typically think of a company that makes things. And then we're going to have overhead. If we make things, there's going to be three types of things within production that's going to be direct labor, direct material and overhead. So overhead, Of course, is that kind of tricky thing that we have because the problem is that we can't apply the overhead if it's a job cost system to a specific to a specific job, if it's a process cost system to a specific process, I'll think about a job cost system because it's easier for me to do so. So if we think about it, we can't apply the overhead cost to a specific job and therefore we put it into the overhead. So the overhead is kind of this dumping ground for us to put these costs that we know that should go into the job. So we know it should go into inventory, in other words, but we can't apply it to inventory because we don't know which inventory or in this case, which job, which reflects the inventory we're making. We don't know which one to put it to. So we have to put it into overhead.

Why does that help us? Because we're going to later on allocate it to the jobs based on some kind of allocation. We're just going to say we're going to put it here and we'll figure it out later and we'll use some kind of estimate to put it into the actual job. And then later, Of course, we're going to have to figure out how to do that. We're going to allocate it out. Now, when we allocate it out, we don't allocate actual overhead. We allocate an estimate because and there's a few different reasons for that. We allocate an estimate because we don't know what the total costs will be, number one. And, and that's going to be the main reason we use basically an estimate. We don't know what the costs are at the end of the time period.

We're just estimating what they are and we have to record them throughout the time period even so. So for example, we're using the utility bill in the factory right now and we're allocating part of the overhead being utility that's used in the factory that's going into the inventory. But we haven't paid the utility bill yet until the end of the month. So we don't know exactly what the utility bill is. That should be part of the overhead that we're going to allocate. So we have to use this estimate. And Of course, any time we use an estimate, it's not going to be precise unless we're perfect, which most of us fall a little short of.

So we're not we're probably going to have therefore an underapplied or overapplied overhead, meaning we're going to track the actual overhead that we incur in direct labor, indirect material, all other things that are in the factory that are going to help us convert the materials to the finished goods, and then we're going to allocate it using some kind of estimate. So if you think about a T account, we're going to debit everything for the actual costs in overhead. It's going to add up kind of like inventory has a debit balance. It's kind of like inventories there. It's holding the inventory with a debit because it's an asset type account when it goes in the inventory at least. And then we're going to allocate it.

We're going to credit out of the overhead and we're going to put it into the work in process because we can apply it to a job. At that point, we'll use some type of estimate to apply it to the job and we'll put it into work in process, which will then be supported by the jobs. So if you think about that, if the debits are greater than the credits, when we allocate out to the jobs, then we're going to be off the debits being higher than the credits. That means we had more actual costs than we applied out. Therefore it would be under applied so we would have a debit balance remaining if it were under applied. If, on the other hand, when we applied it out using our estimate, the credit was larger than the debits, we're left with a credit balance in the overhead account.

We would have then applied out more of the overhead costs than we actually had at the end of the month. We would be able to see this only at the end of the month and therefore we would have over applied, leaving us with a credit balance in the overhead. Now, conceptually, this kind of makes sense. We can say, okay, I know we're going to be underapplied or overapplied. That makes it an estimate. We're not going to be perfect. I get all that. But should it be a debit balance or a credit balance? What does it mean to be a debit or a credit? Is it underapplied or overapplied? If it's a debit or a credit? And then what do we do with it? Well, the only way to really do that is to actually draw t accounts.

So if you see a question like this, questions draw out the T account and put in direct labor overhead and direct materials on the left side and then put on the right side the allocation that you're going to have and that'll help you to kind of think about, well, what does it mean if it's a debit balance at the end, whatever the estimate is, if it's off by an estimate, we're just going to clear it out to zero because we need to start over next time period. So although this isn't really a clearing account, this overhead account, because we're not closing it out to retained earnings or in other words, it's not a temporary account because we're not really closing it out to retained earnings. It is temporary in the sense it's only temporary, though, since we are going to be forced to close it out by closing it out someplace, in our case, to the cost of goods sold generally so that we can start the process over. So whatever's left in overhead, what do we do? How do we deal with this under overapplied overhead? Whatever it is, we're going to make it zero.

We're going to write a journal entry to make it zero. If it's small, if it's immaterial, then we're just going to close it out to the cost of goods sold. Why? Because that's the easiest thing to do. Okay. So first, why is it the easiest thing to do? Because the cost of goods sold. We want to close it out to an income statement account because the income statement accounts will then roll into retained earnings and in essence disappear. So we won't be dealing with them. They're not permanent accounts. They're temporary. Once it goes away, then we won't have to deal with it kind of in the future. Cost of goods sold is the most logical place to put it because logic.

Oh yeah, the, you know, the inventory will eventually get to the cost of goods sold when it gets to the income statement, meaning the overhead would then go to work in process, then finished goods, then be sold and moved to finally cost of goods sold. So that's the logical ending point that it would get to. Our problem, Of course, is we don't know if it should be in the cost of goods sold or still in process or still in finished goods. But we're just going to say it's small, it's in material. That's our justification for doing the easy thing, writing it off to the cost of goods sold because it will not affect decision making given the dollar amount that we are talking about now. Now, if the dollar amount is large, if we're saying, Oh, that's material, we were off by a lot, then, then we can't. We shouldn't just write it off because it's going to be affecting the financial statements.

So in that case, we would want to try to figure out and go back in and try to figure out, okay, how much of this overhead do we believe based on we'd have to think about how much would still be in work, in process, how much would still be in finished goods and how much had yet had already been sold, and get more detail to try to be more precise about this number. Again, if it's small, it's not worth the time and effort to do that because it's immaterial. We'll just write it off to the cost of goods sold, which hopefully will be the normal practice. So then Of course, what will the journal entry look like? Well, again, if the debits on the T account for overhead are greater than the credits, that means we had more actual costs than what was applied out. And therefore if we under -apply, we're left with a debit balance.

So we're going to credit the overhead account to make it go to zero and we're going to debit the cost of goods sold. And again, the cost of goods sold here is nothing but just whatever we got to do. So you can't really think of why we're doing it to the cost of goods sold. We're doing whatever we need to do to get overhead to go to zero. In this case, we needed to credit overhead to make it go to zero. So we had to debit the cost of goods sold. If, on the other hand, we look at our overhead account and the debit side, the actual costs are less than the credit side. The amount we allocated then we have over applied. So if we're over-applied, we have a credit balance. How do we make it go to zero? We do a journal entry while doing the opposite thing to the overhead account. We debit it, we debit overhead to make it go to zero and we credit the cost of goods sold.

And that's a little bit unusual because again, you're going to say the cost of goods sold shouldn't be credited. That's unusual. Cost of goods sold only goes up. It's like an expense that only goes up in a debit. But this is an exception to the rule in that it's immaterial. Therefore, we're doing whatever we do to make the overhead account go to zero and putting it to the cost of goods sold. If it's a credit, so be it.

Don't miss out!

Visit the website below and you can sign up to receive emails whenever Gaurav Sanjiv Kalangan publishes a new book. There's no charge and no obligation.

https://books2read.com/r/B-A-EPFBB-FVDVC

BOOKS 2 READ

Connecting independent readers to independent writers.

Also by Gaurav Sanjiv Kalangan

Learn Options Strategies Options Basics & Greeks For Stock Trading By Technical Analysis
Bitcoin, Altcoins & ICOs Learn the Basics of Digital Coins from Zero
Time Management This Is How I Work 300 Percent Faster
How To Build And Implement A Winning Pricing Strategy
Networking For Introverts: Gracefully Exiting A Conversation
Accounting 101: Learn Cost Accounting From A To Z

www.ingramcontent.com/pod-product-compliance
Lightning Source LLC
La Vergne TN
LVHW052031200926
848481LV00005B/1644
* 9 7 9 8 2 2 4 2 4 4 4 0 9 *